Set the Record Straight!

For the nation's 31 million African-Americans, it can happen at any time: reading the newspaper, watching the nightly news, or chatting with a co-worker, and suddenly they're on the spot—confronted by an ignorant or stereotyped comment but lacking the hard facts they need to fight back. This book provides that information. For example: Most Americans believe that blacks make up the majority of the welfare population, but the truth is that well over half of the welfare recipients are white. Similarly, most American drug users are white, but the media tends to focus its coverage on black inner-city drug use.

Don't Believe the Hype contains verbal ammunition for the battles over race that are fought in the media—and in our private lives—every day.

Farai Chideya worked as a reporter in *Newsweek*'s Washington bureau for four years; she is currently an editor at MTV News. A graduate of Harvard University, she lives in New York City.

ABOUT THE AUTHOR

FERGUS M. BORDEWICH spent a large part of his childhood traveling among Indian reservations in the 1950s and 1960s. An international correspondent for *Reader's Digest*, covering China, Southeast Asia, the Middle East, and Europe, his articles have appeared in the *Atlantic Monthly*, *New York*, the *New York Times Magazine*, and other publications. His first book, *Cathay: A Journey in Search of Old China*, was published in 1991. He lives in New York's Hudson Valley.

CONTENTS

Part III: Money and Power

Part IV: The Structures of Society

Introduction

We should expect more from the media, but not unless we make an effort to monitor it ourselves.

Four summers ago, a few months after America entered the World War, there arrived in New York from the island of Jamaica, a coal black Negro of the purest African type, whose muscular, chunky, short body was burdened with a negligible load of tangible assets, but whose prognathic-jawed, broad-nosed, kinky-haired head was fairly bursting with an idea that was as great and as heavy as it was intangible.

—From a partially positive 1920 article on
Marcus Garvey in the publication *World's Work.*[1]

M UCH has changed in American journalism since the excerpt from the article above was written. At the very least, anyone in the mainstream media who spent time mocking blacks for their "strange" features would be a journalistic pariah, censured by both colleagues and America at large. Cartoonish portrayals and ethnic slurs are the easiest type of journalistic bias to identify. But what about the more substantive issues of how African-Americans are portrayed in print and on television today?

It would be nice to say that the media now treats African-Americans fairly across the board. But the fact of the matter is blacks are far from equitably represented in the stories, programs, and advertisements we see, hear, and read today. For example, in June 1994, *Time* magazine darkened accused murderer O.J. Simpson's mug shot, then ran the image on its cover. For many African-Americans following the already intense and controversial news coverage of the trial, this was too much to bear.[2]

This book is designed to give readers a chance to question the depictions of race that have become standard in newspapers and on the nightly news, a map through the modern realities and misconceptions about race. Chapter by chapter, I provide facts about the African-American community, facts which often run counter to prevailing depictions.

As a journalist and an African-American, the issue of monitoring the media's accuracy on race is not just important, but personal. I grew up being encouraged to challenge the "givens" of race in America. In fact, I've cribbed the quote at the top of this preface from a paper my mother wrote about Marcus Garvey in 1967. The paper, for a graduate program in journalism, analyzed the mainstream media's coverage of the African pride pioneer. Now a public school science teacher, my mother crusaded for fair depictions of African-American issues even before she became a journalist. As a college student in Indianapolis in the sixties, she fought against anti-civil rights bias in the local press. She wrote a series of pro-integration letters to one of the Indianapolis papers, which printed them—along with her home address. As a result, she received hate mail, in addition to letters of support from some readers.

So questioning the racial status quo is something of a tradition in my family. As a journalist, I spend much of my time keeping track of current articles and broadcasts. When coverage of an African-American issue struck me as biased, slanted, or incomplete, I often found I had surprisingly little idea where to go to find the facts behind what I saw as inaccuracies. I decided to write this book in part to fill the gaps in my own knowledge. Because of my profession, I've been privileged to have access to the books, publications, and experts that have allowed me to challenge the "facts" about race in America. The chapters that follow are written in a spirit of inquiry and a desire to share with you the information I've uncovered.

I also hope, perhaps naïvely, that this book can help blacks and whites understand each other a little better. White Americans are often turned off by what they see as the stridency or complaints of African-Americans, who say they've been wronged by negative portrayals. Blacks are often angry that, even when they can prove media bias in specific instances, like the Simpson photo in *Time*, mainstream depictions of the black community are too often still taken as gospel.

Black America and white America still live separately. Most whites live in overwhelmingly white neighborhoods; most blacks live in majority-black ones. Americans of different races still tend not to live together, socialize together, or chart their paths in this society together. What we know about one another, then, is often secondhand, passed through a filter—the filter of the media. I use the term "filter" because the media doesn't depict everything that goes on in America—that would be impossible. So stories are picked and chosen—filtered—for their ability to be fresh, important, entertaining, *new*—"news," in fact. The news media tends in general to focus on extremes—people who have done extremely bad things, and people who have done extremely good ones. But when many non-black Americans draw their primary experience of an entire community from the media's stories about blacks, there are bound to be problems. For African-Americans, the media's filtering is even more acute. Blacks tend to show up in stories on crime and celebrities, but get left out of everyday news. Anyone who tries to imagine African-American life from media accounts will get the high end (Oprah Winfrey and Michael Jordan) and, too often, the low end (crime and welfare), but will miss the middle.

Perhaps we can find middle ground again by questioning our assumptions about race, no matter how solid those assumptions (like blacks being the heart of the drug problem) may seem to be. This book, despite being chockablock with facts, probably raises as many questions as it answers. It's not a "last word" on race; no book can be. But my sincere hope is that it will help us think twice about making assumptions based on what we see and hear and read. When it comes to the media, questioning is the answer.

Notes to Introduction

1. Truman Talley, "Marcus Garvey, The Negro Moses," *World's Work* vol. XLI (December 1920), p. 153, cited in unpublished graduate paper by Cynthia Chideya, "Marcus Garvey and the Press," Syracuse University (December 1967).
2. Cover of *Time* magazine, 6/27/94.

TEST YOUR RACIAL ISSUES IQ

This quiz challenges you to find out for yourself (whether you're black or white) how your perceptions have been shaped by how the media portrays issues of race and African-Americans.

1. According to a 1993 study, what percentage of network news about African-Americans is negative in tone?
   A. 80%
   B. 60%
   C. 50%
   D. 25%

2. What percentage of newspaper reporters are black?
   A. 20%
   B. 12%
   C. 9%
   D. 5%

3. What percentage of U.S. newspapers don't have any black reporters on staff?
   A. 53%
   B. 45%
   C. 33%
   D. 15%

4. How many poor black families and poor white families are there in America?
   A. 5 million black families, over 2 million white families
   B. 3 million black families, 3 million white families
   C. Over 2 million black families, 5 million white families
   D. 4 million black families, 5 million white families

5. Between 1980 and 1990, in terms of the rate of increase for children born to single mothers:
   A. The black rate grew nine times as much as the white rate
   B. The white rate grew nine times as much as the black rate
   C. Both rates are increasing rapidly
   D. The black rate is increasing and the white rate is decreasing

6. The typical benefit for a family receiving welfare is:
   A. $9,800 per year
   B. Under $7,500 per year
   C. Under $5,000 per year
   D. $3,500 per year

7. The average size of a family on welfare is:
   A. A mother and five children
   B. A mother and three children
   C. A mother and two children
   D. A mother and one child

8. How long, on average, have the families on welfare been receiving benefits?
   A. 5 years
   B. 3 years
   C. 22 months
   D. 18 months

9. What percentage of the total U.S. Government budget goes to welfare and to Social Security?
   A. 10% to welfare, 20% to Social Security
   B. 8.5% to welfare, 33% to Social Security
   C. 2.5% to welfare, 19% to Social Security
   D. Less than one percent to welfare, 20% to Social Security

10. In a phenomenon called "tipping," white residents of a neighborhood tend to move out when a certain percentage of their neighbors are black. What percentage of black neighbors causes "white flight"?
    A. 20%
    B. 15%
    C. 8%
    D. 4%

11. What is the best predictor for whether a student will score well on the college entrance exam, the Scholastic Aptitude Test (SAT)?
    A. Gender
    B. Race
    C. Family income
    D. Private school attendance

12. How do black, white, and foreign students stack up in terms of receiving funding for a graduate degree?
    A. Foreign graduate students get three-quarters of their funding from grants, whites get less than half, and African-Americans get a quarter of their costs paid
    B. African-Americans get three-quarters of cost in grants, whites get less than half, and foreign students get one quarter of costs
    C. White students get three-quarters of cost in grants, blacks get less than half, and foreign students get one quarter of costs

13. In married-couple families with children, what percentage of black and white wives hold jobs outside of the home?
    A. 42% of black wives, 55% of white wives
    B. 68% of black wives, 50% of white wives
    C. 71% of black wives, 68% of white wives

14. How much money does a full-time employee working for the minimum wage make relative to the poverty line for a family of three?
    A. $2,000 more than the poverty level
    B. $500 more than the poverty level
    C. $2,000 less than the poverty level
    D. $500 less than the poverty level

15. What percentage of the 71,000 Americans employed as professional athletes of some type are African-Americans?
    A. 60%

B. 25%

C. 10%

D. 7%

16. What percentage of professional football players in the NFL are black?

    A. 75%

    B. 60%

    C. 25%

    D. 10%

17. During the 1990–91 season, what percentage of black and white NBA basketball players scored over 10 points per game?

    A. Over 50% of black players, less than 20% of white players

    B. 33% of black players, 25% of white players

    C. 75% of black players, 44% of white players

    D. Over 33% of black players, over 10% of white players

18. How many coaches in the NFL, the NBA, and major-league baseball are black?

    A. 4 of 28 NFL coaches, 12 of 27 NBA coaches, 3 of 26 major-league baseball coaches

    B. 2 of 28 NFL coaches, 5 of 27 NBA coaches, 4 of 26 major-league baseball coaches

    C. 0 of 28 NFL coaches, 8 of 27 NBA coaches, 1 of 26 major-league baseball coaches

19. What are the chances of a black high school basketball player making the NBA?

    A. over 24,000 to 1

    B. over 7,600 to 1

    C. over 2,400 to 1

    D. over 760 to 1

20. What are the chances of a black college senior on the basketball team making the NBA?

    A. 1,500 to 1

    B. 150 to 1

    C. 15 to 1

    D. 1.5 to 1

21. When the first people of African descent came to the British colonies that became America, they were:
    A. Slaves
    B. Indentured servants
    C. Free
    D. Free, and later enslaved

22. Which state was the first to abolish slavery, and in what year?
    A. Massachusetts, 1695
    B. Rhode Island, in 1712
    C. Vermont, in 1777
    D. Maryland, in 1790

23. The first person to die in the American Revolution, during the Boston Massacre in 1770, was:
    A. A free white man
    B. A free black man
    C. A white indentured servant
    D. A black slave

24. In what year did Patrick Francis Healy become the president of George-town University, and the first African-American to head a white institution of higher learning?
    A. 1774
    B. 1832
    C. 1874
    D. 1932

25. How much prison time do African-Americans receive for drug and weapons violations compared to whites convicted of the same crime?
    A. The same amount of time
    B. 5% less time
    C. 5% more time
    D. 50% more time

26. Powder cocaine (largely used by whites) and crack cocaine (largely used by blacks) contain roughly the same amount of the drug per gram. How much of either substance must an individual be convicted of possessing to be sentenced to a mandatory minimum of five years in jail under federal law?
    A. 500 grams of powder or crack cocaine

    B. 50 grams of powder cocaine or 5 grams of crack cocaine
    C. 500 grams of powder cocaine or 5 grams of crack cocaine
    D. 5 grams of either powder or crack cocaine

27. What percentage of America's drug users are black, and what percentage are white?
    A. 50% black, 35% white
    B. over 25% black, 50% white
    C. 12% black, 50% white
    D. 12% black, 70% white

28. From ages 12 to 34:
    A. Blacks and whites are equally likely to have tried drugs
    B. Blacks are four times as likely to have tried drugs as whites
    C. Blacks are twice as likely to have tried drugs as whites
    D. Blacks are less likely to have taken drugs

29. How many African-Americans were there in Congress in 1994?
    A. Between 20 and 30
    B. 30
    C. 40
    D. 50

30. What percentage of managers in broadcast news are black?
    A. 2%
    B. 6%
    C. 12%
    D. 20%

31. What percentage of senior personnel at America's magazines are black?
    A. 2%
    B. 6%
    C. 12%
    D. 20

ANSWERS

1. B	7. C	12. A	17. A	22. C	27. D
2. D	8. C	13. B	18. B	23. B	28. D
3. B	9. D	14. C	19. B	24. C	29. D
4. C	10. C	15. C	20. C	25. D	30. B
5. B	11. C	16. B	21. B	26. C	31. A
6. C					

PART I

Round One:
Nature v. Nurture

one

When Is a Fact Not the Truth?

I used to think that eleven o'clock on Sunday [morning] was the most segregated hour in America because that's when we all dressed up and went to our own churches. But I've changed my mind. . . . The most segregated hour comes at about four P.M., when [newspaper editors] sit down and decide . . . what is news.

—Ben Johnson, a black assistant managing editor at the
St. Petersburg Times, as quoted in the *Los Angeles Times*[1]

You might have been reading along with me on June 1, 1993, when the *Wall Street Journal* editorial page bashed "welfare mothers" by describing their so-called opposites, senior citizens, who "are patriotic, they do not have illegitimate children, they do not commit crimes, they do not riot in the streets, [and] their popular entertainments are decent rather then degrading." Or in February 1990 when CBS humorist Andy Rooney was quoted as saying: "I've believed all along that most people are born with equal intelligence, but blacks have watered down their genes because the less intelligent ones are the ones that have the most children. They drop out of school early, do drugs, and get pregnant."

It may be one of the best-kept secrets in America: the "liberal media" is not terribly liberal. American journalism is often misleading, myopic, and unreliable when it comes to detailing the lives of African-Americans. Powerful columnists like *U.S. News and World Report*'s John Leo rail about "the demonizing of white men."[2] "Like guerrillas moving down from the hills to attack the cities," he writes, "the race-and-gender people are no longer just sniping from marginal positions. . . . With the aid of an ever-credulous press corps, they are now pumping their doctrine into the general culture." But even on public television, the supposed nexus of the liberal media, these "guerillas" are nowhere to be found. In fact, a study by watchdog group Fairness and Accuracy In Reporting reveals, fully 90 percent of the guest sources on PBS's the "MacNeil/Lehrer News Hour" and, in the networks, on ABC's "Nightline," were white.[3]

An extensive study of how network news covers African-Americans came to equally disturbing conclusions. Northwestern University professor Robert Entman found that black experts only showed up as experts in fifteen of 2,000 minutes of news not specifically covering racial issues. (They were half of the experts on race-based stories.) More devastating, African-Americans are almost always shown as sources or victims of trouble. Fully 46 percent of stories involving blacks showed them as criminals or victims of crime, poverty, and discrimination, or, as the study puts it: "as threats to or non-contributing victims of American society." In all, nearly 60 percent of network news about blacks was negative.[4]

The African-Americans who are shown succeeding, on television and in newspapers and magazines, are often the superstars—entertainers and athletes who lead lifestyles far beyond the means of most black or white Americans. The entire hardworking, typical center of the black community drops out of media coverage.

The problem with this skewed presentation is not simply that it is incorrect. The larger dilemma is that many white Americans have little to base their knowledge of African-Americans on but what they see, hear, and read in the media. The vast majority of Americans still live and socialize, if not work, predominantly among people of their own race. Given that fact, the repeated images of blacks as unproductive and often dangerous members of this society can have a deep effect on racial attitudes and tensions.

In journalism's game of connect the dots, "black" has come to symbolize crime, reckless childbearing, moral turpitude—"pathology." African-Americans have come to symbolize the worst America has to offer. Demographic "facts" don't sufficiently explain the pervasive stereotyping of blacks. Consider this comparison: African-Americans are a mere 12 percent of America's population. The majority of violent crime is committed by whites, but violent criminals are *disproportionately* likely to be black (over 40 percent of violent criminals are black). The majority of enlistees in the army are white, but a disproportionate number of enlistees are black (over 30 percent of army soldiers are black).[5] Those are, on their face, two unrelated facts, but they illustrate a point. Blacks have become a symbol of crime in America, yet not a symbol of patriotism. (In fact, most Americans consider blacks *less* patriotic than whites.[6]) The same stereotyping that occurs for blacks works in reverse for whites. Whites have *not* become symbols of mass murder, though serial killers are disproportionately likely to be white. No one talks of the Jeffrey Dahmer, Ted Bundy, Jim Jones, or Joel Rifkin killings as "white" crimes. The only recent mass murder by an African-American, Colin Ferguson, received a disproportionate amount of news coverage.

As much as facts can be manipulated, facts are also a powerful way to destroy stereotypes. Facts that don't fit the "conventional wisdom" on race, facts that we as readers and viewers can use to write letters to the editor—or just to inform our own thoughts and conversations—empower us. *Don't Believe the Hype* contains factual ammunition for the battles over race that are fought in the media—and in our private lives—every day.

Many of the facts in this book contradict the images of African-Americans seen in the news. But more than that, they round out the simplistic notions of how race affects our actions and perceptions, shedding light on a more complicated reality.

_____ Defining "The Media"

What is the media, anyway? For the purpose of this book, "media" doesn't just mean newspapers, magazines, and the television news. Advertisements, television shows, and politicians' statements are equally powerful ways that Americans learn facts—and stereotypes—about African-Americans. During the 1988 presidential campaign, Republican organizations supporting George Bush put out advertisements about a black murderer who, on furlough from a Massachusetts prison, raped and brutalized a white wife and husband. The "Willie Horton" ads became infamous for exploiting white fear of black criminals for political gain. But perhaps the worst part of the saga was that even the articles decrying the ads did not offer statistics to counter the myth that blacks are at the heart of America's crime problem. Nobody bothered to point out that the majority of America's violent criminals are, in fact, white.

Top Five Reasons
Why the Perception Does Not
_____ Equal the Reality

1. *Journalism is one of the most segregated professions in America.*

In the broadcast industry, only six percent of management jobs are held by African-Americans.[7] And according to the American Society of Newspaper Editors, only five percent of newspaper reporters are black; forty-five percent of newspapers have no non-white reporters.[8] Even at major publications, the numbers can be startling. At *Newsweek* magazine, where I was a reporter for four years, well under five percent of writers and reporters are black.

2. Journalists and others in the media are human—they work from what they know.

When it comes to doing "real people" articles—like a photo essay on a day in the park or a story on buying a new car—many reporters go to communities that they are familiar with. Because the overwhelming majority of reporters are white, the everyday goings-on in black neighborhoods tend to be severely underreported.

3. It's easy to get stories from the ghetto.

The adage goes, "If it bleeds, it leads." When it comes to stories of deviance and degradation, white reporters go more easily to black neighborhoods because, among other reasons, they aren't likely to feel personally conflicted about the people they're portraying in a negative light. Although the vast majority of drug users are white, it's easier to focus on inner-city crack use than it is to examine middle-class cocaine and heroin addicts.

There is also a tendency to see African-Americans as less than human in their emotions. For example, during the reporting of the murder of white Bostonian Carol Stuart, which at first was wrongly blamed on a black man, several articles repeated the idea that Boston's blacks were "desensitized" to hearing negative news about their community. But when reporters bothered to interview residents, members of the local African-American community revealed their deep pain—pain at the violence in their everyday lives, and at the stigmatization of their neighborhood.

4. *White journalists are presumed to be objective; black journalists, quite often, are presumed not to be objective about racial issues.*

Therefore white journalists often have more latitude to freely express their views on race. For example, when Andy Rooney made the statement about blacks being less intelligent, Howard Rosenberg of the *Los Angeles Times* quickly defended him, saying: "Those are not the words of a racist. . . . This is nothing but a blunt, coarse way of stating an essential truth."

Among the other sins of racial reporting are taking comments out of context and using polarized rhetoric. Some articles on President Clinton's nominee for head of the Justice Department's Civil Rights Division, Lani Guinier, for example, took a snippet of a discussion which made it seem as if she called former Virginia governor Douglas Wilder "inauthentic" (i.e., an Uncle Tom). In fact, she was talking about the disproportionate influence white voters often have over black politicians, who must be very careful not to alienate their skittish white constituency. And, too often, media organizations use terms that have been popularized by politicians. Newspapers often use the term "preference program" (used by conservative politicians like Jesse Helms) when they mean affirmative action.

5. *Once something becomes "conventional wisdom," even if it's misleading, it gets repeated over and over again.*

For example, the statement "There are more black men in prison than in college"[9] turns up again and again in stories on black crime. But very rarely is it noted how misleading the statement is. In 1991, there were 136,000 black males aged 18 to 24 in prison, and fully 378,000 black males the same age in college. Comparing black male prisoners of all ages (a staggering half a million) to the overwhelmingly young college population gives a very false perception.[10] Language can also become "conventional wisdom." Words like "gang" are consistently used to describe groups of young black men—even when they have absolutely no gang affiliation.

A final thought: If the media creates the facts, who critiques the media? The answer to that question is too few people and organizations. Media outlets are supposed to be authorities, so in order to question their judgement, critics have to gather authoritative facts. In addition, media organizations often don't take kindly to criticism. The newspapers, political organizations, public relations firms, and film and television producers are used to being the ones who set the agenda, not the ones who answer for it. When the *Boston Herald* was criticized for overlooking positive stories in the black community, editor Kevin Convey tried to explain his paper's failings by saying that the events "were things we never got a phone call or press release about." Of course, the whole point of journalism is having the ability to find stories independently.

_____ When Is a Fact Not the Truth?

Can something be a fact and still not be true? When "truth" means giving a clear picture of a situation, what seem like solid statistics and hard numbers can often be interpreted to give totally different impressions. Take the controversy over welfare. Many people would be surprised by the fact that 39 percent of mothers receiving welfare are black and 38 percent are white. Stating the statistics that way shows a virtually equal *number* of black and white women receiving Aid to Families with Dependent Children (AFDC). But stated another way, the statistics can show that blacks are seven times as *likely* to be on welfare as whites, as a proportion of the population. Yet one other way of stating the facts is to say that over 30 percent of the seven million black *families* or 20 percent of the ten million black *households* receive AFDC.

Another way that facts aren't "true" is when individual stories, each of them correct, don't add up to an accurate big picture. Continuing with the example, if a newspaper does fifteen profiles of women on welfare, and each woman is black, the individual stories may each be correct but the message the entire series conveys is not accurate. Photographs can be just as misleading as words, either by being pictures of only African-Americans day after day, or simply by being misused. Both *Newsweek* and *Time* ran mug shots of former football star and accused murderer O. J. Simpson on the cover of their issues dated June 27, 1994. But while *Newsweek* printed Simpson's photograph in naturalistic colors, *Time* magazine retouched the photograph to make Simpson's eyes seem more deeply hooded, and his skin seem blotchy and darker than it is. It seems that when an African-American does not fit the crudest stereotype of what a black criminal looks like, members of the media may alter the evidence to convey the worst impression.

The Media and You

Too often, the American media tolerates and perpetuates stereotypes about African-Americans. But recognizing that this is the case does not mean that the media is not doing a solid job most of the time. For the most part, what we read—even if we think "This can't be for real"—*is* for real, for better or worse. But often we expect the impossible; we expect the media to be correct a hundred percent of the time. Of course it isn't. Even the sources in this book, the best available, are bound not to be perfect. I use information from some of the same newspapers I later criticize. I use U.S. Census data, which is widely believed to undercount African-Americans. I use academic studies, papers, and articles, which are bound to be influenced by the views of the researchers and authors who wrote them. The common thread of all these sources is that they aren't perfect, but they're the best we've got.

In the final analysis, it's up to us as reader and viewers to keep the media honest, to not simply rely on (or reject out of hand) any one source of information. That's hard work! But the next time—and there will be one—that you see or read something that makes you want to scream and write a letter, this book will help you find the facts you need to say what you want to say. Pointing out times that the media has misrepresented the African-American community can only make the media better. Pointing out the issues and problems facing the African-American community, no matter how painful, can only make the community better. The media belongs to all of us. If we want it to work, *we* have to work.

Notes to Chapter One

1. David Shaw, "What's the News? White Editors Make the Call," *Los Angeles Times* (12/13/90).
2. John Leo, "The Demonizing of White Men," *U.S. News & World Report* (4/26/93): 24.
3. Lionel McPherson, "Focus on Racism in the Media," *Extra!* (July/August 1992).
4. Robert Entman, "Representation and Reality in the Portrayal of Blacks on Network Television News," *Journalism Quarterly* 71, no. 3 (Autumn 1994): 509–520.
5. Andrew Billingsley, *Climbing Jacob's Ladder* (New York: Simon and Schuster, 1992) : 198–200.
6. Tom W. Smith, *Ethnic Images*, (National Opinion Research Center: University of Chicago, December 1990).
7. 1992 Federal Communications Commission employment survey.
8. "Newsroom minorities top ten percent, ASNE 1993 survey shows,"

news release from the American Society of Newspaper Editors (3/30/93).

9. Seth Mydans, "The Courts on Trial," *New York Times* (4/8/93).
10. Author's interview with Alan Beck, U.S. Bureau of Justice Statistics, October 1993.

two

Black America at a Glance:

A Statistical Overview of the African-American Community

> *[T]he average American thinks that America is 32 percent black, 21 percent Hispanic, and 18 percent Jewish—although the actual figures are 12 percent black, 8 percent Hispanic, and less than 3 percent Jewish.*
>
> —From a 1990 Gallup Poll.[1]

THE fact that most of this country's citizens wildly over-estimate how many African-Americans there are says a lot about the changing composition of American society—and even more about the beliefs and fears that inspires. In 1992, African-Americans were 12.5 percent of the American population, a community totaling 31.4 million people. But the high profile of black Americans is due in large part to the media—to the countless, ceaseless images of African-Americans in newspapers, magazines, and on television. Some of this visibility is positive: for example, the successful African-American journalists, musicians, athletes, talk show hosts, and other celebrities seen on television every day. Much of it is negative: the constant and disproportionate media attention on black criminals, black poverty, and anything else that falls under the umbrella of "the black problem" in American society.

The statistical portrait of black America is far more complex than the extremes often projected by the media. For example, there are many more black accountants than there are black athletes, many more young black men in college than in prison, vastly more self-supporting African-American mothers than ones on welfare. Every day, more African-Americans join the middle classes, leading lives that parallel those of the "everyday working people" profiled on the pages of local newspapers and nightly newscasts. Too often, however, the role of typical Americans in the media is delegated to whites. And certainly regardless of their socioeconomic standing, the lives of African-Americans deserve to be treated with the same attention to detail and nuance as the lives of white Americans.

Statistics

Population

All population calculations—and the other surveys of income and family type that go with them—are approximate. Every ten years, the U.S. Census Bureau performs a large, comprehensive decennial census. Every month, the bureau calculates similar statistics in a Current Population Survey (CPS). The CPS tends to show that African-Americans are a larger proportion of the U.S. total than the decennial census does. In fact, the 1990 census is estimated to have missed about three million Americans, most of them blacks and other minorities living in big cities. Census undercounts are both important and controversial. The bigger the population of a city or state, the more money they receive from the federal government and the greater their number of representatives in Congress. Because of this, many cities have argued, so far unsuccessfully, that the federal government should use census figures which are adjusted for the undercount.[2]

Provided below are numbers and percentages for the U.S. total, black and white populations from both the 1992 CPS and the 1990 census. Both the black and white figures include Hispanics, who may be of any race.

1992 Population Estimates from the Current Population Survey:[3]

	Number	Percent
Total U.S. Population	251,447,000	100%
African-American Population	31,439,000	12.5%
White Population	210,257,000	83.6%

1990 Population Estimates from the 1990 Census:[4]

	Number	Percent
Total U.S. Population	222,561,000	100%
African-American Population	25,819,000	11.6%
White Population	188,052,000	84.5%

Population is also calculated by the number of families (two or more people who live together and are related by birth or marriage) and households (residences of families, single individuals, and unrelated persons). Here are the figures for 1992:[5]

	Families	Households
Black	7.9 million	11.2 million
White	57.9 million	75.9 million

Geographic Distribution

Because of historical patterns and continuing segregation, blacks and whites tend to live in very different areas. The majority of blacks, 54 percent, live in the South, as opposed to only 32 percent of whites.[6]

The majority of blacks also live in central cities: 56 percent compared to only 26 percent of whites. Over 75 percent of all Americans live in metropolitan areas—major cities and their surrounding smaller cities and suburbs. Whites, however, are much more likely to live in suburbs and surrounding areas.[7]

Marriage, Births, and Family

Marriage. In 1992, 38 percent of black women were married, dropping from 45 percent in 1980. For black men, the figures are 42 percent in 1992 and 49 percent in 1980.[8]

Family composition. Forty-seven percent of black families are married couples, 46 percent are female-headed, and 7 percent are male-headed. For whites, the corresponding figures are 82 percent married couples, 14 percent female-headed, and 4 percent male-headed.[9] In 1992, 36 percent of black children lived with both parents, versus 77 percent of white children.[10]

Births. The majority of black children are born to single mothers. In 1990, 67 percent of black children were born to unmarried women, versus 20 percent of white children.[11]

Education

High School. In recent years, the African-American community as a whole has become increasingly likely to have completed a high school education because of the increased graduation rates of younger blacks. In 1992, 68 percent of blacks twenty-five and over had a high school diploma; in 1980, that proportion was only 51 percent.[12]

College. In 1992, 12 percent of blacks and 22 percent of

whites had at least a bachelor's degree. In 1980, those numbers were 8 and 18 percent.[13]

Employment, Income, and Poverty

Black social class structure. African-Americans have both made gains and suffered losses in the American economy since the 1960s. According to one analysis, the black upper class has been rising and the middle class stable, but many formerly of the working class have become poor. Here is a comparison of black family income levels between 1969 and 1986:[14]

Income	1969	1986
Upper class ($50,000+)	5%	9%
Middle class ($25,000–$49,999)	27%	27%
Working class ($10,000–$24,999)	42%	34%
Working poor (under $10,000)	13%	12%
Non-working poor	13%	18%

By 1992, 15 percent of black families earned over $50,000 per year, versus 34 percent of whites.[15] Only one percent of African-Americans and four percent of whites earned over $50,000 individually.[16]

Employment and unemployment. There are 14 million African-Americans in the labor force—that is, either working or actively looking for work. Twelve million are employed and two million are unemployed. In all, African-Americans are 10 percent of all people employed in the United States—but 21 percent of the total unemployed. In 1992, the black unemployment rate was 14 percent, versus 6 percent for whites.[17]

Earnings and education. Average yearly earnings for African-Americans with a bachelor's degree is $30,910, or 66 percent higher than the $18,620 earned by blacks with a high school diploma.

Poverty. There are a staggering 5 million white families and 2.3 million African-American ones living in poverty in this country. These numbers provide a classic example of how statistics can be interpreted differently. It is true that there are over twice as many poor whites as poor blacks, but also that blacks are three times as *likely* to be poor as whites. Overall, 30 percent of black families and 9 percent of white families are poor; the figures for individuals are 33 percent for blacks, 11 percent for whites. Regardless of how the numbers are presented, they indicate that poverty is not simply a "black" problem.[18]

Working poor. Again, the majority of America's working poor are whites, but blacks are more than twice as likely as whites to be working poor. Fifteen percent of blacks, versus 6 percent of whites, earn income below the poverty level (about $7,000 for an individual, $14,000 for a family of four). There are 1.2 million black women and 800,000 black men among the working poor. Among whites, the figures are 3.5 million men and 3.3 million women.

Life Expectancy

Due to factors ranging from violence to poor access to health care, African-Americans live an average of six years less than whites. Black men and women live an average of 66 and 74 years; white men and women live an average of 72 and 80 years.[19] Because African-Americans tend to live shorter lives than whites, the black population as a whole is significantly younger than the white population. The average age of African-Americans is 28 years. For whites, the figure is 34 years.[20]

As evidenced simply by the figures presented in this chapter, the African-American experience of today is complex, often difficult, and frequently at variance with both stereotypes and media coverage. What the bare numbers cannot explain are the reasons, both contemporary and historical, why black and white Americans often lead very different lives. The following chapters of this book attempt to provide this much-needed context.

Notes to Chapter Two

1. George Gallup, Jr., and Dr. Frank Newport, "Americans Ignorant of Basic Census Facts," *The Gallup Poll Monthly* (March 1990): 2.
2. Barbara Vobejda, "Court Won't Adjust 1990 Census Totals," *Washington Post* (4/15/93).
3. The Bureau of the Census: Claudette E. Bennett, *The Black Population in the United States: March 1992* (September 1993): 2.
4. Ibid.
5. U.S. Department of Commerce, *Money Income of Households, Families, and Persons in the United States: 1992* (October 1993): xii.
6. *The Black Population in the United States: March 1992*, p. 2.
7. U.S. Dept. of Census Press Release CB91–66, (2/21/91).
8. *The Black Population in the United States: March 1992*, p. 2.
9. Ibid., p. 2.
10. Ibid., p. 2.
11. National Center for Health Statistics, "Advance Report of Final Natality Statistics," *Monthly Vital Statistics Report*, vol. 41, no. 9, supplement, p. 9.
12. *The Black Population in the United States: March 1992*, p. 8.
13. Ibid, p. 1.
14. Andrew Billingsley, *Climbing Jacob's Ladder* (New York: Simon and Schuster, 1992): 46.
15. *The Black Population in the United States: March 1992*, p. 26.
16. Ibid, p. 42.
17. Ibid, p. 9.
18. Ibid, p. 18.
19. Ibid, p. 16.
20. Ibid, p. 1.

three

Sex, Love, and Family Values

[T]he black story [of out of wedlock births], however dismaying, is old news. The new trend that threatens the U.S. is white illegitimacy. . . . [T]he brutal truth is that American society as a whole could survive when illegitimacy became epidemic within a comparatively small ethnic minority. It cannot survive the same epidemic among whites.

—Charles Murray, author of *Losing Ground*, in a
Wall Street Journal editorial.[1]

Restoring fatherhood might do more than the twenty next-best things we could think of to give our children the chance they deserve—the chance they must have if we are to arrest the disastrous slide of recent years.

—African-American columnist William Raspberry
of the *Washington Post.*[2]

MANY African-Americans agree, as William Raspberry says, that improving the fortunes of the black family could solve some of the gravest problems facing the community. But at the same time, the constant focus of white pundits and politicians on the black out-of-wedlock birth rate seems less out of concern than condemnation. Too often, the black birth rate is seen as pathology; the white rate, as in the Murray editorial above, is a motivator, a common social problem that all Americans must pull together to stop. At this point in time, the white out-of-wedlock birth rate is rising faster than the black rate and by 1992 was 22 percent—a trend that until recently was all but ignored. African-Americans who would like to believe that this emerging focus on whites as well as blacks offers a chance for a less racially charged dialogue on the subject have so far been disappointed. Underlying articles like Murray's is the implication that only a perceived racial self interest—a threat to the white community—will truly mobilize a national effort to combat this problem.

Statistical Overview: African-American Birth Rates _____ and Black Families

Marriage rates. Among African-Americans, marriage rates have declined sharply. In 1980, 45 percent of black women were married; by 1992, that number had declined to 38 percent. Because black women outnumber black men, and because black men are more likely than black women to marry someone of another race, the corresponding figures for black men are 49 percent in 1980 and 42 percent in 1992. The percentage of divorced black men and women also rose over that time span, from 9 to 11 percent for women, and from 6 to 8 percent for men.[3]

Many black women find it difficult to find a mate. Due largely to deaths from violence, there are only eighty-five black men for every 100 black women in the 25 to 44 age group.[4]

Single-mother births. Two thirds of black children are now born to single women, one third to married couples. In 1990, 20 percent of white children were born to single women.[5] In 1992, only 36 percent of black children lived with both parents, compared with 77 percent of white children. The numbers are dropping for both races, though much more sharply for blacks. In 1980, those figures were 42 percent for black children and 83 percent for white children.[6]

Family composition. Forty-seven percent of black families are married couple ones, 46 percent are female-headed, and 7 percent are male-headed. For whites, the corresponding figures are 82 percent married couple, 14 percent female-headed, and 4 percent male-headed.[7]

There are clear benefits to raising children in a two-parent black family. Black children raised in married-couple households achieve higher educational levels, in part because of greater economic resources.[8] Although black married-couple families may be the ideal, many single-parent families raise well-adjusted, productive individuals. The greatest problems arise when poverty, youth, and single parenthood intersect.

Fertility rates. Since the post-World War II baby boom, both black and white fertility rates, the number of women aged 15 to 44 per thousand who have a child, have dropped sharply. The 1990 rate was 68 for white women and 87 for black women. While the white birth rate is beginning to rise again, the black rate is staying stable.[9]

Race determination. Mixed race children are now categorized at birth by the National Center for Health Statistics by the race of their mother. Previously, they were categorized by the race of the non-white parent if one parent was white, or the race of the father if both parents were of color. This change results in more mixed-race children being categorized as white.[10]

Abortion. Through the age of eighteen, white teenagers are more likely to have abortions than black teens. Overall, black women have over twice as many abortions as white women.[11] The difference is that married black women are far more likely to have abortions than white women. This may be due to black married women's poor access to or use of birth control.[12] Education is also a predictor of who chooses to get an abortion. The least educated—and poorest—American women are least likely to abort a pregnancy. Both black and white women with less than a high school education are the least likely to have an abortion. White women with a high school diploma and black women with college degrees are most likely to have abortions within the racial groups.[13]

One of the paradoxes of the debate over out-of-wedlock births is that the women who can least afford to have children are also those who can least afford *not* to have them. Since 1978, poor women have been banned from using federal funds, such as Medicaid, to receive abortions. (In 1977, there were nearly 300,000 federally funded abortions; in 1990, that number dropped to just 165 performed because the mothers' lives were in danger.) In late 1993, President Clinton signed a federal directive ordering states to fund abortions for women who claim they have been victims of rape or incest, even if they did not fill out a police report. The Clinton directive doesn't affect most poor women who need funding to receive abortions, and it is also being contested by state officials, including governor Robert Casey of Pennsylvania.[14]

Some poor women now pay for abortions themselves; some of them have children out of wedlock, unplanned and sometimes unwanted. A study by the Guttmacher Institute estimates that 20 percent of poor women now bear unwanted children. For example, after Michigan banned the use of state Medicaid for abortions in 1988, abortions dropped by 23 percent and the number of children registered before birth on the welfare rolls by women receiving Medicaid rose by 31 percent. Abortions are simply too expensive for many women to afford; in Washington, D.C., the least expensive abortion costs more than $250, or well over one-third of the monthly minimum wage.[15]

Out-of-Wedlock Births
and the Black Family

The 1965 report *The Negro Family*, released by Assistant Secretary of Labor (now Senator) Daniel Patrick Moynihan, said that single-mother families were "the fundamental source of the weakness in the Negro community," and that poverty and black out-of-wedlock births were a "tangle of pathology." Moynihan's ideas were immediately seized upon and cited by those who argue black family structure is *by nature* and *by culture* weak and "pathological."[16] A highly touted 1986 article by Nicholas Lemann on "The Origins of the Underclass" stated: "High illegitimacy ... is a peculiarity of black *culture* [emphasis added], and within that, of the black lower class, and within that, of isolation; out-of-wedlock childbearing in ghettos is one aspect of life over which the people there have the most control."[17]

Today, people and publications ranging from conservative politicians to the most mainstream of newspapers often speak of black family life in terms of cultural pathology. For example, a 1990 editorial in the *Philadelphia Inquirer* suggested that offering women on welfare money to use the Norplant contraceptive, which is inserted in the arm and lasts up to three years, "could be invaluable in breaking the cycle of [black] inner city poverty."[18] The article was criticized for the idea of offering women money (some argue, coercing them) to use the contraceptive—but also for specifically targeting the black community. (The paper later apologized.) The reality is that in terms of sheer numbers, most poor children and poor Americans in general are white. That does not diminish the crushing impact of poverty on the black community, but it means that "solutions" like the one in the *Philadelphia Inquirer* ought to have broader applications than to one race alone.

Q & A: Illegitimacy and African-American Families

Q: *Aren't births to single African-American women just one symptom of the cycle of pathology and poverty that exists in the black community?*

A: America is at a turning point regarding out-of-wedlock births as a "black" pathology or problem. At the moment, African-American children are three times as likely to be born to an unmarried mother as white children. That ratio has held true at least since 1950, possibly for over a century, though in the past the numbers for both blacks and whites were much lower.[19] But the numbers are rapidly shifting. Between 1980 and 1990, the birth rate for white unmarried women climbed nearly 100 percent, while the black rate rose by only 12 percent. Though the gap is still vast—22 percent of white children were born to single women in 1991, as compared with 68 percent for black children, the racial gap is shrinking.[20]

Not only is single motherhood not just a black issue, it's not just an American issue. In Western Europe, from 1970 to 1986, out-of-wedlock births went from 7 to 20 percent of the total in France, 8 to 21 percent in England, and 1 to 23 percent in Austria. In Sweden and Denmark, where cohabitation laws give unmarried couples virtually the same rights as married couples, out-of-wedlock births rose to 48 and 43 percent respectively.[21] And the numbers are still rising: in the 1990s, France and Britain's out-of-wedlock rate rose to 30 percent and 28 percent.[22]

Q: *Didn't slavery cause the higher black out-of-wedlock birth rate?*

A: Although the report *The Negro Family* asserted that the trend towards single motherhood was a result of a weakness in the black family dating black to slavery,[23] most current historians believe that the majority of black families during slavery were headed by two parents. Despite the fact that almost all slaves were forbidden to legally marry, and that countless families were broken up by slave trading, many men and women made commitments to each other in legally unrecognized ceremonies ("jumping the broom") and lived out their entire lives as "married" family units. During the thirties, the majority of former slaves interviewed as part of the Federal Writer's Project remembered both their mother and father, indicating that black families during that era tended to be intact.[24]

Until recently, married-couple families were the norm in the black community. In 1960, for example, nearly 80 percent of black families were headed by married couples. Many sociologists believe that the decline in two-parent black families is a result of several factors including the increased unemployment of black men and growing female independence.[25] Robert Griswold, a historian whose book *Fatherhood in America* looks at the relationship between men as breadwinners and men as fathers, says that men who can't find work lose self-worth, become less involved with their children, and do not form stable families. "I think that the rates of female headedness [in black families] are very strongly tied to inability of African-Americans to find decent jobs in so much of the economy," he states. "It depends on one's politics, I suppose. Depending on who you listen to, people will argue it is irresponsibility on the part of black men. I think that's absurd."[26]

Q: *Isn't welfare to blame—or African-American women— for taking welfare?*

In November 1993 author Charles Murray, appearing on "This Week with David Brinkley," stated that per-child welfare payments act as an incentive for single women to bear children, a common belief among political conservatives. Said Murray, "I'm going to say that welfare is largely to blame. Not entirely. But look: In 1960, a young woman had a small cash payment, and that was it, and she got it under very restricted circumstances. And by ten years later she had a whole variety of new services, she had also much larger cash payment, she had much easier conditions in getting it."[27]

A: In 1992, the average monthly benefit for the typical family receiving welfare, a mother and two children, was just $388—or well under five thousand dollars for an entire *year* of benefits.[28] Even Murray qualified his statement by saying, "Now, since that time [1960], we haven't had an explosion in welfare. I'm not saying that women live a luxurious life on welfare."[29] No proponent of the "welfare theory" can account for why the out-of-wedlock birthrate began its precipitous rise before the creation of welfare and why that rise has continued despite the fact that the inflation-adjusted value of welfare benefits has been dropping for well over a decade.[30]

Q: *The reason so many black women are single mothers is because they just don't want to get married, right?*

A: In fact, the majority of black single mothers very much want to be part of a traditional family, and most single mothers did not set out to become pregnant. One study of unmarried pregnant teens, for example, found that only 21 percent of the black teens and 16 percent of the white ones intended to become pregnant.[31] Far from not wanting to be married, many black women have a hard time finding a husband. The pain and frustration of African-American women who can't find a mate was documented in Terry McMillan's best-selling novel *Waiting to Exhale.* Black men face high unemployment rates and are less likely to get college degrees than black women, leaving black women with fewer good marriage prospects. One staggering statistic: in 1988, one-third of black men aged 15 to 24 lived in poverty, compared with one in 100 white men.

University of Chicago sociologist William Julius Wilson documented the trend with the Male Marriageable Index (MMI), a measure which showed that the ratio of employed black men to black women under thirty-five fell steeply in the 1970s and early 1980s. Another study by Wilson found that in regions where black male joblessness increased the most, so did the percentage of black single-mother families. Black single-parent families increased at the same rate that the numbers of men who could find good solid jobs decreased.[32]

Q: *Aren't black single-parent families, particularly those of teen mothers, a result of self-destructiveness on the part of African-Americans?*

Said a front-page *Wall Street Journal* article titled "For Poor Teenagers, Pregnancies Become New Rite of Passage": "[G]enerations of teenage mothers have lost opportunities for education and work because of their own out-of-wedlock children."[33]

A: While it's true that teen mothers decrease their educational and employment opportunities, a provocative 1990 study argues, sadly, that many black girls have less to lose. Black teens are already at risk because of substandard schools and bad employment prospects, and having a child young may not further disrupt what are already bleak opportunities. Some of the study's findings:

FACT: Black teens who refrain from having children benefit depressingly little compared to their white counterparts. On the one hand, black women cope better with teen motherhood, attaining higher levels of education and employment than their white counterparts. On the other hand, black women who don't have children young have fewer job opportunities than similar white women. Together, these two factors make the gap between black teen mothers and other black women comparatively small. Says the study, "[W]hy are already poor women (who are of course disproportionately black) less likely to postpone first births? . . . [T]hey can anticipate smaller average economic rewards for delaying motherhood. Due in large part to the discriminatory structure of labor markets and/or inferior schooling, black women simply do not stand on average to gain that much from conforming to white childbearing patterns."[34]

FACT: Black teenage mothers are more likely to finish their education than white teen mothers. In 1986, 63 percent of African-Americans who gave birth before the age of eighteen completed high school, compared with 89 percent of black non-mothers. For white women, the figures were 52 percent and 93 percent.[35]

FACT: White women have a greater incentive to delay childbirth in order to obtain better jobs. The 1986 study divided women by the desirability of the jobs they found. The study called good managerial and skilled positions "independent primary sector" employment, versus service and support jobs in the "secondary sector." (To put it in simpler terms, the study nicknamed "secondary sector" work like burger-flipping and toilet-scrubbing "the arena of bad jobs.")

African-American women who waited until at least their twenties to have children were more likely to be unemployed or underemployed than their white counterparts. The table below illustrates how black and white teen mothers and non-teen mothers fared in the job market.

The Smaller Payoff for Black Women Who Wait to Have Children
Percent with Good "Primary Sector" Jobs

	Black	White
Teen Mothers (first birth at 17 or younger)	15%	9%
Waited Until at Least 18 to Have Children	21%	27%

In addition, black women who became teen mothers were 35 percent more likely to be unemployed than black women who waited to have children. For white women, the differential was 62 percent.[36]

Why do black women who avoid teen motherhood not benefit as much as white women who wait to have kids? Among the reasons: poor education in substandard schools, segregation (blacks are more likely to live in inner cities far from new suburban jobs), and employment discrimination all mean that black women, whether they are teen mothers or not, are less likely to get good jobs. Low-paying "secondary sector" jobs usually don't lead to anything better, even if a worker gets more education. In other words, if you're flipping burgers, it doesn't matter if you have a GED, a high school diploma, or are taking community college courses. Concludes the study, "[A]n important strategy for reducing teenage childbearing and its associated problems is the upgrading of education and jobs for poor women."[37]

Q: *Why are African-Americans so sexually irresponsible?*

A: Recent studies refute the idea that African-Americans are "sexually irresponsible," and indicate that in many areas, African-Americans are more responsible than Americans as a whole. Although there are more black out-of-wedlock births, the discrepancy may in part be due to African-Americans having less access to abortion and birth control. And the two studies summarized below show that young African-Americans are keenly aware of the risks of sexual activity—and they're *more* likely than whites to have changed their behavior to try to prevent the spread of HIV, the virus that causes AIDS.

A 1993 report on the sexual behavior of young men found that both black and white men had intercourse an average of once a week, and while black men had more different sexual partners than white men, they were also more likely to use condoms, which can help stop the spread of AIDS. The study by the Battelle Human Affairs Research Center on sexual behavior said that the total number of different sexual partners for men aged 20 to 39 averaged 7.3—6.6 for whites and 10.2 for blacks.[38]

Just as black men are more likely to use condoms, a study by the Centers for Disease Control found that black, Hispanic, and low-income women are more likely than white and higher-income women to have made changes in their sexual behavior to avoid AIDS.[39] The fastest AIDS infection rates are among

young women of color, many of whom get the virus from sex
with IV drug-using men. Black and white IV drug users are
equally likely to have unprotected sex—56 percent never use
condoms.[40]

Q: *Why don't the leaders of the black community stop
whining about prejudice and start being honest about
black sexual irresponsibility? They might actually solve
some problems that way.*

For example, an article in the *New Orleans Times-
Picayune* claimed that black "sexual irresponsibility" was the
cause of crime. "While black leaders and intellectuals regularly call for gun control to combat the black crime problem, I
rarely hear any of them condemn the sexual irresponsibility
that results in the staggering black illegitimate birth rate, the
most significant precursor of that crime problem," it stated.
". . . Until the problems of sexual irresponsibility and illegitimate births in the black community are seriously addressed,
this country will continue to be beset by the resulting and
growing crime problem."[41]

A: It's a myth that African-Americans have their heads in
the sand when it comes to the problems facing the black family. Within the African-American community, the problems
facing black children of single mothers are a constant topic of
conversation. More importantly, countless black individuals,
leaders, and foundations are devoting huge amounts of energy
to trying to solve problems in the black family. Among the efforts is the Washington, D.C.–based National Black Child Development Institute's "Parent Empowerment Project," which
offers parenting classes and assistance in getting a job to low-
income residents of Anacostia, D.C.[42] The Children's Defense
Fund, run by Marian Wright Edelman, is running the Black
Community Crusade for Children, which helps organize com-
munity- and church-run mentoring and tutoring programs,

anti-violence initiatives, immunization drives, and the like. Leaders in the black community are not waiting for anyone to come in and solve these problems for them. At the same time, there is little hope of making progress unless we all pull together. For the benefit of all citizens, America must extend the same concern now being mustered for the rising numbers of children born to white single mothers to black children and single mothers as well.

Notes to Chapter Three

1. Charles Murray, "The Coming White Underclass," *Wall Street Journal* editorial (10/29/93).
2. William Raspberry, "The Trouble with Fatherless Households," *Washington Post* (9/22/93).
3. *The Black Population in the United States: March 1992*, p. 2.
4. Dr. Jeffrey M. Johnson, "Stony the Road They Trod: The African-American Male," *Runta: The National Urban League Research Department Fact Sheet* (June 1990).
5. National Center for Health Statistics, "Advance Report of Final Natality Statistics," *Monthly Vital Statistics Report*, vol. 41, no. 9, supplement, p. 9.
6. *The Black Population in the United States: March 1992*, p. 2.
7. Ibid.
8. William D. Bradford, "Wealth, Assets, and Income of Black Households," (College Park, MD: Department of Finance, University of Maryland College Park, September 1990).
9. National Center for Health Statistics, "Advance Report of Final Natality Statistics, 1990," *Monthly Vital Statistics Report*, vol. 41, no. 9, supplement, (2/25/93): 6.
10. Ibid, p. 5.
11. National Center for Health Statistics, "Induced Terminations of Pregnancy: Reporting States, 1988," *Monthly Vital Statistics Report*, vol. 39, no. 12, supplement, (4/30/91): 1–3.
12. Ibid, p. 4.
13. Ibid, p. 5.
14. Frank J. Murray, "Clinton's order on abortion rebuffed," *Washington Times* (1/19/94).

15. Stephanie Mencimer, "The Welfare Mommy Trap," *Washington Post* (1/9/94).
16. Daniel Patrick Moynihan, *The Negro Family* (U.S. Department of Labor, 1965).
17. Nicholas Lemann, "Origins of the Underclass," *Atlantic*, 258 (June 1986): 31–55.
18. *The Philadelphia Inquirer*, "Poverty and Norplant" editorial (12/12/90).
19. Andrew Hacker, *Two Nations Black and White, Separate, Hostile, Unequal* (New York: Scribners, 1992): 68; Margaret L. Usdansky, "For Many Blacks, Family Tree Long Splintered," *USA Today* (1/17/94).
20. National Center for Health Statistics, *Advance Report of Final Natality Statistics, 1990*, p. 9; National Center for Health Statistics, Monthly Statistics Report, Vol. 42, No. 3.
21. Paul Taylor, "Nonmarital Births: As Rates Soar, Theories Abound," *Washington Post* (1/22/91).
22. Charlotte Grimes, "For Single Mothers, It's Déjà Vu All Over Again," *St. Louis Post-Dispatch* (1/13/94).
23. Moynihan, *The Negro Family*, pp. 15–17.
24. Andrew Billingsley, *Climbing Jacob's Ladder* (New York: Simon and Schuster, 1992): 105–110.
25. Anne M. Nichols-Casebolt, "Black Families Headed by Single Mothers," *Journal of the National Association of Social Workers* (January/February 1988).
26. Author's interview of Robert Griswold (August 1993).
27. Transcript of "This Week with David Brinkley," (11/28/93).
28. U.S. Department of Health and Human Services, *Characteristics and Financial Circumstances of AFDC Recipients, Fiscal Year 1991* (1993): 2.
29. Transcript of "This Week with David Brinkley," (11/28/93).
30. Isaac Shapiro and Robert Greenstein, "Selective Prosperity: Increasing Income Disparities Since 1977," (Washington, D.C.: The Center on Budget and Policy Priorities, July 1991).
31. Nichols-Casebolt, "Black Families Headed By Single Mothers."
32. Nichols-Casebolt, "Black Families Headed By Single Mothers"; and Johnson, "Stony the Road They Trod: The African-American Male."
33. Eileen White Read, "For Poor Teenagers, Pregnancies Become New Rite of Passage," *Wall Street Journal* (3/17/88).
34. Elaine McCrate, "Labor Market Segmentation, and Relative Black/White Teenage Birth Rates," *Review of Black Political Economy* (Spring 1990): 37–53.

35. Ibid.
36. Ibid.
37. Ibid.
38. Martin Walker, "Startling New American Sex Study Tells It Straight," *The Guardian* (April 16, 1993).
39. Gina Kolata, "Drop in Casual Sex Tied to AIDS Peril," *New York Times* (5/15/91).
40. National Institutes on Drug Abuse, *Drug Abuse Among Racial/Ethnic Groups* (Washington, D.C.: Government Printing Office, January 1993).
41. Gordon M. Fitzpatrick, "Illegitimate Birth Rate and Youth Crime," *Times-Picayune* (8/9/93).
42. The National Black Child Development Institute, *The Black Child Advocate*, vol. 20, no. 3, (Washington, D.C.: Fall 1993).

four

The Myth of the Welfare Queen

Some women on welfare are more concerned by the feeding of their drug habit than by the gut instinct to feed their children.

—A statement by Congresswoman Nancy Johnson of Connecticut.[1]

Smith is a walking statistic: a single welfare mother of five who dropped out of high school at seventeen, pregnant with her first child.

—From an article in the New York newspaper *Newsday.*[2]

JUST as black men are stereotyped as criminals, black women in the American media are typecast as welfare mothers. America's newspapers are filled with images of slovenly, ne'er-do-well women and their multitudes of children—families who are nearly always African-American. Yet this image is startlingly at odds with the majority of families receiving Aid to Families with Dependent Children (AFDC), or welfare. Although the welfare crisis is very real, it is nothing like the social and financial armageddon described by its critics. In fact, most women who are forced to rely for a time on welfare work for a living most of the time, and the AFDC program is less than one percent of the entire federal budget.

The stereotype of the "welfare queen" has a clear racial component. Although nearly all of the women pictured in stories on welfare are black, blacks and non-Hispanic whites constitute a virtually equal number of women receiving assistance. (When the figures are broken down by race alone and not ethnicity, as they are in many census listings, whites constitute the solid majority of those on welfare.) So why the pervasive stereotyping? One problem is geography—another is journalistic myopia. White women on welfare tend to live in the suburbs and in rural areas, farther from reporters' eyes. Even when articles and broadcasts state that women on welfare are of all races, they often slip up on visuals. An April 12, 1992 segment of "This Week with David Brinkley" paid lip service to the issue of race by stating: "Most welfare recipients are white, not black; most live in the suburbs, not the inner city; and the notion that they live high is nonsense. . . . Nevertheless, the image of 'welfare queens' getting a free ride on society's back persists." Then the segment proceeded to illustrate welfare with repeated images of inner-city blacks. Politicians regularly rely on welfare as an explanation for all urban ills. In 1992, White House chief of staff Marlon Fitzwater said that the "Great Society" programs begun in the sixties (which include everything from Head Start to welfare) were a cause of the Los Angeles riots.[3]

Welfare is an easy target for both racial and non-racial smears because it has come to symbolize a sort of anti-American Dream, a complete lack of work ethic and responsibility. Americans see welfare as giving money to people who are somehow unworthy or undeserving. One *New York Times*/CBS News poll asked people about assistance for the poor: two-thirds said there was too little. But when those polled were asked about welfare, only 23 percent said the amount of assistance was too little.[4] In fact, the typical woman on welfare is someone who has worked and will work most of her life, has only one or two children, and uses welfare as a fallback when she's unemployed.

Top Twenty Facts:
_____ The Real Face of Welfare

Race

1. The population of families on AFDC covers all races. Thirty-nine percent of the families receiving welfare are black; 38 percent are non-Hispanic white; 17 percent are Hispanic, and 3 percent are Asian.

2. In a strict racial breakdown, the majority of welfare recipients are white.[5]

3. Hispanic origin is an ethnicity and not a race. Some Hispanic-Americans choose not to mark a race on census forms; 90 percent of those who do designate a race select white.

Overall Numbers

4. In 1991, there were 4,374,708 families on welfare.[6]

5. In the midst of the recession, in 1992 the welfare rolls topped a record five million families.[7]

Family Size

6. The average family on welfare consists of a woman and two young children.[8]

7. Over 40 percent of families on AFDC have only one child, as opposed to less than 4 percent with five or more children.[9]

8. Over 60 percent of children who receive welfare are five years old or less.[10]

9. Men are 11 percent of the adults on welfare.[11]

10. Fifty-three percent of children on welfare come from families where the parents never married; 33 percent come from broken marriages.[12]

Teen Mothers

11. Over two-thirds of women on welfare are between the ages of twenty and thirty-four. Less than 9 percent are teenagers; less than 2 percent are under the age of 18.[13]

Duration of Benefits

12. Families receiving welfare have been on assistance for an average of twenty-two months.[14]

13. Over half of families have been on the rolls for two years or less, and only 20 percent of families have been on welfare for more than five years.[15]

Benefits Received

14. The average payment for a family of three was a mere $388 per month or $4,656 per year—less than half of the $10,860 poverty level.[16]

15. The average monthly income for AFDC households of three (which includes all types of benefits plus any earned income) was $456—still just half of poverty-level income for a family of three.[17]

16. Eight percent of families on AFDC also earned income, averaging $330 per month.[18]

17. Some surveys have shown that many women on welfare do work in the underground economy—baby-sitting children, sewing, working off the books. Currently, women who work

legally have their welfare checks reduced by the same amount as their earnings, providing little incentive to find employment. And those who work off the books are considered welfare cheats, even if their income is meager. The federal officials orchestrating welfare reform are considering ways to encourage poor women, even those who earn sub-poverty incomes, to enter or stay in the workforce.[19]

18. In 1972, a woman with income totaling three-fourths of the poverty level could have supplemented her earnings with AFDC in most states. Today, she can no longer get assistance.[20]

Housing

19. The vast majority of families receiving welfare live in private housing and receive no rent subsidies. Less than 10 percent live in public housing.[21]

Child Poverty

20. The U.S. child poverty rate is twice that in Canada, and four times that of most Western European nations.[22]

Questions and Myths About Welfare

Q: *Isn't a lot of the criticism of women on welfare coming from political conservatives, not the media itself?*

A: Much of the time, the media aids and abets the efforts of conservatives to attack women on AFDC. One example is an editorial conservative Irving Kristol wrote for the *Wall Street Journal*. Unlike "op-eds" (the short pieces opposite the editorial page of a newspaper), which may reflect opinions not shared by the paper's editorial page staff, guest editorials do reflect opinions approved or endorsed by those at the newspaper. Among Kristol's statements apparently endorsed by the *Journal*: "The emergence of a growing and self-perpetuating 'urban underclass' that makes our cities close to uninhabited is a demonstrable consequence of the present, liberal-inspired welfare system."[23]

Q: *But isn't it true that the money America gives women on welfare just means they won't look for jobs? Why not cut or eliminate their benefits?*

A: A study in the *Journal of Population Economics* indicates that the supposed generosity of welfare benefits is not to blame for the "underclass"—and the stinginess of the benefits may even contribute to the perpetuation of poverty.

In Europe, where benefits are much more generous than in the United States, women and their children are less likely to live in poverty and more likely to escape it. Researchers theorized that the European women were already closer to the mainstream of society and didn't find it such a leap to make it into the world of work. If, as many critics of welfare say, the amount of benefits are what is keeping women on welfare, then European women, with their generous benefits, should be *more* likely to stay on assistance than Americans. In the United States, only 15 percent of poor African-Americans and 22 percent of poor Americans overall rose out of poverty in a year; in France, where benefits are more generous, the number was 32 percent.[24] Another study comparing public assistance in Europe and America found that the vast majority of single-mother families in most Western European countries do not live in poverty. In addition to more generous assistance, European governments are more likely to fund child care and higher-quality public housing which does not isolate single mothers in "underclass" areas. As Mary Frances Berry, chair of the U.S. Commission on Civil Rights, has stated: "It's cheaper to blame mothers for the problem. . . . If you bash single mothers and blame them, you don't have to spend any money."[25]

Q: *Don't black teenagers get pregnant as an attempt to escape abusive family situations and poverty? Why don't they just get married instead?*

A: The sad fact is that given the current job market, marriage does not guarantee economic security. One study found that almost two thirds of poor single mothers came from poor homes themselves, thus "one cannot conclude that much of poverty could have been avoided had families stayed together." While remarriage provides a way off the welfare rolls for many whites, that institution may not necessarily lift black women out of poverty and off the AFDC rolls.[26]

Q: *Don't the kids who grow up in welfare families just end up on welfare themselves?*

A: Although some families are dependent on welfare from one generation to the next, there are many more adults and children on welfare who move from dependence to independence. African-American author and former *New York Times Book Review* editor Rosemary Bray was raised much of her life on welfare. She and her four siblings now are all productive, employed members of the American economy. In an article for the *New York Times* magazine, Bray stated: "[I]n spite of a wealth of evidence about the true nature of welfare and poverty in America, the debate has turned ugly, vicious, and racist. The 'welfare question' has become the race question and the woman question in disguise. . . . I know that the welfare system is designed to be inadequate, to leave its constituents on the edge of survival."[27]

Women who have received AFDC almost invariably talk about the stigma attached to receiving welfare. California Congresswoman Lynn Woolsey, who is white, received welfare and food stamps after a divorce left her alone to raise two young sons. She got off assistance when she remarried. "And the discomfort when I purchased food with stamps and clerks judged me," she remembers; "they thought I should be buying cheaper food."[28]

Myth: *Welfare is a high-cost program that is bleeding this country dry.*

In January 1994, federal investigators said that the cost of running the nation's welfare programs was growing twice as fast as the number of recipients.[29]

Reality: Welfare is a minuscule part of the national budget. In 1991, welfare accounted for *less than one percent* of the United States' federal outlays.[30] In fact, the report above was grossly misleading—the federal investigators did not adjust the cost of welfare for inflation. When an advocacy group caught the error, they found that, adjusted for inflation, the costs of running AFDC are completely in line with the rise in families receiving benefits.[31]

The fact remains that welfare and food stamps combined are still *less than two and a half percent* of the federal budget. By comparison, Social Security, a benefits program whose recipients are doubtless deserving but, for the most part, not poor, made up fully 20 percent of the cost of running the federal government in 1991; national defense was 24 percent of costs.[32] Benefits programs that might be considered "welfare" for non-poor Americans—programs such as subsidies for beekeepers and other business tax breaks—are at least five times a greater proportion of the federal budget than "welfare" programs for the poor.[33]

Myth: *Black inner-city residents have accounted for the rise in the welfare rolls.*

Reality: In fact, the percentage of black families on welfare as a percentage of the whole has dropped in the past two decades. In 1973, 46 percent of welfare recipients were black, 38 percent white, and 13 percent Hispanic. By 1992, blacks constituted 39 percent of welfare rolls.[34]

Myth: *Reforming welfare is as easy as simply cutting off benefits.*

Reality: Unfortunately, there are no easy solutions. The proposal to put a two-year cap on welfare won't necessarily reduce the rolls dramatically. Most women receive welfare for less than two years, but low wages and sporadic employment means they will go on and off assistance for years. Including repeated stays on welfare, one-third of women receive assistance for eight years or more.[35]

By June 1994, President Clinton unveiled his plan to "end welfare as we know it"—a 431-page bill which at the time of this book's writing is awaiting debates and a vote before Congress. Among the proposals contained in the bill are making women who don't get off welfare within two years take a minimum-wage government-sponsored job, ultimately cutting all funding to women who don't find private-sector work, and allowing states to deny increased benefits to women on welfare who give birth to additional children. Although the plan provides grants to fight teenage pregnancy and money for job training and child care, critics are skeptical that some of the mothers on welfare, particularly those with little education or training, will be able to find work before their benefits run out. Is the government willing to let children go hungry, these critics ask, if their parents fail to follow the government's directives? Critics with the opposite viewpoint, including some African-American conservatives, believe that Clinton's plan contains too many second chances for women who don't want to work. It remains to be seen what legislation will pass, and what its effect will be. But there is one certainty: America will have to provide a "carrot"—improved education and employment opportunities—as well as a "stick" in order to end welfare dependency.[36]

Notes to Chapter Four

1. Jason DeParle, "Plan for Welfare Limits Questioned About Its Own," *New York Times* (11/17/93).
2. D. J. Hill, "Proud but Often Powerless, Wyandanch Residents Try to Stabilize Their Community," *New York Newsday* (9/23/90).
3. Michael Wines, "White House Links Riots to Welfare," *New York Times* (5/5/92).
4. Robin Toner, "Politics of Welfare: Focusing on the Problems," *New York Times* (7/5/92).
5. U.S. Department of Health and Human Services, *Characteristics and Financial Circumstances of AFDC Recipients: Fiscal Year 1991* (1993).
6. Ibid, p. 5.
7. DeParle, "Plan for Welfare Limits Questioned About Its Own."
8. *Characteristics and Financial Circumstances of AFDC Recipients: Fiscal Year 1991*, pp. 1–4.
9. Ibid.
10. Ibid, p. 1.
11. Ibid, p. 2.
12. Ibid, p. 1.
13. Ibid, p. 42.
14. Ibid., pp. 1–4.
15. Ibid.
16. Ibid, pp. 2–3, 9; and U.S. Department of Commerce, table on poverty threshold, 1991 figures, *The Statistical Abstract of the United States: 1993*, p. 441.
17. Ibid.
18. Ibid.
19. Associated Press, "A New View on Welfare, Work," *Chicago Tribune* (7/9/93).
20. Isaac Shapiro and Robert Greenstein, "Selective Prosperity: In-

creasing Income Disparities Since 1977," (Washington, D.C.: The Center on Budget and Policy Priorities, July 1991).

21. *Characteristics and Financial Circumstances of AFDC Recipients: Fiscal Year 1991*, pp. 1–4.

22. Shapiro and Greenstein, "Selective Prosperity: Increasing Income Disparities Since 1977."

23. Irving Kristol, "A Conservative Welfare State," *Wall Street Journal* (6/14/93).

24. Spencer Rich, "Challenging A Theory On Welfare," *Washington Post* (8/12/93).

25. Charlotte Grimes, "For Single Mothers, It's Déjà Vu All Over Again," *St. Louis Post-Dispatch* (1/13/94).

26. M. J. Bane, "Household Composition and Poverty," in S. H. Danziger, *Fighting Poverty* (Cambridge, MA: Harvard University Press, 1986): 231; cited in Anne M. Nichols-Casebolt, "Black Families Headed By Single Mothers," *Journal of the National Association of Social Workers* (January/February 1988).

27. Rosemary Bray, " 'So How Did I Get Here?' " *New York Times Magazine* (11/8/92).

28. Lois Romano, "Rep. Woolsey, On the Needy Edge," *Washington Post* (7/15/93).

29. Associated Press, "Errors are Found in Report on Welfare Costs," *New York Times* (1/12/94).

30. U.S. Department of Commerce, tables 512 and 583, *Statistical Abstract of the United States, 1993*, pp. 330, 371.

31. Associated Press, "Errors are Found in Report on Welfare Costs."

32. U.S. Department of Commerce, tables 512 and 583, *Statistical Abstract of the United States, 1993*, pp. 330, 371.

33. Herbert Stein, "Who's Subsidizing Whom?" *Wall Street Journal* (9/15/93).

34. *Characteristics and Financial Circumstances of AFDC Recipients: Fiscal Year 1991*; and William M. Welch, "States Forging Ahead on Welfare Reform," *USA Today* (8/13/93).

35. DeParle, "Plan for Welfare Limits Questioned About Its Own."

36. Jason DeParle, "From Pledge to Plan: The Campaign to End Welfare—A Special Report," *New York Times* (7/15/94).

five

Where Home Is

'[I]t is like in America when blacks move into a neighborhood, and whites are forced to leave,' he said.

—Japanese Minister of Justice Seiroku Kajima in 1990, making an analogy in a speech on how prostitution ruins a neighborhood.[1]

ALTHOUGH in theory blacks and whites have had every opportunity to live side by side since the sixties, the two races still lead deeply divided lives. The persistence of segregation affects African-American families in countless ways—the ability to move into the middle class, the accessibility of jobs, personal safety, the proximity to good schools.

This chapter focuses particularly closely on the misguided fears of black neighbors. The term "black neighborhood" has become synonymous with crime, degradation, and declining buildings. Too often—though certainly not to the extent that most non-black Americans fear—this is true. What is not usually mentioned are the extenuating circumstances, the reasons why black neighborhoods decline.

_____**Fact Overview**

Black Geographic Distribution, Neighborhoods, and Homes Segregation

The vast majority of African-Americans live in neighborhoods that are disproportionately black relative to the racial and ethnic mix of the entire city or region.

1. One-third of blacks live in racial "ghettos"—areas of intense racial segregation.[2]

2. Blacks are segregated to some degree in all of the thirty major cities with the highest black population.[3]

3. In fifteen of those thirty cities, African-Americans are "hyper-segregated." The black population in these cities tends to be clustered in the central (inner-city) areas, isolated from white neighborhoods, have more people concentrated in a smaller area than white families are, and, overall, have few black families living in majority-white areas and most living in majority-black ones, even when the city itself is not majority black. These "hyper-segregated" cities include: Baltimore, Maryland; Philadelphia, Pennsylvania; Dallas-Ft. Worth, Texas; and Chicago, Illinois.[4]

Even Affluent African-Americans Are Still Segregated

4. Income does not remedy the effects of racial discrimination in the housing market—and that discrimination is specifically targeted against blacks. African-Americans earning over $50,000 per year are more likely to be segregated than an Hispanic-American earning just $2,500 per year.[5]

5. Said an *American Demographics* analysis, "Forty-three percent of U.S. counties have above-average concentrations of

minority households (blacks, Asians, and Hispanics). But only 5 percent of counties have above-average concentrations of affluent households for all three of these groups. Through a combination of settlement patterns and segregation, affluent minorities often don't mix."[6]

6. Seven of the twenty counties with the most affluent black households are in New York and New Jersey. Six more are in the Baltimore/Washington area. None are in the Deep South.[7]

Geographical Distribution

7. The majority of blacks (54 percent) live in the South, as opposed to only 32 percent of whites.[8]

8. The poorest black households are in rural areas, with average incomes of just $15,316 per family.[9]

9. The wealthiest black households are in suburbs of major cities, with average family incomes of $32,192.[10]

Renting Versus Owning

10. More whites realize the dream of owning a home than blacks. Forty-two percent of African-American householders own their homes, and 56 percent rent. By contrast, 67 percent of whites own their own homes.[11]

Q & A: Black Neighborhoods and Housing Patterns

Q: *Aren't things better now than in the past regarding segregation?*

A: No. In the 1800s, for example, Northern cities were not segregated because there were few blacks, whom whites accepted into various craft, professional, and labor niches. It was not until the great outflow of African-Americans from the South to the North that whites became fearful, and race riots ensued which pushed blacks into the ghetto.

In southern cities, black servants lived in cramped housing on alleyways near the genteel homes of their white employers. Their lives certainly were not integrated, but the geographic areas were, resulting in, at the very least, a more common language.

The segregation index—the percentage of blacks who would have to move to white neighborhoods in order to insure even integration—was just 29 for free blacks in northern cities in 1860. By comparison, the segregation index of several cities today is over 85.[12]

Q: *Don't African-Americans now have equal access to the best housing they can afford, just like other Americans?*

A: No. Fifteen percent of black families now earn more than $50,000 per year. Yet, as stated above, a black person earning $50,000 per year is more likely to live in a predominantly black neighborhood than an Hispanic-American earning just $2,500 per year is to live in a mostly Hispanic neighborhood.

Q: *Don't African-Americans live in black neighborhoods because they want to be with people like themselves, not because of white prejudice?*

A: Unfortunately, study after study has demonstrated that the resistance of white Americans to black neighbors can be extreme. In one poll, 73 percent of whites said they would be unwilling to move into a neighborhood that was 36 percent black. Twenty-seven percent of whites said they would be unwilling to move into a neighborhood that was just 8 percent black. Other studies clearly indicate that most African-Americans would ideally prefer to live in more racially mixed neighborhoods.

White fear of black neighbors is not just a theory, either. It actively shapes how and where we live. In a phenomenon called "tipping," once neighborhoods become more than 8 percent black, white residents start to move out. Since America is 12 percent black, the 8 percent threshold makes true integration all but impossible.[13]

Both poor and middle-class African-Americans suffer from the refusal of whites to live near blacks. Unlike their poor white counterparts, the majority of whom live in suburban and rural areas, poor blacks live in the most abject conditions possible in decaying central cities. Middle-class African-Americans, even ones with good income and credit records, often cannot purchase a home in the suburbs, or can only move to increasingly segregated (and often increasingly underserved) black areas outside of central cities.[14]

Q: *Well, the Fair Housing Act, barring racial discrimination in housing rentals and sales, was passed back in the sixties. Hasn't that eliminated housing bias?*

A: No. In 1989, the Department of Housing and Urban Development (HUD) did a study using "testers" (individuals who posed as house and apartment seekers) which found that whites received much more favorable treatment:

1. Forty-five percent of the time, rental housing was more available to whites.

2. Thirty-four percent of the time, the white testers found it easier to find a home to buy.

3. Forty-six percent of the time, white individuals got more help in financing the home they wanted to buy.

4. Seventeen percent of the time, they were offered better, lower rates and terms on their loan.[15]

Q: *Since African-Americans tend to earn less than non-black Americans, doesn't the difference in income explain the difference in housing?*

A: No. A black family with the same income and financial history as a comparable white family doesn't have the same chance of getting a loan to buy a home. "Redlining" is a term for the illegal bank practice of not making loans in certain neighborhoods, particularly black ones. In 1992, the Federal Reserve Bank of Boston studied its own lending practices, and found that they rejected the mortgage applications of non-whites sixty percent more often than for whites with the same level of income and the same credit history. The study also found that, even accounting for economic differences, white neighborhoods received twenty-four percent more loans than black ones.[16] One reason it's so difficult for individuals applying for mortgages to determine if they've been the victims of redlining is because fewer than twenty percent of applicants have flawless credit histories. Therefore, most potential borrowers are in a gray zone, where the bank agent relies heavily on his or her personal feelings about how credit-worthy the loan applicant is. In the gray area, apparently it matters if you're black or white.

Q: *How does redlining affect black neighborhoods?*

A: Redlining often means that black home buyers have to pay higher prices to finance their homes. Just as check cashing companies proliferate in black neighborhoods that don't have enough banks, private mortgage companies go into black neighborhoods and charge more interest than banks. That may leave homeowners with less money for expenses like home repairs or may even mean that some buildings in the neighborhood become vacant because potential home buyers can't find any institution willing to make a loan.

This affects African-Americans of all income levels, even

wealthy ones. Spencer Boyer, a senior law professor at Howard University with a net worth of $1.2 million, was profiled by the *Washington Post* because he could not get a $50,000 bank home-equity loan. Although like most Americans he had made a few late payments on bills, his credit was still rated in the highest possible category.[17]

As part of their 1993 series of articles on lending discrimination, the *Washington Post* completed a computer-assisted study of 130,000 deeds for the sale of area homes which found that "race—not income or housing characteristics—was the decisive factor in determining where local banks and thrifts made home loans in the Washington area." One suburban black neighborhood in Prince George's County with an average household income of $65,000 got *fewer* bank loans than poor white neighborhoods in the D.C. area. American Security Bank, which has almost all of its branches in the District of Columbia, made only ten of its 1,325 mortgage loans for 1991 in predominantly black neighborhoods. Banks help shape the neighborhood. American Security admits its strategy is to lend to multi-family or apartment buildings. Single-family homes are often the best way to keep a neighborhood stable and healthy, while renters in apartment buildings may not have the same commitment to the community.[18]

There are some signs that the federal government is getting more serious about cracking down on mortgage bias. In November 1993, the Federal Reserve board blocked a large bank merger because of concern over possible mortgage bias. The board failed to approve the Shawmut National Corporation's acquisition of the New Dartmouth Bank because Shawmut may not have complied with fair-lending laws.[19]

Q: *Is the media's coverage of modern-day segregation biased?*

A: The media has sometimes been reluctant to call a spade a spade—or rather, racism racism—when it comes to housing discrimination. As one analysis of media coverage pointed out, a 1991 *Washington Post* article "on white flight ever avoids using the term 'racism'—instead talking about 'whites who have migrated' to live among 'neighbors racially like them.' "[20] (The same paper later did the survey of Washington mortgage bias outlined above.)

Q: *It's not the fault of white Americans when black families move in and run a neighborhood down. How can African-Americans possibly blame neighborhood declines on "white flight"?*

A: When the white families "flee" an influx of black families—who, at least at first, are of the same socioeconomic class—the rushed exodus often devalues the housing, and the socioeconomic character of the neighborhood changes. The black families who moved into the majority-white neighborhood in order to live with other middle- or working-class people often find themselves in the same hodgepodge of poverty they just left.

This segregation has a deep impact on the lives of black families and the achievement of black children. Says the 1993 book *American Apartheid:* "Because of racial segregation, a significant share of black America is condemned to experience a social environment where poverty and joblessness are the norm, where the majority of children are born out of wedlock, where most families are on welfare, where educational failure prevails, and where social and physical deterioration abound. Through prolonged exposure to such an environment, black chances for social and economic success are drastically reduced."[21]

Even some conservatives admit as much. In a 1993 editorial titled "The Coming White Underclass," author Charles Murray wrote: "In raw numbers, European-American whites are the ethnic group with the most people in poverty, most illegitimate children, most women on welfare, most unemployed men, and most arrests for serious crimes," says the editorial.

"And yet whites have not had an 'underclass' as such, because the whites who might qualify have been scattered among the working class."[22] (Segregation's effect on African-American employment is discussed in chapter 10.)

Q: *Does segregation affect African-Americans in the suburbs?*

A: Yes. Even when African-Americans do make it to the suburbs, their experience is very different from that of suburban whites. For example, Prince George's County, a suburb of Washington, D.C., with one of the largest concentrations of well-off African-Americans, seems extremely integrated at first glance; it is 51 percent black and 43 percent white. However, the majority of census tracts in Prince George's County are segregated, either 70-plus percent white or 70-plus percent black.[23]

Q: *Isn't the federal government pouring lots of money into the inner city to help poor blacks? Why isn't that working?*

A: Contrary to popular opinion, the U.S. government is not devoting large sums of money to inner-city communities. In fact, as America's inner cities have become increasingly segregated and predominantly African-American, government funding has dropped precipitously. In the decade between 1982 and 1992, federal aid to cities was cut in half. Of course, the problem lies not just with the government, but with private businesses. For example, black city neighborhoods rarely see the kind of clean, well-run supermarkets with reasonably priced goods that white suburban areas have.

Q: *Don't private businesses like supermarkets avoid black neighborhoods because they can't make a profit there?*

A: The lack of businesses in black neighborhoods betrays bias, not good business sense. For example, First National Supermarkets recently built or rebuilt nine inner-city Cleveland supermarkets. Contrary to what many supermarket chains must expect from the urban market, First National's stores have been profitable. Their eleven urban Ohio stores, out of a total of forty-one, are a third of Ohio division sales. Many cities have lost half of their grocery stores since the sixties.[24]

Q: *Why aren't African-Americans putting enough effort into improving their own neighborhoods? They seem to be waiting around for white America to save them.*

A: Across the country, residents of black neighborhoods are taking charge of their own destiny. In Baltimore and other cities, black residents risk their lives by forming community associations and videotaping drug deals near their homes. Sometimes drug dealers even infiltrate neighborhood associations to find out who their "enemies" are. In the summer of 1994, the city of Cleveland, Ohio, sponsored a summit on violence aimed at helping community activists find solutions to the drug and crime problems in their communities. Among those attending were a sixty-year-old African-American woman who boldly tells dealers to leave local street corners, and another black woman whose teenage daughter was beaten in retaliation for the mother's anti-gang activism. In New York, the organization Black Men Against Drugs counsels local youths in conflict resolution and conducts anti-drug sweeps of local apartment buildings. The stories of these and other African-Americans trying to hold their communities together largely go untold in the media.[25]

Too often, though, the idea that African-Americans are waiting around for white saviors is the image that comes across in the media. A 1993 front-page story in the *Wall Street Journal* profiles Mary Lou Holte, a white resident of a now mostly minority Los Angeles neighborhood. "Like many other city dwellers, Ms. Holte is angry and frightened about what is happening about her," the article reads. "Urban life seems to get worse each year.... There are more of 'them'—whoever they might be."[26] The article can afford to be coy, because everyone knows "they" are black.

Q: *Blacks don't seem to want to assimilate. If they just tried harder to blend in to white communities, wouldn't they be accepted just like Italian-, Irish- and Jewish-Americans were before them?*

A: The history of initial separation and eventual acceptance of the ethnic groups above is very different from the continuing rejection of African-Americans as part of majority-white communities. Black Americans have always been segregated in ways that even the most stigmatized white ethnic groups were not. For example, the most segregated white ethnic group in the country was Polish-Americans during the first half of this century. But blacks were, and are, more segregated than any white ethnic group. In fact, today African-Americans are more segregated than any white ethnic group ever was throughout the history of Europe.[27]

Q: *Aren't all poor black areas dominated by people on welfare and other forms of assistance? If they worked, then they could afford to move someplace better.*

A: No. The majority of black lower-income areas are dominated by working-poor and blue-collar families. For example, in the troubled East New York area of Brooklyn, with one of the highest murder rates in the New York area, two-thirds of residents don't receive any kind of public assistance. Residents make a household average of $15,000 per year.[28] In many cases, African-American families working for a living can't find safe, affordable housing.

Q: *How does segregation affect the political power of black neighborhoods?*

A: Most non-black ethnic groups live in at least somewhat integrated neighborhoods. The fact that they share their neighborhood with white Americans or Americans of other ethnicities gives them a base for coalition-building with other ethnic and political groups. The more groups who have an interest in seeing that a neighborhood thrives, the better. African-Americans, however, are too often isolated, not just geographically but also politically. If only African-Americans benefit when money is allocated to an inner-city neighborhood, other groups may resent funding projects for that area. At the same time, most African-Americans will not benefit from funding that goes to suburban or wealthier areas, since even more affluent African-Americans usually live in predominantly black neighborhoods. Segregation affects not just funding, of course, but issues like which neighborhoods receive particularly desirable or undesirable projects like schools, jobs, and waste dumps.[29]

_____ What Is Being Done Well

There are individuals and institutions trying to solve some of the problems of modern-day American segregation. National privately run programs like the Neighborworks Campaign for Home Ownership and the Fund for an Open Society help African-Americans become home owners. Neighborworks not only helps families finance their homes, but also offers money management guidance, counseling, and home renovation advice. Nearly half of the families Neighborworks has helped buy a home are African-American, and over 40 percent have female heads-of-household.[30] The Fund for an Open

Society offers low-income loans to families willing to move into areas where they are in the racial or ethnic minority.[31]

There are also public-run programs, most notably the Gautreaux Assisted Housing Program in Chicago, which relocates African-American families on welfare to predominantly white suburbs. Dorothy Gautreaux, an African-American woman, filed a successful class-action suit which proved that Chicago's public housing system was racially segregated. As a result of Gautreaux's suit, thousands of African-American families have resettled in the suburbs. One study of these families found that the mothers had an easier time finding work, and the children did better in school and were more likely to attend college. The program, begun in 1976, is scheduled to end before the year 2000, but a similar program may start on a national level.[32]

Notes to Chapter Five

1. Eddie Williams, "Japanese Bias, American Blacks," *Washington Post* (10/18/90).
2. Douglas S. Massey and Nancy A. Denton, *American Apartheid* (Boston: Harvard University Press, 1993): 76–77.
3. Ibid.
4. Ibid.
5. Ibid, p. 87.
6. Judith Waldrop and Linda Jacobsen, "American Affluence," *American Demographics* (December 1992): 29–39.
7. Ibid.
8. *The Black Population in the United States: March 1992*, p. 2.
9. Money Income of Households, Families, and Persons in the United States: 1992 (U.S. Department of Commerce, October 1993): 3.
10. Ibid.
11. The Bureau of the Census: Claudette E. Bennett, *The Black Population in the United States: March 1992* (September 1993): 2.
12. Massey and Denton, *American Apartheid*, p. 17.
13. Ibid., pp. 80–93.
14. Ibid., p. 9, and passim.

15. Scott Minerbrook, "Home Ownership Anchors the Middle Class," *Emerge* (October 1993): 42–48.
16. Jonathan Yenkin, "Boston Dispute Could Sway National Loan Bias Debate," *Baltimore Sun* (8/15/93).
17. Joel Glenn Brenner and Liz Spayd, "Law Professor Files Suit Over Loan Rejection," *Washington Post* (7/6/93).
18. ———, "A Pattern of Bias In Mortgage Loans," *Washington Post* (7/6/93).
19. Steven Greenhouse, "Fed Stops Bank Merger; Cities Lending Concerns," *New York Times* (11/17/93).
20. Lionel McPherson, "Focus on Racism in the Media," *Extra!* (July/August 1992).
21. Massey and Denton, *American Apartheid*, p. 2.
22. Charles Murray, "The Coming White Underclass," *Wall Street Journal* (10/29/93).
23. William P. O'Hare and William H. Frey, "Booming, Suburban, and Black," *American Demographics*, (September 1992): 30–38.
24. Dana Milbank, "Finast Finds Challenges and Surprising Profits in Urban Supermarkets," *Wall Street Journal* (6/8/92).
25. Evelyn Theiss, "Residents to Swap Ideas at Summit on Violence," *The Cleveland Plain Dealer* (8/1/94); Mohammad Bazzi, "Grants Help Anticrime Efforts," *New York Newsday* (5/2/94); Park Heights Neighborhood Association, Baltimore, MD (1993).
26. John R. Emshwiller, "Los Angeles Woman Takes on the Hoods Invading Her 'Hood," *Wall Street Journal* (10/22/93).
27. Massey and Denton, *American Apartheid*, pp. 57–59.
28. Dennis Hevesi, "Combatting a Pocket of Crime," *New York Times* (1/4/94).
29. Massey and Denton, *American Apartheid*, p. 14.
30. Neighborhood Reinvestment Corporation, Press Release: "NeighborWorks Campaign for Home Ownership Expands to 54 Locations," (11/10/93).
31. Scott Minerbrook, "Home Ownership Anchors the Middle Class," *Emerge* (October 1993): 42–48.
32. Guy Gugliotta, "Lottery Offers Chicago's Black Welfare Families a Ticket Out of Town," *Washington Post* (2/24/93).

PART II

The Education of Black America

six

Teaching Them Well?

In fact, as is well known by now, the problems of young blacks do not arise in our schools, nor are they remediable there. They are the product of their homes and environments—a terrible social problem, not an educational problem.

—From a 1991 editorial in the *Wall Street Journal.*[1]

SLOW, disruptive, violent, ineducable—these are some of the labels pinned on black America's children. If the individuals are defective, the reasoning goes, then society at large cannot be faulted for the sometimes shaky progress of blacks through America's educational systems. The African-American community is well aware of the need to improve school performance. Said an article in the National Urban League's yearly digest *The State of Black America,* "[M]any black children are underdeveloped. Many are not proficient in the particular brand of English usage that prevails in the marketplace where they must seek employment; they have, at best, rudimentary mathematical skills and so are closed out of the science and technology that drives the modern economy. Too many have not been taught to behave with ethics and humanity."[2] The article called for the black community to redouble and redirect its efforts to prepare children for the twenty-first century.

But too often under-education is portrayed as a black problem and not a national one. In general, Americans are not learning the basic skills they need. A 1993 study by the Department of Education and the Educational Testing Service found that half of American adults are either illiterate or have minimal reading and math skills.[3]

"Born Dumb?": The Attack on Black Intelligence

Myth: *Blacks are by nature less intelligent than people of other races.*

In 1994, Charles Murray and the late Richard Herrnstein published *The Bell Curve*, a book arguing that America is dividing into two societies—one productive, civic-minded and inherently (through nature and possibly nurture as well) high-IQ; the other underachieving, undereducated, crime-prone and low-IQ. The low-IQ/low-achievement underclass, the theorists argue, is reproducing faster than more gifted Americans. In addition, this underclass is disproportionately black.

And in 1990, "60 Minutes" humorist Andy Rooney said, "I've believed all along that most people are born with equal intelligence, but blacks have watered down their genes because the less intelligent ones are the ones that have the most children. They drop out of school early, do drugs, and get pregnant." He was suspended by CBS for what was supposed to be three months, then reinstated early, one month later. Rooney was backed up by at least some of the media. Said Howard Rosenberg of the *Los Angeles Times*, "Those are not the words of a racist. . . . This is nothing but a blunt, coarse way of stating an essential truth."[4]

Reality: Unfortunately, a majority of Americans equate the underclass with low intelligence—and low intelligence with African-Americans. In a poll by the National Opinion Research Center, 53 percent of non-blacks thought that blacks were less intelligent than whites.[5]

The debate over race-based intelligence has been raging for decades despite the fact that the idea that African-Americans are inherently less intelligent is given little credence by most of the scientific community. And not only do the vast majority of scientists think that African-Americans are inherently as intelligent as whites, but the idea of the irrefutable IQ test can be challenged on its face. Biologist Stephen Jay Gould of Harvard says there are no significant biological differences between the races, including intelligence, and measured differences are likely a result of environment.

Many people make the mistake of equating the cycle of poverty with genes—people don't have to be stupid to be poor, and they don't have to be geniuses to be rich. It's undeniable that many of the poorest Americans—black and white—were born in poverty and give birth to children who will be the next generation to live without proper education, jobs, health care, and food. And yes, some drop out of school and/or do drugs. But the cycle of poverty is just what it sounds like—in this country, and most other ones, it is difficult for people at the bottom to climb to the top. Racial discrimination only compounds the problems for low-income African-Americans.

It's also a big mistake to place too much emphasis on IQ measurements. "[The IQ system] properly speaking, does not permit the measure of intelligence," said Alfred Binet, a Frenchman who developed the test in 1905. The test may be more accurate at predicting how well individuals will do in school—but family income is the best predictor of achievement. Does this mean that wealthy individuals are by nature the most intelligent? Or does the passing down of family income, status, and educational and work opportunities form the basis for continuing success? One caveat for those who equate even educational achievement with intelligence: American dropouts include not only slow children but *gifted* children, who become bored and sometimes rebellious.

In fact, intelligence is not an absolute quantity at birth, but depends upon a combination of genetics and environment, especially the level of stimulation given babies and toddlers while the brain is developing. By some estimates, the majority of Americans with mental retardation are not born that way but suffer permanent neurological damage as a result of being understimulated—for example, being left alone in their cribs all day without being frequently touched and spoken to. Exposure to lead and malnutrition are two other factors that may cause brain damage after birth—and they, of course, are both more common among poor, inner-city, minority, and rural children than among wealthy and white children. Factors such as whether the mother smokes or abuses drugs or alcohol affect infants before they are born. A whole host of factors other than genetics determine the future intellectual capacity of America's children.[6]

One scientific study which indicates the effect of individual experience on intelligence was performed on identical twins, who have the exact same genetic makeup and therefore ought to have the exact same I.Q. if genetics alone determine intelligence. Furthermore, if heredity were the sole determinant of intelligence, even identical twins who didn't grow up together ought to have the same I.Q. scores. However, as Carl Senna states in his book *The Fallacy of I.Q.*, "In one of the few studies of separated white identical twins, four of the nineteen pairs had I.Q. differences greater than 15 points—differences that had to be due to environment." To put this back in the context of race, the average difference between black and white I.Q. scores is fifteen points. In addition, the range of I.Q.s among siblings in an average family will typically have a fifteen-point spread. Another study by Craig Ramey of the University of Alabama initially found that children of low-I.Q. mothers tended to have low scores. He put disadvantaged infants into an intensive stimulation program until the age of five, including play with toys, interaction with other playmates, and good nutrition. Children in this program developed normal I.Q. scores, while those in a control group had I.Q.s averaging twenty points lower. When the educational enrichment was continued during school years, only 13 percent of children in the enrichment group failed a grade by age twelve, while fully half of those not given attention had failed a grade or more. Ramey says that three-quarters of all men in prison have low I.Q.s and poor school records. We now know we can do something about this legacy of failure. But by ignoring the opportunity to break the cycle of low achievement, "we are creating a backlog of children who have great criminal potential," Ramey says.[7]

IQ tests also have an uncanny knack for predicting who people in power don't like. At the turn of the century, when Jews, Italians, and Russians were regarded with distaste by Protestant-American society, vast numbers of these immigrants were subjected to testing and labeled "high-grade defectives," or morons. The whole idea of the objectivity of IQ tests comes into question with a look into history. When Americans were first tested, they scored badly. That's because the early IQ test was geared towards European, and not American, cultural standards. American scholars adjusted the tests in order that Americans would test better, but African-American educators don't have the power of being in the majority that revamps the tests to account for cultural differences. The evidence for cultural bias is compelling. Among those who score lower than the norm are southern whites, who arguably have a different culture from the northerners. In one widely studied battery of intelligence tests given by the U.S. Army, northern blacks scored better than southern whites. Rural whites also test lower than urban whites. Yet these white groups are not subjected to nearly the same scrutiny as African-Americans.

IQ tests show up with regularity when African-Americans are pushing for social change. In the fifties, intelligence debates turned up just as African-Americans had succeeded in persuading the U.S. Supreme Court to order the desegregation of America's schools. *U.S. News & World Report* published a 1956 article titled "A Scientist's Report on Racial Differences," which decried integration because of what it saw as the innate inferiority of blacks.[8] One of the most vehement proponents of race-based intelligence, Professor Arthur Jensen of Berkeley, said among other things that dark-skinned blacks were less intelligent than light-skinned ones, and that the U.S. government should take matters into its own hands with eugenics marriage controls.[9]

Nearly forty years later, in 1993, the same publication trumpeted the upcoming publication of Herrnstein and Murray's *The Bell Curve. U.S. News & World Report*'s article implied (in what might be called the "anti-politically correct" ruse) that oversensitive African-Americans and liberals couldn't stand to hear the truth. "[Herrnstein and Murray's] bleak prognosis will mock egalitarian aspirations and challenge postwar liberal orthodoxy at every turn," the article read. "Because African-Americans average 15 points lower than whites do on standardized IQ tests, critics for a generation have condemned such measures as culturally biased."[10] Although many reviews and articles on *The Bell Curve* brought up the idea of liberal censorship, the book received a tremendous reception from the media, including the cover of the *New York Times Book Review* and *Magazine* and of *Newsweek*, and appearances by Charles Murray on television programs like "Good Morning America."

Historically, of course, the idea of race-based intelligence has been used as a way of shirking Americans' commitment to equal opportunity. The reasoning is this: if African-Americans are inferior to begin with, then no amount of equality in schools and employment will make a difference. In his interviews and appearances for *The Bell Curve*, as well as his articles in public forums like the *Wall Street Journal*, Murray has stated that liberal-sponsored social programs like Head Start, welfare and affirmative action are at best ineffective, and at worst encouraging the propagation of low-IQ Americans. The logical conclusion of their research, the authors indicate, would be the cessation of these useless programs. Head Start, in fact, has been a clear success, but the early gains in IQ and achievement are not sustained over time, after the children enter what are usually substandard urban schools. Perhaps this is not a reason for us to despair, merely a call for us as a society to try harder.

Finally, children very often live up to the expectations placed on them. Successful African-Americans have always managed to surmount the lack of high expectations and the lack of equal access to strong public education. Unfortunately, today's African-American students are still facing those same hurdles. We will not see equal achievement in the workplace and in American society until we expect the same level of accomplishment from African-Americans as from white students, and offer them the same opportunities to learn as well.[11]

Just the Facts: Primary and
_____ Secondary Education

Here are statistics on the state of American education: enrollment, funding, and teachers and resources:[12]

1. Sixteen percent of public schoolchildren are black.[13]
2. High school graduation rates for African-Americans have risen sharply in the past two decades. Between 1973 and 1990, the dropout rate for blacks dropped from 22 percent to 13 percent; for whites from 12 percent to 9 percent.[14]
3. In 1992, a total of 68 percent of blacks 25 and over had a high school diploma.[15]
4. By comparison until World War II, the average American did not graduate from high school. The average educational achievement was ninth grade, after which people went to semi-skilled jobs. Even the best students were not required to take more than two years of math and science.[16]
5. In 1991, there were a total of 41.8 million children in U.S. public elementary and secondary schools, and 5.2 million in private schools.[17]
6. Ninety-two percent of blacks and 93 percent of whites aged 16 to 17 are enrolled in school. Blacks are slightly less likely than whites to be enrolled in preschool.[18]
7. There is a growing black presence in elite prep schools. Fourteen percent of the students and 5 percent of the faculty at the 800 member schools of the National Association of Independent Schools (NAIS) are minorities.[19]
8. Federal funding for primary and secondary education is lagging. In 1970, federal funds covered 7.4 percent of expenditures in U.S. public schools. But by 1990, the federal government was pitching in only 5.6 percent of the cost of educating America's children.[20]

9. In 1991, the total cost of running America's schools was $216 billion (or an average of just over $6,000 per pupil) for public elementary and secondary schools, and $18.2 billion at private ones.[21]

10. During the 1990–91 school year, there were 2.6 million public school teachers, 212,000 of whom were black, 87,000 of whom were Hispanic.[22]

Performance, Expectations, Environment: African-American Students in the U.S. Public Schools

Many black children are never given a chance to learn as much and as well as they can. One legacy of the belief that blacks are less intelligent than whites is their disproportionate "tracking" into low-ability classes, most of which offer a substandard education, rather than the remedial help they were designed to. The systems schools use to rank students are far from infallible. In New Jersey, 5,000 high school students were wrongly assigned to remedial classes after taking the Early Warning Test (EWT), which is supposed to predict their performance on yet another test which they need to pass to graduate. Thirty-four percent of the 80,000 students who took the 1992 EWT failed, compared with 26 percent the previous year. There were problems with both the 1991 and 1992 tests, including an inaccurate U.S. map.[23] Some children are kept out of the educational mainstream from day one. Many school districts now test children who are old enough to start first grade for their "readiness" for school. Boys, minorities, and low-income children are disproportionately kept from starting first grade.[24]

Standardized testing is often used to sort children into high and low tracks. These tests are overly reliant on specific bits of knowledge rather than an overall grasp of subject and mastery of actual skills. Some school systems are switching to "portfolio reviews," where children are evaluated by samples of their classwork.[25] The problem with the standardized test system is that the constant comparisons can, unfortunately, compel some schools to "warehouse" problem children in low-ability classes. School systems like New York's rank the worst schools by standardized test scores. If students who score poorly on the tests are put in special education classes, they are no longer counted in the overall scores.[26]

Future black scientists are at a special disadvantage. A National Science Foundation study says that tracking essentially segregates schools by splitting blacks and whites into different classes—more blacks in low-ability classes, more whites in the high-ability track. Taking low-ability classes makes it less likely that black students will learn adequate math and science skills, because these classes have less access to lab equipment and good teachers. The fewer whites there are in a school, the higher the proportion of students placed in low-ability classes. In nearly all-minority schools, 28 percent of math and science classes were low ability versus 9 percent high ability. But in nearly all-white schools, only 7 percent of classes were low ability versus 11 percent high ability.[27]

An analysis of the progress of children through school offers compelling evidence that black students are "turned off" to school over time. In the third grade, the progress of black and white students is roughly equal—about a quarter of children are below grade level. But by eighth grade, almost twice as many black students are below grade level as compared to whites.[28]

Some social scientists go so far as to argue that schools steer children toward certain roles in later life. "Schools teach children of different socioeconomic classes to cultivate the social skills that will ultimately be most important in surviving or succeeding at their anticipated levels in the labor hierarchy," state authors Samuel Bowles and Herbert Ginti.

"[S]chools of privileged children teach them to be self-directed. Schools teach working-class children to obey rules.... In the worst cases, blacks and other minorities are concentrated in schools whose repressive, arbitrary, generally chaotic internal order, coercive authority structures, and minimal possibilities for advancement mirror the characteristics of inferior job situations."[29] In her 1993 book *Lives on the Edge*, author Valerie Polakow makes much the same assertion: that even some preschool teachers assume the worst of their students' intellectual and social abilities, looking on them as little more than future failures.[30]

Educational racism is a problem in other countries where blacks live in a majority-white society. In England, a government-funded report titled *Education for Some* detailed how black students in British public schools were placed in classes below their ability level, discouraged from taking courses that would prepare them for college-qualification exams, and were more likely to be expelled than whites and Asians for the same discipline problems.[31]

Segregation

African-Americans may have gotten some inkling of how difficult a task it would truly be to overcome white prejudice and integrate America's schools in the aftermath of the 1954 *Brown* v. *Board of Education* decision. That Supreme Court ruling ordered America's school systems to desegregate "with all deliberate speed."[32] But rather than integrate, many white communities simply circumvented the ruling by pulling their children out of the public school system and developing private schools. In some areas, local governments shut down the public schools entirely, leaving black students worse off than when they had inferior, segregated schools.[33] Georgia, for example, enacted a law requiring the state to give tuition scholarships to students who wanted to attend private schools. In 1963, 1,200 schoolchildren got the vouchers. Ironically, today some African-Americans are hoping to use this law to send their own children from public schools to private ones.[34]

One of the reasons that black families are contemplating an escape from the public school systems they fought so hard to truly participate in is that depressingly little has changed. In cities across the country, there is "white flight" from the public schools. In Atlanta, the population is 67 percent black but the public schools are 92 percent black. Washington, D.C., is 66 percent black, but the schools are 90 percent black. New York City schools are just 19 percent white; the white population in the Dallas schools has fallen from 57 percent fifty years ago to 16 percent today. It's a never-ending cycle: as white parents take their children out of public schools, they balk at paying for public schools they don't use. The more underfunded the schools, the less they attract white students whose parents can afford to send them elsewhere.[35]

Jonathan Kozol's 1991 book *Savage Inequalities* documents the undereducation of black children with depressing clarity. It also states clearly that segregation is both a cause and a result of poor education. "What startled me most ... was the remarkable degree of racial segregation that persisted almost everywhere.... Most of the urban schools I visited were 95 to 99 percent non-white.... [Yet, m]any people seemed to view the segregation issue as a 'past injustice' that had been sufficiently addressed." A teacher for a time himself, in one school Kozol was fired for teaching the poetry of Langston Hughes—considered both too "advanced" and too "incendiary" for his students, although it was one of the few texts that struck a chord with them. Many urban schools have few or no recreation areas like playgrounds, outdated school books, and teachers who are either undertrained (a reading teacher who isn't trained to teach reading, for example) or the problem teachers dismissed from other schools.[36]

Kozol also takes a sharp look at the aims of those who push tracking and the corresponding less-advanced curricula ("business math" rather than calculus) as a way of preparing poor blacks for "realistic" lots in life. "[T]he business leaders who put emphasis on filling entry-level job slots are too frequently the people who, by prior lobbying and voting patterns and their impact upon social policy, have made it all but certain that few of these urban kids would get the education in their early years that would have made them *look* like college prospects by their secondary years. First we circumscribe their destinies, then we say, 'Let's be pragmatic and do with them what we can.' "[37]

Magnet programs—specialized academic curricula, often specifically designed to bring more white students back into public schools—have their own drawbacks. Montgomery Blair High School in Silver Spring, Maryland, is renowned for its math and science "magnet" program. Though the school is 60 percent black and Hispanic, these students make up less than 15 percent of the magnet program.[38]

One example of how difficult it is to integrate even better-off black areas is Prince George's County. A desegregation order begun in the early 1970s failed to desegregate the system and improve educational achievement. White enrollments plunged from 124,000 white children in 1971–72 to 26,000 in 1990–91. Although the average household income has actually gone up, school spending has fallen behind that of other districts. SAT scores have dropped; fewer than one-third of the county's graduates met the requirements to get into the University of Maryland. Said Franklin Jackson, a black lawyer who runs a tutoring program in the schools: "Back then [before integration], while you had more racial conflict than you do now, there was also much more a commitment to excellence. It's almost like we expect [children] to do worse as the system becomes darker." In July 1994, the Prince George's County Board of Education announced a plan to abandon bussing of students to address segregation. Instead, the district is prepared to spend $350 million to improve neighborhood schools. That may rectify disparities in the quality of education, but probably will leave the racial segregation of students intact.[39]

Race and Teachers

As the percentage of black schoolchildren in some public schools skyrockets, the percentage of teachers who are African-American is dropping. In 1980, 12 percent of American public school teachers were black. Because the recruitment of minority teachers has not kept pace with the growth of school systems, today only 8 percent of public school teachers are black.[40]

Possible Solutions

Many cities are trying to find solutions to the dearth of black teachers. A program in Philadelphia recruits black men from non-teaching backgrounds, including professionals such as engineers and accountants. Prince George's County in Maryland recruits at historically black colleges such as Morehouse and Spelman. The Seattle public school system is sending classroom aides, mostly minority, back to school. A similar program in New York has produced 6,000 teachers, 75 percent of them minority.[41] There are individual success stories as well. Bessie Pender, a Norfolk, Virginia, elementary school teacher, went to school part-time for seven years in order to leave her job as a school custodian. As a result, her salary rose from $10,650 to $26,300.[42]

Some teachers are trying unconventional methods, like incorporating rap lyrics into classroom instruction.[43] One New York City teacher has had success using rap as a classroom tool. Beverly Davidman at Norman Thomas High School in Manhattan occasionally assumes the role of Queen Math Teacher. Since she began rapping, 67 percent of the tenth graders she's taught have passed the June Regents exams in math; in the previous five years, the figure was only 33 percent.[44]

On a broader level, another program trying to make a difference is Teach for America, which sends over 1,000 young college graduates into urban schools. Many of the recruits, who get paid the minimum for first-year teachers, give up in frustration. Ten percent drop out during or after the first year, which is higher than the average for all teachers, but lower than the 25 percent average attrition at the schools to which they're assigned.[45]

Notes to Chapter Six

1. Irving Kristol, "The Tragedy of Multiculturalism," *Wall Street Journal* editorial (7/31/91).
2. Jeff P. Howard, "The Third Movement: Developing Black Children for 21st Century," *The State of Black America, 1993* (The National Urban League, 1993).
3. William Celis, 3rd, "Study Says Half of Adults in U.S. Can't Read or Handle Arithmetic," *New York Times* (9/9/93).
4. Howard Rosenberg, "Is CBS News Guilty Of Andy Rooney–Bashing?" *Los Angeles Times* (2/10/90).
5. Tom W. Smith, *Ethnic Images*, (National Opinion Research Center: University of Chicago, December 1990).
6. Lucille F. Newman, "Early risk factors for impaired learning," *The Brown University Child and Adolescent Behavior Letter*, vol. 9, no. 7 (July 1993): 1.
7. Carl Senna, *The Fallacy of I.Q.* (New York City: The Third Press, 1973): 27; Ronald Kotulak, "Reshaping brain for better future: Scientists learning how to boost I.Q., avert retardation," *Chicago Tribune* (4/15/93).

8. Frank C. J. McGurk, "A Scientist's Report on Race Relations," *U.S. News & World Report* (10/5/56).

9. Carl Senna, *The Fallacy of I.Q.*, p. xi.

10. Gerald Parshall, "Genes, Race, and Intelligence," *U.S. News & World Report* (12/27/93–1/3/94).

11. Frank L. Morris, *The Jensen Hypothesis* (Center for Afro-American Studies Monograph Series, the University of California, Los Angeles) Monograph 2. (Library of Congress entry date 1982); The Chicago Urban League, "A Chicago Urban League Staff Report on 'A Scientist's Report on Race Differences' by Frank C. J. McGurk, Ph.D." (1956); Ezra Brown, "Nakasone's World-Class Blunder," *Time* (10/6/86): 66–67.

12. Bureau of the Census, "School Enrollments and Expenditures," *The Statistical Abstract of the United States: 1993*, 113th edition (Washington, D.C.: 1993).

13. Sarah Lubman, "Efforts to Hire Minority Educators Aim to Narrow Student-Teacher Ethnic Gap," *Wall Street Journal* (9/7/93).

14. U.S. Department of Education, *Dropout Rates in the United States: 1990*.

15. The Bureau of the Census: Claudette E. Bennett, *The Black Population in the United States: March 1992* (September 1993): 8.

16. Deborah W. Meier, "Myths, Lies, and Public Schools," *The Nation* (9/21/92): 271–72.

17. U.S. Bureau of the Census, table 221, *The Statistical Abstract of the United States*, p. 147.

18. Ibid, table 227, p. 151.

19. Sylvester Monroe, "Diversity Comes to Elite Prep Schools," *Emerge* (October 1993): 50–54.

20. U.S. Bureau of the Census, table 225, *The Statistical Abstract of the United States*, p. 150.

21. Ibid, table 222 and 238, pp. 147 and 157.

22. Ibid, table 244, p. 160.

23. FairTest, "New Jersey Students Harmed by Testing Error" *FairTest Examiner* (Cambridge, MA: Spring 1993): 9.

24. ———, "Measuring School Readiness" *FairTest Examiner* (Cambridge, MA: Spring 1993), p. 8.

25. ———, "K–12 Testing Fact Sheet," (Cambridge, MA: Spring 1993).

26. Richard Allington and Anne McGill-Franzen, "Unintended Effects of Educational Reform in New York" *Educational Policy*, (December 1992); Allington and McGill-Franzen, "Flunk 'em or Get Them Classified," *Educational Researcher* (January/February 1993).

27. Gary Putka, " 'Tracking of Minority Pupils Takes Toll,' " *Wall Street Journal* (4/23/90).

28. Margaret C. Simms, "Public Schools: Chance or Choice," (Washington, D.C.: The Joint Center for Political and Economic Studies).

29. Samuel Bowles and Herbert Ginti, *Schooling in Capitalist America: Educational Reform and the Contradictions of Economic Life* (New York: Basic Books, 1979): 25; cited in Elaine McCrate, "Labor Market Segmentation and Relative Black/White Teenage Birth Rates," *The Review of Black Political Economy* (Spring 1990): 37–53.

30. Valerie Polakow, *Lives on the Edge* (Chicago: University of Chicago Press, 1993), passim.

31. John Eggleston, *Education for Some: The Educational and Vocational Experiences of 15-to-18 Year-Old Members of Minority Ethnic Groups* (University of Warwick, England: 1986); cited in Joint Center for Political and Economic Studies, *Focus*, vol. 21, no. 4 (Washington, D.C.: April 1993).

32. Lerone Bennett, Jr., *Before the Mayflower: A History of Black America* (Johnson Publishing Company, 1986): 376.

33. Donald P. Baker, "A School Left Behind," *Washington Post* (8/9/93).

34. *Wall Street Journal* unsigned editorial, "Choice Reality," (9/21/93).

35. Mary Jordan, "In Cities Like Atlanta, Whites are Passing on Public Schools," *Washington Post* (5/24/93).

36. Jonathan Kozol, *Savage Inequalities* (New York: HarperPerrenial, 1992): 2–3 and passim.

37. Ibid, p. 75.

38. *New York Times*, "In a Minority District in Maryland, a Magnet School That Really Draws," (3/3/93).

39. Lisa Leff, "For Schools, Court Order Provided No Shortcut to Excellence," *Washington Post* (9/13/93); David Alan Coia and Jim Keary, "PG schools to end bussing after 21 years," *Washington Times* (7/21/94).

40. Bureau of the Census, table 244, *The Statistical Abstract of the United States: 1993* 113th edition (Washington, D.C.: 1993): 160; and The National Black Child Development Institute, "An Interview with Dr. Asa G. Hilliard, III, Ed.D.," *The Black Child Advocate*, vol. 20, no. 3 (Fall 1993): 6–7.

41. William Celis, 3rd, "Cities Innovate in a Search for Minority Men to Teach," *New York Times* (11/3/93); and Retha Hill, "P.G. Goes the Extra Mile to Find Minority Teachers," *Washington Post* (5/4/94).

42. Michael Winerip, "Putting Down the Mop and Picking Up the Chalk," *New York Times* (9/22/93).
43. Milford A. Jeremiah, "Rap Lyrics: Instruments for Language Arts Instruction," *The Western Journal of Black Studies*, vol. 16, no. 2, (1992): 98–102.
44. Lynda Richardson, "Up Tempo Teaching by Rapping Right Triangles," *New York Times* (11/17/93).
45. Tim Larimer, "Reach Out and Teach Someone," *Washington Post* magazine (2/14/93).

seven

Ivory Towers:

The African-American College and University Experience

The syndrome that ensues is all too familiar: College X, hell-bent on diversity, accepts disproportionate numbers of blacks and Hispanics who don't meet its usual standards. As those students do poorly, even well-qualified students of color experience white stereotyping and resentment. . . . "

—From an article in *The New Republic.*[1]

As evidenced above, African-American college students face the same types of stereotypes that younger black students face. Instead of making progress in recent years, however, the problems of race and the university have reached a crisis point. White students facing a grim job market are increasingly and openly resentful of blacks. Racial tensions on campuses across the country have reached the boiling point. Federal funding for higher education has been shrinking, having a deep and immediate effect on black enrollments. Just as bad as lagging enrollments is the fact that half of black students who enter college do not graduate, an attrition rate far higher than for whites. It is truly a taxing time for America's black collegians.

In many ways, America has not completed the process of integrating higher education. Although some of America's private colleges have served both blacks and whites from the day they opened, segregation was the norm in higher education until just over three decades ago. For example, the University of Virginia did not admit African-American students until 1970.

This chapter is broken into two sections. The first presents information and statistics concerning college admissions, financial aid, graduation rates, and related topics. The second section discusses the media's chronicling of the battles over multiculturalism and "political correctness."

Part I: African Americans and Higher Education: History and Overview

After years of gains, the percentage of African-Americans getting a college education is declining. The percentage of blacks aged 25 to 29 with at least some college rose until 1990, then fell from 13 percent to 11 percent between 1990 and 1992. The white numbers rose steadily, to a total of 23.6 percent.[2] Says a report published by the Joint Center for Political and Economic Studies, "By 1975, black high school graduates between the ages of eighteen and twenty-four had reached parity with whites in rate of college attendance. Black women were attending at a slightly higher rate than white women: 32 percent to 30.7 percent, while black and white men were enrolled at the same rate, 35.4 percent."[3] However, although the gap in black/white SAT scores and high school graduation rates has narrowed, college funding has dropped. Consequently, in 1991, "41.7 percent of white high school graduates went on to college, but only 31.5 percent of blacks did so."[4]

In 1991, total black enrollment in higher education was 1.3 million: 517,000 black men and 818,000 black women.[5] African-Americans are 9 percent of all college students, still significantly below their 12 percent representation in the total population. Because of the difference in graduation rates, in 1990 blacks earned only 6 percent of bachelor's degrees and 3 percent of doctorate degrees awarded in this country.[6] Only fourteen percent of black 25 to 29 year-olds have completed four years of college, versus 30 percent of whites. The discrepancy becomes lower, but does not disappear, for blacks and whites from similar socioeconomic backgrounds.[7]

Almost 80 percent of both blacks and whites attend public colleges; however, whites are slightly more likely than blacks to attend four-year colleges.[8]

Less than half of all Americans finish their college degree in four years. It takes African-Americans an average of 7 years to get a bachelor's degree, 6.2 years for whites.[9]

College graduates by race: In 1992, 12 percent of blacks and 22 percent of whites had at least a bachelor's degree. In 1980, those numbers were 8 and 18 percent.[10] Four percent of blacks and 8 percent of whites had an advanced degree.[11]

Here are 1991 figures for the percentage of those in each race or ethnicity who have completed four or more years of college:[12]

Percent Finished Four Years of College

	Black	White	Asian	Hispanic
Women	12%	19%	36%	9%
Men	11%	25%	43%	10%

Historically black colleges have been a place of strength for black students. There are approximately 100 historically black colleges and universities (HBCUs), schools founded before 1964 expressly to educate blacks. In 1990, over a quarter of a million students attended HBCUs. Black colleges do a better job of graduating black students than white colleges do. While 17 percent of black undergraduates attend HBCUs, fully 27 percent of African-Americans who receive bachelor's degrees get them from HBCUs.[13]

Q & A: Affirmative Action
and the SATs

Q: *Aren't unqualified blacks flooding the university due to affirmative action?*

A: No. Critics of affirmative action aren't even honest about who privileged-admittance programs apply to most often. One of the biggest "affirmative action" programs on campus is not for minorities but for "legacies"—the privileged children of alumni. A 1992 study by the U.S. Department of Education (looking into complaints by Asian-Americans that they were being rejected for less-qualified whites) uncovered some unexpected information. Children of alumni, as well as athletes, consistently received "special preference" over other applicants at some of the nation's top schools, including Harvard, Yale, and Stanford. While the average combined SAT score of Harvard legacies was thirty-five points lower than for all those admitted, legacies were more than twice as likely to get in. Thirty-six percent of Harvard legacy applicants were admitted, versus only 17 percent of all applicants. Clearly underqualified applicants in some cases received the privilege of "special preference." In the study, one Harvard admissions officer evaluated a legacy this way: "Without lineage, there would be little case. With it, we will keep looking. . . . " Some colleges even have outright quotas ("quotas" being the bogey that affirmative action foes decry the loudest). Notre Dame has a quota decreeing that 25 percent of each class be children of alumni. Yet the critics of "special preference" never bring up these policies.[14]

However, when it comes to African-Americans, special recruitment and enrollment programs are lambasted. Affirmative action programs have served a clear function in the higher education of African-Americans. A report by the Joint Council on Political and Economic studies stated that, although black veterans made use of the GI Bill to attend college, blacks and whites did not begin to attend college at the same rates until "1976–77, when affirmative action programs were at their peak." The report also points out that "objections to 'racial preferences' are often raised as a qualifications issue. . . . But the concept of 'equally qualified' in the selection of students for college is an abstraction. Criteria for selection inevitably mix subjective and objective factors as well as personal factors." Affirmative action is just one of a host of factors, including "athletic prowess, other special talents, alumni parents, and geographic locations, which enter into the decision."[15]

Far from being courted as superstars, many college-bound African-Americans are steered away from educational opportunities. In an article in *Emerge* magazine, Leonard A. Slade, a professor of Africana Studies at SUNY Albany, recounted his observations about the educational pitfalls African-Americans face. A teacher summarily told his high school–age daughter that she could not take an advanced math class, though she had earned excellent grades at a previous school. He took the teacher to task, and his daughter took the class. Later, a white principal admitted that he did not tell black students about " 'excellent colleges visiting their high school because it would be a disservice to them if they do not have the grades.' " (Slade's daughter's average was a 93.) For African-American students without parents who have the time, confidence, and knowledge to push for equal opportunities, many potential college opportunities fall through the cracks.[16]

One problem with affirmative action in college is that black students are often recruited, admitted, and then left to "sink or swim." Many black students do come from school systems and educational backgrounds that leave them less-prepared for college curricula, but that does not mean they do not have the innate ability and will to succeed. Historically black colleges have been able to provide the counseling and sometimes remedial education that black students from underprivileged backgrounds need to get a strong start on advanced studies. Majority-white colleges will have to redouble their efforts to guide students through the university in order to see the same results.

Q: *Aren't the administrators of the Scholastic Achievement Test, a college entrance exam, bending over backward to ensure that minorities score well?*

A 1991 *New York Times* op-ed by David Reich, a student at the exclusive Georgetown Day High School, charged that the SAT went out of its way to accommodate minorities. "I emerged from the three-and-one-half hour ordeal struck by the too-large number of questions that emphasized the achievements of minorities, women, and third-world countries; bemoaned the shortcomings of American society, and advanced fashionable causes," Reich wrote. "... Men should complain because they rarely seem to achieve anything unless they are of minority origin."[17]

A: The SAT is a flawed test in general and certainly is not overly accommodating to blacks. Following is a discussion of the most common misperceptions about the test:

1. *The SAT does not accurately predict achievement.* The SAT is designed to predict first-year college grades. But although females get higher grades in both high school and college, they receive lower scores on the SAT. Some researchers for the Educational Testing Service (ETS), which administers the SAT, have admitted that cultural differences can affect performance as well. After the Educational Testing Service added more questions pertaining to minorities in the 1970s, a spokesperson admitted that the passages would make black students more comfortable, and "when people are more comfortable, they'll do better on the test."[18]

2. *The SAT certainly does not predict innate ability,* since coaching programs like the Princeton Review can help test takers dramatically raise their scores. In 1993, Princeton Re-

view SAT prep courses cost $600 or more, a sum few African-American families can afford to spend.[19] In fact, the SAT changed its name from the Scholastic Achievement Test to the Scholastic Assessment Test to deflect criticism.

3. *Many of the questions on the SAT favor well-off kids.* Questions with words that are more familiar to wealthy students are disproportionately likely to be missed by blacks. Some examples are the two analogy questions from past SATs which included "dividend is to stockholder" and "oarsman is to regatta." The "oarsman is to regatta" question was answered correctly by 53 percent of whites and only 22 percent of blacks—and that is a question that *passed* the ETS's screen for racial bias.

4. *Family income is the best indicator of how well a student will score,* superior even to race. In 1992, test takers from families with incomes over $70,000 scored an average 1,000 out of 1,600 maximum; students from families with incomes under $10,000 scored an average 767.[20] By race, 1992 average scores were 899 overall: 945 for Asian test takers, 933 for whites, and 737 for blacks.[21]

5. *The SAT is not universally required.* More than 110 colleges now do not require the SAT.[22]

Q & A: Black Students and Scholarship Dollars

Q: *Don't black students get more funding than white students? After all, it seems like colleges are bending over backward to recruit African-Americans.*

A: On the whole, African-Americans are losing the funding wars, not winning them. Between 1978 and 1988, the percentage of black students who had to rely on loans increased from 10 percent of a total to 28 percent. This lack of college funding may be one reason why black college enrollment rates have stagnated for the past twenty years.[23] And yet the image of black students as recipients of undeserved money persists. For example, a *U.S. News & World Report* article stated, "Many whites bridle at a system of financial aid that they believe often rewards the offspring of well-to-do black families at the expense of less well-off whites."[24]

While 85 percent of college students need some kind of aid—be it loans, grants, work-study, or a combination—the government assistance available to students has been dropping. In 1992, Congress and the President approved a rise in funding for Pell Grants, which in general go to middle-class collegians, to a maximum payment of $3,700 for 1993–94. But under pressure to cut the budget, Congress dropped the maximum to $2,300—a hundred dollars *less* than the previous year's grant.[25]

Family income still to a great degree determines who gets a college degree in this country. In 1991, students with family incomes above $61,600 were five times as likely to graduate by age twenty-four as students from families earning $21,500 to $38,200 per year. Those from wealthy homes were ten times as likely to graduate from college as students from families earning less than $21,500.[26]

Since 1977, federal grants and scholarships fell 62 percent. . . . [I]f you look at students at traditionally black colleges, you find that 42 percent of them come from families with income below the poverty line; a third of them come from families with a total family income less than $6,000 a year. So when it comes to larger economic trends, blacks are like canaries in the coal mine: the first to go when things are going wrong.

—Harvard Afro-American Studies Department chair
Henry Louis Gates, Jr.[27]

Q: *Don't black graduate students really hit the funding jack-pot since they're even scarcer than black college students?*

A: As with undergraduate education, the money available to black students is far less than critics of financial "affirmative action" fear. In fact, African-American graduate students get by far the least funding to complete advanced studies. Foreign students receive the most, followed by white American students.

Foreign graduate students get three times as much funding to get a doctorate degree as African-Americans do. On average, the universities paid three-quarters of education expenses for foreign students, compared to 42 percent for white Americans and just one-quarter for African-Americans. Asian-Americans get more money than any other U.S. ethnic group, but still less than foreign students. The following is a table showing how the three different groups pay for their graduate degrees:[28]

Source of Funds

	University	Personal	Federal
African-Americans	25%	61%	5%
Foreign Students	73%	12%	1%
White-Americans	42%	47%	6%

Consequently, black PhDs are deeper in debt than whites. For example, 26 percent of blacks versus 17 percent of whites are more than $15,000 in debt; on the other end of the spectrum, only 36 percent of blacks versus 45 percent of whites graduate with no debt at all.[29]

_____ The Lack of Black Professors

This graduate underfunding has a profound effect on the faculty of America's colleges and universities. In 1989, the per-

centage of black faculty was 4.5 percent—virtually the same
as it was fifteen years before. Half of those professors were
employed at black colleges, meaning that only 2.3 percent of
professors at majority-white colleges are black. The African-
Americans who are professors are less likely to get tenure and
more likely to remain at the lower levels of the university.[30]
Black professors often are severely overburdened. As some of
the few representatives of their race, they are solicited if not
commanded to join numerous committees, spend extra time
mentoring black students—and, of course, publish or perish
like everyone else.[31]

African-Americans earned a smaller share of the PhDs in
1992 than they did fifteen years ago—the only minority group
for which this is true. In 1977, blacks got 4.5 percent of PhDs.
Today, blacks are awarded only 3.7 percent of all PhDs—less
than one-third of the proportion of blacks in the U.S. population.[32]

That's not just a drop in percentage: fewer African-Americans
in number received PhDs in 1992 than in 1977.[33]

By a narrow margin, blacks still get more PhDs than Asians
and Hispanics, but those two racial and ethnic groups are a
smaller proportion of the American population.[34]

Blacks are also, on average, five years older than their
white counterparts when they get their degrees. The average
black doctoral recipient is just over forty years old, while the
average white recipient is just under thirty-five years old.[35]

The underrepresentation of blacks in some fields is astound-
ing. There are many disciplines, mostly math and science, in
which no African-Americans received degrees in 1992. Among
them: applied math (which produced 92 white PhDs), physics
(101 white PhDs), and cell biology (130 white PhDs). Even in
humanities fields, the numbers were grim. Comparative literature produced no black PhDs in 1992, but 111 whites. There
were only eighteen black PhDs out of the total of over 900
awarded in English and American Language and Literature in
1992.[36]

Racial Tensions on Campus
———— and Black "Self-Segregation"

Q: *Why are black students so oversensitive? They're always demanding special privileges on campus, segregating themselves from whites, and causing trouble.*

The conservative magazine *National Review* put the issue this way: "It is thus in the interest of blacks in general—and perhaps, indeed, the duty of the preferred black in particular—to 'act black' as much as possible. In the school context this usually means, unfortunately, displaying an exceptional sensitivity to possible racial slights and an ability to see malignant racism as the explanation of most historical events and social phenomena."[37]

A: The presence of anti-black sentiment on America's campuses is far from a figment of African-American students' imagination. At the University of Pennsylvania in 1993, during a protracted debate over "politically correct," telephone bomb threats were made to the mostly black residents of DuBois College House, threatening to "blow up the nigger house."[38] Three years earlier, a fraternity at George Mason University held an "ugly woman" contest where one member competed in drag and blackface. Initially, the university suspended the fraternity for two years, but a District Court judge ruled that the blackface was protected under the First Amendment.[39] Almost every majority-white campus includes black students who have been followed around by campus security, endured verbal and sometimes physical racial attacks from other students, and have been taken less seriously by campus faculty.

At the same time, there has been a backlash by black students, who reason that if the universities they pay to attend will not insure their psychological and physical safety, then they will find safety in numbers. The report by the Joint Center on Political and Economic Studies makes clear the pitfalls in both the talk of black "self-segregation" and in black theme houses themselves. "It is disquieting to be taken into a college dining room and be shown row upon row of tables occupied solely by white students and one or two tables of black students, and then ask why blacks insist on segregating themselves," the report states. " . . . [T]he assumption [is] that black students should make concessions to the predominance of whites, and also represent their race." But, it continues, "Settings of this kind can become self-segregating cocoons sheltering black students from reality and enforcing feelings of paranoia rather than girding students to confront the broader world. . . . Black centers may also unwittingly tend to impose a particular point of view upon all black students."[40]

The media is hardly objective about racial tensions on campus. A *U.S. News and World Report* cover story puts much more emphasis on the black rage against a racial incident than it does to the incident itself. "At the University of Massachusetts at Amherst last fall . . . an African-American residential adviser was beaten up by a white visitor and feces were smeared on the door of his room. Enraged, scores of black students rampaged through a twenty-two story dormitory. Police had to warn residents not to leave their rooms."[41]

Even in popular culture, African-Americans are portrayed as mediocre and troublesome students. The lily-white television series "Beverly Hills 90210," which has no regular black characters, introduced in a cameo character none other than an academically unmotivated black basketball player. The ballplayer is befriended by regular white character Brandon, who had to beg him to crack the books. The black student player tries to get Brandon to take a test for him, then, when refused, threatens him, yelling: "I'll mess you up! You're buying yourself a world of hurt!"[42] This kind of patronizing drivel does nothing to help the perceptions—either black or white—

of what life on America's campuses is and, just as important, should be like.

PART II: The Battles Over Multiculturalism and ─────── "Political Correctness"

If some Kleagle of the Ku Klux Klan wanted to devise an educational curriculum for the specific purpose of handicapping and disabling black Americans, he would not be likely to come up with anything more diabolically effective than Afrocentrism.

—Historian Arthur Schlesinger, Jr.,
in his book *The Disuniting of America*[43]

The best defense is a good offense. And that is just what many academics mounted with their no-holds-barred attack on multiculturalism and Afrocentrism. Prominent education experts and media figureheads branded the efforts of African-Americans and other ethnic groups to broaden the curriculum "dangerous," even "un-American." Some of the fledgling efforts at multiculturalism are flawed, but the reality is much more complex than the caricature presented in the media, which also betrays a nasty myopic streak about race.

Following are a few examples of the sensationalistic rhetoric that often plays a part in stories on multiculturalism and "political correctness":

[M]ulticulturalism is a desperate—and surely self-defeating—strategy for coping with the educational deficiencies, and associated pathologies, of young blacks.
[Multiculturalism is an ideology that is] above all, anti-American and anti-Western.

It is an educational—and an American—tragedy.

—Excerpts from a *Wall Street Journal* editorial[44]

Has there been any, from your perspective, horror stories of political correctness, of national note or newspaper note?
  Do you think PC violates academic freedom?
  Do you think PC is a form of censorship?
  Would you call political correctness a sinister development?

—Blatantly leading questions posed to an "expert" on political correctness appearing on John McLaughlin's television program "One on One"[45]

This type of rhetoric is widespread. One story went so far as to call "political correctness" a "crime against humanity."[46]

Multiculturalism Myths and Realities

Q: *Isn't multiculturalism a make-work discipline?*

A: America's history, and the history of the world, is multi- rather than mono-cultural. Multiculturalism is not exclusionary of western culture but a much-needed addition to it. An example of a multicultural approach might be, for example, moving beyond the idea that "Lincoln freed the slaves" to talk about the tens of thousands of African-Americans who fought in the Civil War to free themselves and others. Many proponents of multiculturalism describe the approach as moving blacks, women, and those of other ethnicities from spectators in history to actors in the great drama. Not only is this a noble idea—it is how history actually unfolds. Critics are quick to criticize multiculturalism as propaganda to increase black self-esteem. While a minority of multicultural and Afrocentric programs do err in that direction, on the whole, American history as taught in most schools is inaccurately narrow in its presentation of how this nation grew and developed.

Afrocentrism, like multiculturalism, broadens the scope of history to include people of all races. But Afrocentrism additionally "anchors" black students' education with specific reference points in the African-American and African experiences. This, too, is not difficult to do. African-Americans have affected the development of every discipline, from science (like African-Americans Daniel Hale Williams, who performed the nation's first successful heart operation in 1893 at Chicago's Provident Hospital, and Charles Drew, who developed modern blood plasma science) to literature (from the 1773 publication of Phyllis Wheatley's book of poetry, the second by an American woman, to Nobel Prize–winner Toni Morrison).[47] White Americans are used to seeing the contributions of Americans from their race, while blacks and other minorities don't connect history with their own lives—not because the accomplishments are not there, but because they are not taught.

Q: *Haven't schools and universities always provided more than enough instruction in black history and that of other cultures?*

Dinesh D'Souza, author of *Illiberal Education*, states: "There is little argument about the desirability of teaching the greatest works written by members of other cultures, by women, and by minority-group members. Many academic activists go beyond this to insist that texts be selected primarily or exclusively according to the author's race, gender, or sexual preference, and that the Western tradition be exposed in the classroom as bigoted and oppressive in every way."[48]

A: African-Americans are not arguing that the Western tradition is "bigoted and oppressive in every way." But it is a complete fiction that instruction in "other cultures" has always been available in American education—or even that it is available now. In fact, the one of the definitive references on college curricula, *The College Blue Book*, lists under 150 college and university programs in Black/African-American Studies, versus, for example over 1,000 in English.[49]

In fact, there has never been any kind of monolithic agreement about what constitutes the core of a Western education. Some nineteenth-century thinkers, including Charles William Eliot, who presided over Harvard for forty years beginning in 1869, fought for non-Western studies.[50]

Q: *Don't black students intimidate college faculty and administration by crying "racism" every time they don't like something?*

A: Critics of multiculturalism conveniently ignore the balance of power in American society. As professor Darlene Clark Hine puts it, "[T]o imply that minorities have the institutional means to intimidate thousands of white college teachers and administrators, to impose their multicultural imperatives on hapless white students, is at best grossly dishonest."[51]

Universities often act more out of political expediency than in the best interests of the students. New York's City College Black Studies chair Leonard Jeffries made a speech on July 20, 1991, which blamed Jews for the slave trade and for a Hollywood conspiracy. Before that, he called Caucasians aggressive, unfeeling "ice people" and African-Americans superior "sun people." Yet, only a month before the speech he was reappointed unanimously to his post, and the school's president sent him a letter of congratulations. A federal judge who reinstated him in August 1993 found that the university could have tried to take Jeffries's position away because of bad job performance (i.e., that his statements had hurt the department). Instead, their decision to punish him for his speech violated his First Amendment rights. The media's scrutiny of Leonard Jeffries was far more intense than of Michael Levin, a philosophy professor who was reported to have made statements outside of class that blacks are less intelligent than whites. Levin also successfully blocked efforts by the university to punish him for remarks.[52]

Said the *Washington Post,* "There's an implied subtext to this tale, and it's condescension—by university officials who didn't bother to deal with a continuing embarrassment in what should have been a legitimate department. The losers, aside from CCNY, are serious students of Mr. Jeffries's ostensible subject who are now stuck with Mr. Jeffries."[53]

Black studies departments are often underfunded; in 1990, departments around the country, including those at Harvard, Yale, and Stanford, were understaffed or even directorless. When the chair of Harvard University's Afro-American Studies department died, the department was forced to use temporary department heads for two academic years. The chairman at Stanford quit, complaining that his department was underfunded. Two years in a row, the heads of the Yale departments quit. The need for black studies professors is acute. At the 1990 conference of the Modern Language Association, the umbrella group for humanities professors, a quarter of the positions advertised were for black studies, a field in which there were only twenty untenured PhDs in the country.[54] Today many of these departments have rebounded. For example, Harvard's Afro-American Studies Department is chaired by prominent scholar Henry Louis Gates, Jr., and also features professor and author Cornel West.

It's clear to most observers of the educational system that now is no time to retreat from change and deny America's multicultural past, thus making sure academia's ivory towers remain whiter than ever. What is needed is a greater willingness to preserve the parts of America's educational system which are truthful, fair, and useful, and discard those portions which are biased and limiting. This certainly does not mean lowering academic standards. Means of reaching this goal include hiring greater numbers of African-American professors and developing a greater willingness to give disciplines like African-American Studies the same respect and demand from them the same rigor as other academic fields.

Notes to Chapter Seven

1. Jim Sleeper, "Anti-anti-racist," *The New Republic* (6/28/93).
2. Bureau of the Census, "School Enrollments and Expenditures," *The Statistical Abstract of the United States: 1993*, 113th edition (Washington, D.C.: 1993), table 230: 152.
3. Deborah Carter and Reginald Wilson, "Minorities in Higher Education: Eleventh Annual Status Report, 1992" (Washington, D.C.: American Council on Education, 1992): 41–45; cited in The Committee on Policy for Racial Justice, *The Inclusive University* (Joint Center for Political and Economic Studies Press, 1993): 5 and 48.
4. Carter and Wilson, "Minorities in Higher Education: Eleventh Annual Status Report, 1992," p. 42.
5. National Center for Education Statistics, *Trends in Enrollment in Higher Education by Racial/Ethnic Category: Fall 1982 through Fall 1991* (March 1993).
6. Bureau of the Census, "School Enrollments and Expenditures," *The Statistical Abstract of the United States: 1993*, 113th edition (Washington, D.C.: 1993), table 295: 185.
7. U.S. Department of Education, National Center for Education Statistics, *The Condition of Education* (Washington, D.C.: June 1992): 62.; cited in the Committee on Policy for Racial Justice, *The Inclusive University*: 23.
8. National Center for Education Statistics, *Trends in Enrollment in Higher Education by Racial/Ethnic Category: Fall 1982 through Fall 1991* (March 1993).
9. Bureau of the Census, "School Enrollments and Expenditures," *The Statistical Abstract of the United States: 1993*, 113th edition (Washington, D.C.: 1993), table 295: 185.
10. Bureau of the Census: Claudette E. Bennett, *The Black Population in the United States: March 1992* (September 1993): 1.
11. Bureau of the Census, "School Enrollments and Expenditures," *The Statistical Abstract of the United States: 1993*, table 232: 152.

12. Ibid, table 231, p. 152.
13. National Center for Education Statistics, *Historically Black Colleges and Universities 1976–90* (July 1992): vii.
14. Connie Leslie with Pat Wingert and Farai Chideya, "A Rich Legacy of Preference," *Newsweek* (6/24/91): 59.
15. The Committee on Policy for Racial Justice, *The Inclusive University* (Joint Center for Political and Economic Studies Press, 1993): 16–18.
16. Leonard A. Slade, Jr., "A School of Thought on Fighting Racism," *Emerge* (October 1993): 80.
17. David Reich, "The SAT Goes PC," *New York Times* (6/3/91).
18. FairTest, *FairTest Examiner* (Cambridge, MA, Spring 1993): 1–7; FairTest release "Is the SAT Biased?"; and The Chicago Urban League, "A Chicago Urban League Staff Report on 'A Scientist's Report on Race Differences' by Frank C. J. McGurk, Ph.D." (Chicago: 1956): 25.
19. Gary Libman, "Practical View: Multiple Choice for SAT Student," *Los Angeles Times* (9/9/93); and Judi Russell, "Prep Courses Can Boost Scores, for a Price," *Times-Picayune* (10/11/93).
20. *FairTest Examiner*, pp. 1–7.
21. The College Board, *College Bound Seniors: 1993 Profile of SAT and Achievement Test Takers* (Princeton, NJ: 1992).
22. *FairTest Examiner*, pp. 1–7.
23. Scott Jaschick, "Student Aid Changes Affect Blacks More, A UCLA Study Finds," *Chronicle of Higher Education Almanac* (September 5, 1990); cited in The Committee on Policy for Racial Justice, *The Inclusive University* (Joint Center for Political and Economic Studies Press, 1993): 23.
24. Mel Elfin, "Race on Campus," *U.S. News & World Report* (4/19/93): 52.
25. The Committee on Policy for Racial Justice, *The Inclusive University*, pp. 23–24.
26. Thomas G. Mortenson, "Report on Public Policy Analysis of Opportunity for Postsecondary Education," *Postsecondary Education Opportunity* (March 1993), cited in *The Inclusive University*, p. 4.
27. Henry Louis Gates, Jr., "African American Studies in the Twenty-first Century," *The Black Scholar*, vol. 22, no. 3.
28. National Research Council, *Summary Report 1992: Doctorate Recipients from United States Universities* (National Academy Press, 1993): 25–26.
29. Ibid.
30. Deborah Carter and Reginald Wilson, "Minorities in Higher Educa-

tion: Tenth Annual Status Report, 1991" (Washington, D.C.: American Council on Education, 1991): 23–24, 63.

31. The Committee on Policy for Racial Justice, *The Inclusive University* (Joint Center for Political and Economic Studies Press, 1993): 45.

32. National Research Council, *Summary Report 1992: Doctorate Recipients from United States Universities* (National Academy Press, 1993): 5 and 72.

33. Ibid.

34. Ibid.

35. Ibid, pp. 54–55.

36. Ibid, pp. 44–47.

37. Graglia, "Affirmative Discrimination," *The National Review.*

38. Dale Russakoff, "Penn Is Abandoning Speech Code," *Washington Post* (11/17/93).

39. *Washington Post*, "Fraternity Skit Ruled Constitutional" (5/12/93).

40. The Committee on Policy for Racial Justice, *The Inclusive University*, p. 42.

41. Ibid.

42. Mark Lorando, "One Show's Adventures in Political Incorrectness," *Times-Picayune* (12/24/93).

43. Arthur Schlesinger, Jr., *The Disuniting of America* (New York: Penguin, 1992).

44. Irving Kristol, "The Tragedy of Multiculturalism," *Wall Street Journal* (7/31/91).

45. PBS, transcript of "John McLaughlan's One on One," (July 6–7, 1991): 1 to 2–2.

46. *Wall Street Journal* editorial, "Restoring Liberal Education," (5/10/93).

47. Lerone Bennett, Jr., *Before the Mayflower: A History of Black America* (Johnson Publishing Company, 1986).

48. Michael Bérubé, "Public Image Limited," *Village Voice* (6/18/91): 31–38.

49. *The College Blue Book*, 23rd edition (New York: Macmillan, 1991): 434, 372–73, 605–610.

50. William H. Honan, "On 'New' Strife Over Core Studies and What History Teaches," *New York Times* (9/22/93).

51. Darlene Clark Hine, "The Black Studies Movement: Afrocentric-Traditionalist-Feminist Paradigms for the Next Stage," *The Black Scholar*, vol. 22, no. 3.

52. Richard Bernstein, "Judge Reinstates Jeffries as Head of Black Studies for City College," *New York Times* (8/5/93).

53. *Washington Post*, editorial without byline, "Pity His Students," (9/8/93).

54. Farai Chideya and Mark Starr, "Dashed Hopes at Harvard," *Newsweek* (5/14/90): 56; *New York Times*, "Yale's Black Studies Said to Founder" (12/11/89).

PART III

Money and Power

eight

Affirmative Action and Employment Discrimination

Compensating for past discrimination against some people can create fresh discrimination against others. When companies make extraordinary efforts to hire or promote minority workers, they may penalize white workers.

—From the *Business Week* cover story "Race in the Workplace: Is Affirmative Action Working?"[1]

WHEN an African-American succeeds—in being admitted to an Ivy League school, getting a prized job, or breaking through a corporate glass ceiling— "affirmative action" is the whispered put-down. This chapter addresses the myth that affirmative action gives a great and widespread advantage to African-Americans in education and employment, and explores the charges and countercharges of discrimination against blacks and "favoritism" for minorities.

One of my most poignant revelations concerning white resentment of affirmative action occured when I found out that one of my superiors at *Newsweek* had told more than one job applicant: "I would hire you in a second if you were black." (He states, "I don't recall" making those statements, though he adds that he believes black job seekers at *Newsweek* are given higher consideration than whites.) At the same time he made this statement only four reporters, one staff writer, and one editor out of 200-plus editorial employees at *Newsweek* were black. Of course, the job seekers had no idea that *Newsweek* had such a shoddy record concerning black hires. No doubt they left their interview with a sense of resentment toward the African-Americans they assumed had an unfair advantage over them. (After I left, *Newsweek* hired two new African-American reporter/writers.)

_____ Q & A: Affirmative Action

Q: *Doesn't affirmative action only benefit African-Americans?*

A: No. It doesn't even *primarily* benefit African-Americans. Although affirmative action is usually described in a racial context, the program covers groups—African-Americans, other racial and ethnic minorities, and women—who have experienced continuing patterns of discrimination. Since the push for affirmative action in the seventies, white women have made the most progress in becoming adequately represented in the workplace.

An examination of the discrimination claims filed with the Equal Employment Opportunity Commission (EEOC) shows that race-based claims (not all of which were filed by African-Americans) are just a fraction of the total. Here is a breakdown of the different types of claims filed in fiscal year 1993:[2]

Grounds for Claim	Number of Claims in 1993
Race	31,695
Gender	23,919
Age	19,884
Disability	15,230
Religion	14,490
National origin	7,454
Retaliation	12,627
Equal pay	1,334

Q: *Doesn't affirmative action promote "reverse discrimination," with unqualified blacks getting jobs ahead of qualified whites?*

A: No, but politicians ranging from President George Bush to Senator Jesse Helms have certainly manipulated white fears of losing jobs to black "quotas." Helms may have won reelection in 1991 expressly because of such fears. In a tight race against African-American politician Harvey Gantt, Helms ran a last-minute ad showing white hands holding job rejection slips. A voiceover said, "You needed that job, and you were the best qualified. But it had to go to a minority because of a racial quota." Helms won by a margin of only 4 percent.[3]

Part of the reason that politicians can incite panic with anti-affirmative action talk is that no one knows the program's exact scope. Many workplaces that claim to have affirmative action policies make little or no effort to recruit blacks and other minorities. Others that *don't* have stated affirmative action policies make a significant effort to hire and retain women and people of color.

It can be stated with certainty, however, that affirmative action is certainly not giving an overall workplace advantage to blacks. For example, a study discussed at greater length in the second half of this chapter found quite the opposite: twenty percent of the time, potential employers blocked black job hunters from advancing to the same interview or hiring level as whites with the exact same qualifications.[4]

During periods when American government and industry have taken affirmative action seriously, the program has proven effective in countering the prevailing bias against African-Americans. The black middle class has grown only during periods when a strong economy was complemented by affirmative action programs: one or the other simply isn't enough. In the 1950s, the economy was growing, but segregation and workplace bias kept the black middle class from growing. The 1960s brought both a strong economy and the beginnings of affirmative action: the black middle class nearly doubled. In the 1970s, there was a deep recession but affirmative action programs continued, and the black middle class stayed stable. And the 1980s brought economic growth again, but there was a backlash against affirmative action under President Ronald Reagan: the black middle class lost ground. In summary, African-Americans are the most vulnerable workers in bad economic times and don't prosper even during good times unless the government and private industry actively guard black workers' rights.[5]

Q: *Isn't affirmative action a remedy for "past discrimination?" When will it end? After all, African-Americans will always be able to talk about the past.*

A: Most critics of affirmative action make the easy argument that the discrimination of the past can't be atoned for forever. This argument obscures the fact that job discrimination is very much a *current* problem. The federal government defines affirmative action as ". . . action taken first to remedy patterns which show flagrant underutilization of minorities or women as a consequence of past discrimination perpetuated in present . . . systems, and secondly, to prevent future . . . discrimination which would prolong these patterns."[6] This description makes it clear that the program's focus is very much on the present.

As long as "past discrimination" is the sole standard, it will be easy for critics to portray affirmative action as unfairly penalizing whites, as opposed to correcting ongoing discrimination against blacks. An article titled "Affirmative Action: The Road to Serfdom" uses just this tactic. It offers several arguments in favor of affirmative action, then knocks them down. Tellingly, it does not mention current discrimination.[7] One *Wall Street Journal* op-ed says of an affirmative action program in Birmingham, Alabama: "One would think that more than a decade of active court supervision should have rectified the racist past or, at least, *absolved the city of responsibility* for the vestiges of racism." (Emphasis added.)[8] Does the desire for equal opportunity have a time limit? Apparently the author of the article thinks so.

The color of your skin—something which, of course, no one can choose—is a clear advantage or disadvantage in the workplace. It's no wonder that white Americans feel resentful of being stripped of this advantage. One analogy for the position of whites in affirmative action might be this: Tax time has come, and you mistakenly get an extra fifty dollars in your IRS refund. That same fifty dollars is mistakenly debited from someone else's check. It wasn't your fault the IRS gave you the money. Yet even if you didn't realize you'd benefitted from this, the federal government (if vigilant) would still make you give the money back. It's difficult to think about the issue of race in these terms, but in the American job market, being born white is still a clear and unearned advantage. And the value of skin color over a lifetime is far, far more than fifty dollars, as evidenced by the staggering racial homogeneity in the top jobs in American industry. For example, a 1991 survey by the consulting firm Korn/Ferry found that white males still control 95 percent of top corporate positions.[9]

Media Impact on the Public's Views of Affirmative Action

1. The media uses polarized anti-affirmative action rhetoric.

News organizations have been increasingly likely to use the terms "preference" or "racial preference" (popularized in anti-affirmative action speeches by, among others, President George Bush) when discussing affirmative action.

2. *The American public doesn't support polarized affirmative action rhetoric.*

In one poll, 70 percent supported the use of the term "affirmative action" while only 46 percent supported the term "racial preference program."[10]

3. *The media's choice of words has a deep impact on readers.*

One poll of young Americans first asked if they supported or opposed colleges and employers giving "special consideration" to minorities; they were then asked the same questions using the phrase "special preference." When pollsters used the second, politically negative term, the rate of whites who opposed affirmative action rose from 51 percent to 64 percent on education, and from 65 percent to 78 percent on jobs. Blacks were affected as well: just over 50 percent supported affirmative action, but they rejected it by a slight majority when it was called "special preference."[11]

4. *The press sometimes takes the comments of public figures out of context to make the speakers seem anti-affirmative action, even when they're not.*

For example, during a 1992 speech at Yale, Senator John Kerry called inner cities a "violent, drug-ridden, rat-infested reality ... ruled not simply by poverty, but by savagery," and said that civil rights should not focus solely on affirmative action. A March 1992 *New York Times* editorial which lauded the speech wasn't shy about whose interests it was representing. "[T]he economic future of the children of white America will increasingly depend on the talents of non-white Americans," it read. But the *Times* and other organizations reporting the speech didn't mention that Kerry supported affirmative action, calling it a program that has "made our country a better, fairer place to live."[12]

> Blacks and whites must face the fact that affirmative action has made no significant difference in the way whites look at blacks. . . . Before and since affirmative action, most white people see another white as competent until proved incompetent and a black person as incompetent until proved competent.
>
> —From a report by the Joint Center for Political and Economic Studies.[13]

_____ Employment Discrimination

Affirmative action was created, of course, to remedy employment discrimination. Thus any discussion of affirmative action would be incomplete without a discussion of the continuing workplace bias against African-American job seekers.

A comprehensive 1990 study by the Urban Institute found that black job applicants experience discrimination in one out of five searches. Researchers used "testers"—ten black and ten white male college students matched for their age, physical size, and qualities like the ability to speak articulately. The testers were coached on interview skills and memorized fictitious résumés which gave them equivalent educational and job backgrounds. The matched pairs then applied for 476 randomly selected, entry-level, private-company positions advertised in the *Washington Post* and the *Chicago Tribune*.

(Washington was picked because its job market was growing, Chicago because its wasn't.)

"In 20 percent of the cases a white applicant was able to submit an application when a black could not, the white received a formal application when a black did not, or the white was offered a job when the black was not," the research concluded. "[I]n a small share of cases, blacks were 'steered' by potential employers to less desirable positions than their white counterparts." In addition, the researchers found evidence of a "glass ceiling," stating, "Discrimination against blacks appears to be worse in jobs offering the highest wages and income potential.... The researchers concluded that the type of job for which a black applicant applies is the most important predictor of discrimination."[14]

The EEOC, which is supposed to investigate and prosecute discrimination claims, has a backlog of *70,000 cases.* The EEOC files less than 500 bias suits each year, but receives tens of thousands of new suits each year.[15]

In other cases, African-Americans simply find their workplaces are insensitive to minority issues. In September 1993, AT&T printed a cartoon in the employee magazine, *Focus,* which depicted a phone user on each continent of the globe—all human, except for Africa, which had a gorilla standing on it. Black AT&T employees were appalled. Even though chances are 99 to 1 that the illustrator does *not* think Africans are gorillas, it still betrays the widespread stereotype of Africa as a place where the "primitive" people have almost nothing in common with the Western world. The company apologized for the illustration.[16]

___Legal Decisions and Regulations

1. *The Supreme Court has made it increasingly difficult for black workers to challenge corporate bias (an expensive and daunting task to begin with).*

A 1989 Supreme Court decision overturned a previous ruling which said that companies, when challenged in discrimination suits, had to prove that hiring tests were actually related to job performance (i.e., you couldn't give a swim test for being a gas station attendant).[17]

2. *Victims of racial bias in the workplace can no longer win large monetary awards.*

In the 1970s, victims of racial bias could win large monetary awards. But that is no longer the case, and as a result, many people who want to file discrimination suits can't find lawyers who will take them on contingency—that is, for a percentage of the award (if they win) rather than a fee up front.

3. *A survey by the National Employment Lawyer's Association revealed that 44 percent of these lawyers rejected over 90 percent of the job discrimination cases potential clients brought to them.*

4. *The law is easier on age discrimination victims, who are usually white male executives.*

They can receive up to twice the amount of back pay they lost because of discrimination. In addition, these white execs are more "sympathetic" figures to judges and juries, and they often have the funds to pay up front for legal representation.[18]

There is hope for progress in eliminating employment discrimination if Americans remain vigilant, willing to punish discriminatory behavior, and open to constructive solutions. The Shoney's restaurant chain agreed to pay $132.5 million to settle a suit by black employees and job seekers who said they had been denied employment and promotion because of race.[19] The company's chief stockholder, Raymond L. Danner, resigned after being accused of making surprise visits to restaurants and reprimanding them if they had too many "niggers" working there.[20]

An Eye Toward the Future

Increasingly, business and civic leaders within the African-American community are looking at how African-Americans can find new and better niches within not just America's economy but the world economy as well. In July 1994, the head of the Urban League stated that the changing world economy, and not just racism, was responsible for the income gap between blacks and whites. Although racism is still a powerful factor in American life and our economy, he said, "[W]e must not let ourselves and, especially, our children fall into the paranoid trap of thinking that racism accounts for all that plagues us."[21] As America adjusts to a changing workplace that is increasingly oriented toward computer skills, temporary and freelance workers, and multinational corporations, black America is adjusting as well. Many of the same young adults who may find some employers prejudiced toward their race are also more likely to have come from economic backgrounds and attended the schools least likely to provide them with the survival skills, such as computer literacy and foreign language proficiency, best suited to the workplace of tomorrow. Whether this society will seize the opportunity to train young people of all races to compete in the world economy, and by extension foster equality between black and white Americans, remains to be seen.

Notes to Chapter Eight

1. Howard Gleckman, et al., "Race in the Workplace: Is Affirmative Action Working?" *Business Week* (7/8/91): 50–63.
2. Author's interview of Equal Employment Opportunity Commission information officer (1/27/93).
3. Priscilla Painton, "Quota Quagmire," *Time* (5/24/91).
4. Margary Austin Turner, Michael Fix, and Raymond J. Struyk, "Hiring Discrimination Against Young Black Men," *The Urban Institute Policy and Research Report* (Summer 1991): 4–5.
5. Andrew Billingsley, *Climbing Jacob's Ladder* (New York: Simon and Schuster, 1992): 139.
6. The Potomac Institute, *Affirmative Action: The Unrealized Goal* (Washington, D.C.: 1973): 1; cited in The Committee on Policy for Racial Justice, *The Inclusive University* (Joint Center for Political and Economic Studies Press, 1993): 15.
7. Steven Yates, "Affirmative Action: The New Road to Serfdom," in *The Freeman*, vol. 40, no. 12 (December 1990): 461–472.
8. Michael S. Greve, "The New Civil Rights Agenda," *Wall Street Journal* (9/8/93).
9. Sylvester Monroe, "Does Affirmative Action Help or Hurt?" *Time* (5/24/91).
10. Lionel McPherson, "Focus on Racism in the Media," *Extra!* (July/August 1992).
11. People for the American Way, *Democracy's Next Generation II: A Study of American Youth on Race*, (Washington, D.C.: People for the American Way, 1992).
12. Janine Jackson, "Press Finds 'New Candor' In Old Stereotypes," *Extra!* (July/August 1992).
13. The Committee on Policy for Racial Justice, *The Inclusive University* (Joint Center for Political and Economic Studies Press, 1993): 18.

14. Turner, Fix, and Struyk, "Hiring Discrimination Against Young Black Men."
15. Equal Employment Opportunity Commission press release, "EEOC Reports Job Bias Charges On Record Pace Through 3rd Quarter," (8/9/93).
16. Cindy Skrzycki, "AT&T Apologizes for Racist Illustration," *Washington Post* (9/17/93).
17. Terry Eastland, "George Bush's Quota Bill" *Policy Review* (Summer 1991): 45–49.
18. Steven A. Holmes, "Workers Find It Tough Going Filing Lawsuits Over Job Bias," *New York Times* (7/24/91).
19. National Association for the Advancement of Colored People press release, "NAACP and Flagstar Reach $1 Billion Historic Accord to Expand Opportunities for Minorities," (Baltimore, MD: 7/1/93).
20. Lynne Duke, "Cofounder of Shoney's Quits Following Racial Bias Suit," *Washington Post* (3/12/93).
21. Desda Moss, "Urban League Chief: Racism not only factor in economic disparities," *USA Today* (7/25/94).

Sixty Cents to the Dollar:

Black Employment Patterns and Wages

Per-capita black income (income of all working African-Americans divided by the total number of women, men, and children) was $9,170 in 1992, about 60 percent of the $15,510 for whites.

—U.S. Census Bureau[1]

F ROM the dawning days of this country's history, the intertwined phenomena of race and economics have helped define the African-American experience. African-Americans came to this country as economic chattel, and have been working to escape the lowest tiers of the American economic system ever since. The title of this chapter is derived from a bleak statistic about black earnings: the income of black families has rarely gone above sixty cents to the white dollar. Behind the statistics are people, African-Americans who must find ways to continue to support themselves and their families even as workplace bias constricts their opportunities to earn a living and advance their careers. If there is positive news, it is this: The vast majority of African-Americans are, in fact, participating in the pursuit of the American Dream, typical hard-working citizens. This chapter illustrates some aspects of that struggle particular to African-Americans.

When America has it tough, black America has it tougher.

The early 1990s brought a recession and declining job prospects for even well-educated Americans. And between 1977 and 1988, the average after-tax income of the richest one percent of Americans more than doubled, to over $400,000. At the same time, the middle class hung on for dear life and the poor got poorer. In fact, the total combined income of the top one percent—the 2.5 million richest Americans—was almost as big as that of the 100 million people at the bottom. Reagan-era changes in the tax code also meant that the richest one percent paid 18 percent less in taxes.[2]

A 1992 *New York Times* op-ed by Clayton Yeutter, President George Bush's counselor for domestic policy, tried to refute these figures, making no mention of the historic employment inequalities which face black Americans. "Our greatness as a nation arises from the fact that people rise and fall on the strength of their abilities," he said.[3] For the most part that is true. But one of the facts of race in America is that African-Americans face greater challenges in finding ways in which to develop and display those abilities.

Statistical Overview: Black Earnings and Occupations

1. Black families of every description earn significantly less than white families.

Median black family income in 1992 was $21,550, just 57 cents to the white dollar of $37,780.[4]

2. Black married couples where both spouses work are the closest to income equality with similar white families:

They earn 83 cents to the white dollar.

3. *Married couple families where only the husband works make 64 cents per white dollar,*[5]

and female-headed black families have sixty cents for every dollar of similar white families.

4. *A higher percentage of black married couples are two-earner families:*

68 percent of black wives work, versus 61 percent of white wives. In families with children under eighteen, 68 percent of black wives and only 50 percent of white wives work full-time.[6]

5. *Most black couples must both work in order to be in the American middle class.*

In fact, on average, a white husband alone earns only ten thousand dollars less than a black working wife and husband do combined.

The following tables show the average 1992 income for different types of families, and the proportion they make up of the total black and white populations:[7]

	Average Earnings	Number	Percentage*
All Black Families	$21,161	7.9 million	100%
Ones headed by:			
married couples	$34,196	3.7 million	47%
both work	$41,799	2.4 million	30%
husband works	$21,035	1.3 million	16%
female headed	$11,956	3.7 million	47%
male headed	$20,678	0.5 million	6%

*Percentages are rounded.

	Average Earnings	Number	Percentage
All White Families	$38,909	57.9 million	100%
Ones headed by:			
married couples	$42,738	47.6 million	82%
both work	$50,653	27.9 million	48%
husband works	$31,013	19.7 million	34%
female headed	$20,130	7.8 million	13%
male headed	$29,671	2.4 million	4%

Black family poverty is due in part to the fact that female-headed families earn less than married-couple families, and are proportionately much more of black America. (The median income for all American families was $36,812. For female-headed households, the average was just $17,221.)[8]

The income of black single-mother families has also dropped. The typical black female-headed family has changed, from mostly "married-but-separated" and "widowed" in 1970, to mostly "single" and "divorced" in 1987. For every dollar of median income a divorced woman had in 1987, a never-married woman had just fifty-nine cents.[9]

The recent tough economic times have been hard on all Americans, but particularly on African-Americans. While white and Hispanic incomes stayed steady, the income of black families fell 5 percent in 1992.[10] In 1993, the *Wall Street Journal* analyzed Equal Employment Opportunity Commission (EEOC) statistics from over 35,000 companies and found that African-Americans were the only racial group to lose jobs overall during the 1990–91 recession. At white-collar corporations like BankAmerica and ITT, blacks lost jobs at twice the white rate. Overall, blacks lost 15 percent of the total number of jobs that were cut at the 35,000 firms, but got only 11 percent of the total number of jobs added. African-Americans lost jobs in blue-collar occupations, which are shrinking, but also in the service sector, which is growing. Though blacks gained white-collar and managerial jobs, they're still underrepresented, and earn less than whites. Black managers and executives make only seventy-seven cents on the white dollar. Stated Carol Massey, the president of the Los Angeles Chapter of the National Black MBA Association, in the *Journal*'s article, "[R]ecession in America means depression in the black community."[11]

Economic hard times are hitting even college-educated Americans. According to Michigan State University's College Employment Research Institute, at least 35 percent of recent college graduates now take jobs that don't require a degree, up from 15 percent five years ago. The job market of the 1990s is the worst since World War II.[12]

A large minority of families, both black and white, don't include anyone earning a paycheck. Forty-two percent of black families and 26 percent of white ones have no employed members. (Of course, these totals include people such as retirees.) Only 52 percent of black families, versus 66 percent of white families, have at least one person employed full-time.[13] African-Americans are at least twice as likely to be unemployed as whites. In 1992 and 1993, the white unemployment rate was generally around 6 percent while the black rate was 13 to 14 percent. Twenty percent of whites and 22 percent of blacks have been unemployed for over half a year—and this does not include "discouraged" workers who have stopped looking altogether.[14]

In terms of *individual earnings*, black men earn significantly less than white men, but black and white women earn roughly the same salaries. However, these figures don't tell the whole story. More black women are single heads of household who must support an entire family alone, while white women are more likely to be married and have a husband with steady income. Following is a table of earnings by race and gender reflecting overall median earnings and the average for full-time, year-round workers. Whites are slightly more likely to have full-time, year-round work than blacks: 67 percent of white men, 52 percent of white women; 60 percent of black men, and 56 percent of black women have these steady jobs.[15]

	Median Earnings	For Full-time, Year-round[16]
Black Males	$15,490	$22,080
Black Females	$12,210	$18,720
White Males	$22,730	$30,270
White Females	$12,990	$20,790

The African-American workforce is majority-female by a thin margin (50.6 percent); women make up 44.7 percent of the white workforce.[17]

Job distribution. This table shows percentages by race and gender for employment in different categories of jobs. African-Americans are more likely to hold blue-collar and un-skilled jobs than whites, one of the reasons for lower overall black incomes.[18]

	Black M	Black F	White M	White F
Managerial and professional	14%	20%	27%	29%
Technical, sales, support	17%	38%	21%	45%
Service	19%	28%	9%	17%
Craft, production, repair	15%	2%	20%	2%
Operators, laborers	31%	12%	19%	7%
Farming, forestry, fishing	4%	0.3%	5%	1%

___ Q & A: African-American Income

Q: *If African-Americans are equally educated and qualified for a job, won't they earn the same income as whites?*

A: Unfortunately, African-Americans earn less on average than white Americans with the same qualifications. Black men who have finished college earn 80 percent of what their white counterparts do, while black men who have had some college earn 83 percent of what similar whites do. One case in point: black male attorneys between the ages of thirty-five and forty-five earn seventy-nine cents on the white male dollar.[19] And the jobless rate for black college graduates is over twice as high as the white rate—higher than the disparity between high school graduates.

Q: *How do black women fare in the workplace?*

A: Black female college graduates earn slightly (less than one percent) *more* than their white counterparts. This may be because more African-American women are the sole earners for their families, and thus must put an extremely high priority on advancing their careers. It may also be because many employers feel that black women are diversity "two-fers"— African-Americans *and* women—and thus may favor them over black men.[20]

Q: *How about black men?*

A: The situation for black men is far less promising. Black men overall earn sixty-one cents to the white male dollar; employed black men earn seventy-three cents to the white dollar. Although the earnings gap between black and white men shrank between 1930 and 1970, since then it has remained almost the same.[21]

Writes Andrew Hacker in *Two Nations,* "[E]ven when black men reach the same academic level as white men, their incomes stay several steps behind. . . . Hence, the advice so often offered to blacks, that they should stay in school, seems valid only insofar as it informs them that with additional education they will move ahead of others of their own race."[22]

Q: *Have African-Americans made inroads in corporate America?*

A: Certainly, *individual* African-Americans have. But overall, African-Americans are rare in the upper echelons of white-collar professions. A 1987 *National Law Journal* survey of the nation's 250 largest law firms found that fewer than 2 percent of lawyers and less than 1 percent of partners—a mere 157 of the nearly 20,000 partners total—were black. A 1988 survey by Public Advocates, Inc., a San Francisco–based public-interest law firm, showed that fewer than one quarter of one percent of partners in the nation's biggest accounting firms were black: thirty-seven out of 20,000. None of these thirty-seven African-American partners were in top jobs.[23]

_____ Q & A: The Working Poor

Q: *What does it mean to be working poor?*

A: A working-poor individual or family consists of one or more people who are employed, but still don't make a living wage as defined by the U.S. government's poverty line. For example, a full-time minimum wage worker earns $2,000 less than the poverty threshold for a family of three.

Q: *What percentage of African-Americans are working poor, versus whites?*

A: African-Americans are twice as likely to be working poor as white Americans: 15 percent of the black community work for below poverty-level wages, versus 6 percent of whites.[24] However, in sheer numbers, there are more white working-poor Americans.

Q: *Is there a difference in the way poor whites and poor blacks are characterized in the media?*

A: Unfortunately, yes. Poor blacks profiled in news reports are usually receiving government assistance, while poor whites are usually portrayed as working poor. For example, a front page article in the *Wall Street Journal* stated: "America's working poor are mostly white, mostly high-school educated, and disproportionately rural."[25] The article did not mention that proportionately more African-Americans are working poor, nor that, depending on whether the figures are broken down by Hispanic origin as well as race, whites make up either the majority or 38 percent of women on welfare. Though a racial comparison is never explicitly made, this article plays on a subtle tension between the implicit image of blacks on welfare and hard-working, poor whites.

Of course, individuals within the media sometimes take pains to discuss the prevailing assumptions about poor African-Americans. A perceptive column by David Broder in the *Washington Post* commented on the stereotype of blacks as lazy and reminisced about Jesse Jackson's speeches about the working poor during the 1988 campaign: "Most poor folks are not on welfare.... They clean the streets. They cut the grass. They rake the leaves. They work hard every day."[26]

Q: *It often seems as if inner-city African-Americans aren't even trying to find work anymore. Is this the case?*

A: Time and time again, African-Americans line up at the mere hint that there may be jobs. For example, in November 1993 in Detroit, over 10,000 unemployed people, most of them black, filled out applications for jobs at a proposed casino which probably will never open. The will is there; African-Americans as well as whites are looking for the way.[27]

_____Segregation and Jobs

Most African-Americans live in majority-black neighborhoods, which has a profound ramification on employment prospects. Segregation is one of the root causes of the cycle of urban decay and continuing black underemployment. Working-class African-Americans with blue-collar jobs formed, and still tend to form, the spine of black neighborhoods. As manufacturing jobs dry up, the neighborhood becomes less stable. Black communities are usually underserved by services like stores and banks, but as the neighborhood declines, new businesses become even less likely to locate there. The existing businesses in black neighborhoods suffer if the average income in black neighborhoods drops and also if businesses close and their employees are no longer around to make purchases. Finally, residents find it hard to commute to new jobs, which are disproportionately suburban.

The situation is very different for low-income white Americans, who are much more evenly spread among cities, suburbs, and rural areas. Although they are poor, they often don't live in "underclass" neighborhoods, which have low job opportunity and high levels of illegal activity.

Given the lack of opportunities in black neighborhoods, black workers often have to travel long distances to find work. Predictably, the business community chooses to address the problems of residential segregation only when they need more low-wage workers. In Philadelphia, suburban businesses looking for cheap labor have turned to running a special bus for inner-city workers. For example, a black husband and father profiled in a *Wall Street Journal* article takes a commuter train at 6 A.M., gets to a suburban office park ten miles away from his job, then has to take a special bus, which costs fifty cents, to his final destination.

The article enthusiastically endorses this as a solution to urban joblessness, stating: "Giving people a chance to 'reverse commute' to the suburbs is cheaper and quicker than trying to lure businesses into downtown neighborhoods, or attempting to transplant large numbers of inner-city residents to suburban housing." Although this is certainly one part of the answer, transportation alone will not provide long-term opportunity for inner-city blacks.

One expert cited in the story, Mark Alan Hughes, did a study for the Urban Institute which found that from 1976 to 1986, two-thirds of job growth in America's largest metropolitan areas occurred outside the central city. Said Hughes, "In many ways this is less threatening than school bussing or forced integration. It leaves the decision as to where to live up to the household." Unfortunately, the issue isn't so simple as choice, since many potential black home owners (who are heavily steered to black neighborhoods through discriminatory housing practices) don't have one.[28] Writes Andrew Hacker in *Two Nations*, "[A] real obstacle to workforce equity stems from the difficulties blacks have in finding housing in areas where jobs open up."[29]

Employers can be quite ruthless in seeking out the "whitest" areas in which to create new jobs. Toyota located an assembly plant in Harlan County, Kentucky, which is 95 percent white; Honda located its plant in an area of rural Ohio which is 97 percent white.[30] Other employers are closing the businesses they do have in black areas. In 1993, Stride-Rite Shoes, a corporation well known for the minority scholarships they offer, moved their headquarters to a white area from Roxbury, an inner-city Boston neighborhood where unemployment is estimated to be 70 percent.[31] Finally, sometimes entire cities progress while leaving blacks behind. Milwaukee pulled out of a recession by cutting back on manufacturing and expanding the service and hotel jobs. But while these changes helped the city as a whole, the plan devastated black neighborhoods which relied on blue-collar jobs. Milwaukee's black unemployment rate is 20 percent, five times as high as whites'. According to a University of Chicago study, Milwaukee is also one of the nation's five most segregated cities.[32]

_____ **Black-Owned Businesses**

Although African-Americans are less likely than whites to be self-employed (7 percent of white men versus 3 percent of black men),[33] it is far from true that African-Americans are not entrepreneurial.

1. The largest black-owned firm is TLC Beatrice International Holdings, which has 1.6 billion dollars in sales per year. Businessman Reginald Lewis's TLC group bought out the Beatrice food products company in 1987 and brought up profits in the huge corporation. Lewis died of brain cancer in 1993, but his family retains control of the company.[34]

2. The second largest black business is Johnson Publishing Company, with over a quarter of a billion dollars in receipts each year. The company was created from the ground up by John Johnson, who founded and edits *Ebony* magazine, among many ventures.

3. Other prominent black-owned businesses include Park's Sausages, McCall's Patterns, and BET Holdings, Inc., which owns the Black Entertainment Television cable station.[35]

4. Blacks are also moving into very non-traditional business areas as well. In 1993, Milestone Media, a black-owned comic book company, began publishing several titles to strong popular demand.[36]

5. However, despite these successes listed, it is extremely difficult for future black entrepreneurs to get the funding they need. A study by University of Vermont economist Timothy Bates found that African-Americans are less likely to get commercial loans than whites, and the ones who do get loans on average 40 percent lower than for comparable white borrowers.[37]

6. A major source of seed money for African-American businesses is settlements from discrimination suits against former employers. For example, Anita L. Holt won $415,000 from Life Care Services Corp. when, while applying for a promotion in 1990, a senior vice-president told her he wouldn't

review her application because putting a black in an administrative position was too great a "business risk." Holt had received glowing evaluations and had a master's degree in public health. She now co-owns a retirement-care consulting firm.[38]

Military Service

The military has a historical role in black achievement: by one estimate, a quarter of black middle-class families owe their status directly or indirectly to the military.[39]

Today, African-Americans make up a disproportionately high percentage of America's armed forces. Black women total 29 percent of all women in the armed forces (army, navy, air force, marines). Black men total a slightly smaller proportion of all men in the armed forces, but constitute well over 30 percent of all men in the army.[40]

The fact that African-Americans are disproportionately likely to serve in the military does not result in positive characterizations as patriotic. Instead of non-blacks seeing African-Americans as more willing to serve their country, one study found that 51 percent thought blacks were less patriotic.[41]

The African-American community sends some of its best citizens to the U.S. armed forces. A 1982 Brookings Institution study found that 42 percent of eligible African-Americans entered the armed forces, as compared with 14 percent of eligible whites. African-Americans are more likely to reenlist, and are less likely to be discharged for undisciplined behavior. Another indication of the prime black talent pool which enters the military is that black veterans earn more in the civilian workforce than non-veterans; the reverse is true for whites.[42]

Q & A: African-Americans
in the Military

Q: *Why do so many African-Americans join the military?*

A: Many African-Americans find greater opportunities in the armed forces than in the private sector. The armed forces require basic instruction in race relations and black history; evaluations include a category for race-relations skills.[43] This means that African-Americans are insured a modicum of fairness when it comes to their employment and prospects for advancement. Today, however, the military is being downsized under President Clinton, potentially cutting back this traditional avenue for African-American employment. The vast majority of African-Americans support military downsizing if it increases the funds spent on domestic problems.[44]

Q: *Is the military an oasis of racial equality?*

A: Not completely. African-Americans make up nearly a third of armed forces enlistees but only about ten percent of officers. African-Americans are 5.6 percent of marine officers, 4.7 percent of naval officers, 5.6 percent of air force officers, and 11 percent of army officers. In addition, the Department of Defense's analysis of 1993 officer selections stated that "minorities, and particularly blacks, appear less likely to get promoted from captain to major than are whites."[45]

Q: *How have military officials reacted to the disproportionately low numbers of African-American military officers?*

A: Some officials have become defensive rather than offering constructive solutions. In late 1993, General Carl Mundy, the commandant of the marine corps, stated on the television program "60 Minutes": "[I]n the military skills, we find that the minority officers... don't do as well."[46] In fact, the only evidence to support his statement was a study which tested 1,000 whites and only 85 African-Americans in nineteen categories of military skills. Although African-Americans scored slightly lower in seventeen of nineteen categories, statisticians proclaimed the gaps between the scores so low as to be insignificant.[47]

Q: *Have African-Americans reached the top ranks of the U.S. military?*

A: Yes, many have. Over 100 African-Americans have been made generals. The most high-profile black officer in recent years is Colin Powell, who was made Chairman of the Joint Chiefs of Staff by President Bush and also served under President Clinton.[48]

Organizations Looking
to the Future

There are several institutions and organizations trying to raise black entrepreneurship. With a grant from the Dow Jones & Company, historically black Clark Atlanta University has started a Center for Entrepreneurship that will supplement its MBA program, and hopefully help future African-American business owners realize their dreams.[49] And the nonprofit Women's Self Employment Project lends money to low-income women with business plans. With loans averaging less than two thousand dollars, they have helped fund businesses like a full-service trucking company, which was created by a former welfare recipient. If there is a brighter economic future in store for the African-American community, it may be because of the combined efforts of individuals and institutions to foster black business leadership as well as overall employment.

Notes to Chapter Nine

1. The Bureau of the Census: Claudette E. Bennett, *The Black Population in the United States: March 1992* (September 1993): 10.
2. Isaac Shapiro and Robert Greenstein, "Selective Prosperity: Increasing Income Disparities Since 1977," (Washington, D.C.: The Center on Budget and Policy Priorities, July 1991).
3. Clayton Yeutter, "When 'Fairness' Isn't Fair," *New York Times* (3/24/92).
4. The Bureau of the Census: Claudette E. Bennett, *The Black Population in the United States: March 1992* (September 1993): 10.
5. Ibid, pp. 12–14.
6. U.S. Department of Labor, *Employment and Earnings* (October 1993): 70.
7. U.S. Department of Commerce, *Money Income of Households, Families, and Persons in the United States: 1992* (October 1993).
8. Ibid, p. xi.
9. The Bureau of the Census, *The Black Population in the United States: March 1992*, pp. 12–14.
10. U.S. Department of Commerce, *Money Income of Households, Families, and Persons in the United States: 1992* (October 1993): xi.
11. Rochelle Sharpe, "In Latest Recession, Only Blacks Suffered Net Employment Loss," *Wall Street Journal* (9/14/93); and The Bureau of the Census, *The Black Population in the United States: March 1992*, p. 2.
12. Julie Amparano Lopez, "College Class of '93 Learns Hard Lesson: Career Prospects Are Worst in Decades," *Wall Street Journal* (5/20/93).
13. U.S. Department of Labor, *Employment and Earnings*, p. 68.
14. Ibid, p. 66.
15. U.S. Department of Commerce, *Money Income of Households, Families, and Persons in the United States: 1992*, pp. 12–14.
16. Ibid.
17. Andrew Hacker, *Two Nations Black and White, Separate, Hostile, Unequal* (New York: Scribners, 1992): 115.
18. The Bureau of the Census, *The Black Population in the United States: March 1992*, p. 10.

19. Hacker, *Two Nations*.
20. Ibid.
21. Ibid.
22. Ibid, p. 96.
23. Walter L. Updegrave, "Race and Money," *Money* (December 1989): 152–172.
24. The Bureau of the Census, *The Black Population in the United States: March 1992*, p. 2.
25. Tony Horwitz, "Minimum-Wage Jobs Give Many Americans Only A Miserable Life," *Wall Street Journal* (11/2/93).
26. David S. Broder, "Now the 'Character Question' Has Been Written in Fire," *Washington Post* (5/5/92).
27. James Bennett, "Mere Hint of Jobs Draws Crowds in Detroit," *New York Times* (11/12/93).
28. Rick Wartzman, "Good Connections: New Bus Lines Link the Inner-City Poor with Jobs in Suburbia," *Wall Street Journal* (9/24/93).
29. Hacker, *Two Nations*.
30. Ibid.
31. Joseph Pereira, "Social Responsibility And Need for Low Cost Clash at Stride Rite," *Wall Street Journal* (5/28/93).
32. Isabel Wilkerson, "How Milwaukee Has Thrived While Leaving Blacks Behind" *New York Times* (3/19/91).
33. Hacker, *Two Nations*, pp. 100–116.
34. Richard Ringer, "Shareholders Hail Changes at Beatrice," *New York Times* (1/7/94).
35. Andrew Billingsley, *Climbing Jacob's Ladder* (New York: Simon and Schuster, 1993): 293.
36. *New York Times* editorial, "WHOOSH! New Superheroes Liberate the Old-Boy Network," (8/4/93).
37. Updegrave, "Race and Money."
38. Michele L. Norris, "Retirement Firm Settles Racial Discrimination Suit," *Washington Post* (3/24/93).
39. Billingsley, *Climbing Jacob's Ladder*, pp. 193–200.
40. Ibid.
41. Tom W. Smith, *Ethnic Images*, (National Opinion Research Center: University of Chicago, December 1990).
42. Billingsley, *Climbing Jacob's Ladder*, pp. 193–200.
43. Ibid.
44. E. J. Dionne, "In Poll, Blacks Defy Political Stereotyping," *Washington Post* (7/9/92).
45. John Lancaster and Barton Gellman, "Marines: Racial Figures Back Mundy; Validity Disputed," *Washington Post* (11/16/93).

46. Howard Kurtz, "The Shot Not Heard Round the World," *Washington Post* (11/12/93).
47. Lancaster and Gellman, "Marines: Racial Figures Back Mundy; Validity Disputed."
48. Billingsley, *Climbing Jacob's Ladder*, pp. 193–200.
49. Joint Center for Political and Economic Studies, "Creating a Black Wealth-Producing Class," *Focus*, vol. 21, no. 1 (Washington, D.C.: January 1993).

ten

Saving and Spending

Timberland is being adopted by a consumer [i.e., blacks and other "urban youth"] that we didn't know existed relative to our target audience. . . . [of] honest working people.

> —Jeffrey Swartz, executive vice-president of hiking boot manufacturer Timberland. Timberland boots had become popular with African-Americans—a fact which apparently made the company uncomfortable.[1]

IT'S a uniquely galling situation: African-Americans are sometimes shunned by the very companies that profit most from black consumers. Companies ranging from Timberland to Denny's restaurants, heavily patronized by African-Americans, have sought to distance themselves from the black community, sometimes being merely insensitive, occasionally being outright discriminatory. In addition, African-Americans face a higher cost of living than whites, due in large part to residential segregation. Insurance costs more in black neighborhoods; suburban grocery stores are often better and cheaper, meaning residents of black neighborhoods either pay more in transportation or turn to expensive corner stores; even necessities like bank branches are few and far between, meaning many African-Americans turn to check-cashing services instead.

The Perils of Spending:
_____ Race and the Black Consumer

When the executive vice president of Timberland made the comment on page 133, the company had just shown the highest quarterly revenues in its twenty-year history. Despite the fact that black, urban consumers helped push the corporation to new heights, it's obvious that Timberland wants no part of being associated with black consumers. The *New York Times* article quoted Julia Chance, fashion editor for hip hop magazine *The Source:* "I think that they think that if their clothes are celebrated in the black, urban community, with all its ills, that it will cheapen their brand names."[2] The next month, the *Times* published a reader's letter in response to Timberland's statement. "I am an African-American woman 64 years of age," the letter from Violet E. Gill read. ". . . . Mr. Swartz described Timberland's primary consumers as 'honest working people' . . . . I would like Mr. Swartz to know that the majority of the African-Americans in the inner city are 'honest working people.' Wake up, Timberland. If you don't want our money, some other establishment will gladly accept it."[3]

In the 1950s, African-American students began staging sit-ins at lunch counters in order to gain the right to equal service. But even today, some establishments have still not met that benchmark. In 1993, African-Americans filed a series of lawsuits against the Denny's restaurant chain. In March of that year, several black customers in San Jose, California, filed suit against Denny's, alleging they were made to pay a cover charge and prepay for food while whites were not. In April, the chain agreed to a federal consent decree saying they would reinforce their equality policies. But the very next month, six black secret service agents filed suit because they went without food and service at an Annapolis restaurant while agents at the next table, all white except one, were served. The restaurant's manager was fired. (The simple fact that all but one of the black agents were eating together, and all of the whites were doing the same, indicates the ongoing role race plays in America.)[4]

The Financial Health of
_____ Black Households

On average, African-Americans have only one-tenth the net worth (savings and assets minus debts) that white Americans do. Even middle-class black families had a net worth only one-third that of comparable white households: (approximately $18,000 for the black families versus $55,000 for the white ones). Net worth reflects not only earnings, but family savings accumulated over time. This wealth has a profound effect on middle-class milestones like attending college and buying a first home. White Americans are more likely to have wealth to pass from one generation to the next. The lack of inherited income is compounded by the fact that African-Americans earn less than whites with comparable résumés and are more conservative in investing the money they do have (in, say, bonds versus stocks, which ultimately brings a lower return).[5]

It takes money to make money. The assets of wealthy families often provide a primary source of income, with commercial real estate, stock, and businesses providing job opportunities and dividends. All of this adds up to a cluster of wealth at the top of American society. In 1989, the one percent of American families who earned the most in yearly income owned 37 percent of the country's wealth. The ten percent of families earning the most owned nearly 70 percent of America's wealth. The top one percent of Americans alone owned nearly 50 percent of publicly held stock, 45 percent of commercial real estate, and 62 percent of business assets.[6]

The gap in black/white net worth is in part due to slavery,

in some families, up to a twelve-generation period during which most black families labored without earning (and certainly without saving) any income. African-Americans have been free (130 years) only half as long as they were enslaved. And, said an article in *Essence*, "We [African-Americans] also tend as a people to invest in the trappings of success—clothes, expensive cars, electronic equipment, household gadgets, fine liquor—rather than the substance of success. This is due largely to a history of deprivation that has resulted in our needing to make a visible statement about economic success once we achieve it."[7]

Black middle-class families are far more financially vulnerable than comparable white ones. The assets like homes and cars that African-Americans have are financed by more debt. Wealth in the black community is more dependent on high educational achievement than it is for whites, since African-Americans earn less at every educational level, yet the percentage of blacks getting graduate and professional degrees has been declining. This trend means that the next generation of African-Americans may be even worse off in relation to whites.[8]

Most Americans count their home as their most valuable possession, but segregation means that African-Americans build less home equity. Because overwhelmingly whites will not move into black neighborhoods (and will move out of neighborhoods that are getting "too" black), black sellers have fewer potential buyers for their houses. Black home buyers can't count on getting a big return on their housing investment. Looking at black and white neighborhoods with similar socioeconomic profiles illustrates how little wealth blacks accrue from buying a home. For example, over the five years from 1984 to 1989, the 90 percent black Brookland/Catholic University neighborhood in Washington, D.C., appreciated only 8 percent—from an average of $83,300 to $90,200. Dupont Circle, an 83 percent white Washington neighborhood, went from $58,000 to $115,600—99 percent appreciation. In Atlanta, the 97 percent black neighborhood Ben Hill appreciated 46 percent; North Highland, which is 93 percent white, appreciated 67 percent. The home equity that builds up in homes in white neighborhoods provides more money for college and retirement and contributes to how well the neighborhood is kept up, since owners can make repairs with money from home equity loans.[9]

Low appreciation rates in black neighborhoods are not the only problem. Home and car insurance rates are higher in black neighborhoods. For example, residents of overwhelmingly black Detroit pay about 50 to 70 percent more than residents of the mostly white suburbs of the city. There are not as many shops and supermarkets in central cities, and prices are usually higher. Ironically, suburban supermarkets often have the lowest prices on staple goods like laundry detergent and basic foods, although the residents have more income.[10]

Bank Access and African-Americans

The conservative *National Review* published a 1993 article subtitled: "Are bankers letting racism interfere with profits? Now that *would* be news." It derides the story of a woman on welfare, who pays a check-cashing store six dollars to cash two benefits checks. "In fact, this is the market at work," the story reads. "Check-cashing firms can make a profit from people like this, whereas a bank branch could not. Or is the woman supposed to get a mortgage?"[11]

Banks can *make money off of providing service to poor Americans—not only that, they're mandated by law to do so.* Banks, which are insured by the federal government, are required by law to provide service in poor and minority neighborhoods. But the law doesn't have any direct requirements or penalties, so banks almost never get punished for underserving minority neighborhoods.

African-Americans have poor access to banks and financial services, which costs black families time and money. The *Washington Post* did a computer analysis which showed that white neighborhoods have three times as many bank branches per person as black ones. The Anacostia section of the District of Columbia, which is an overwhelmingly low-income, black area of 70,000 people, has only two bank branches. In the mostly white Chevy Chase area, by contrast, there are eight banks along a single one-mile stretch. But this type of discrimination doesn't necessarily follow financial logic. The most profitable of 26 branches of one local bank, American Security, is in an underserved black community. In fact, that branch made more home equity loans than any other. Residents in areas where there are too few bank branches have to go to expensive check-cashing services. Most check-cashing services charge two to three dollars per check (as compared to, say, fifty cents or free depending on the type of bank account).[12] However, some check-cashing services are practically loan sharks, taking a huge fee in exchange for not depositing a customer's check for two weeks. In 1993, one Virginia company of that type charged $28 for a $100 cash advance. The real pitfall is late fees: one customer paid over $800 for a $200 advance that was two months late.[13]

Race, not income, is the problem. Prince George's County, which has a large and affluent black suburban population, has fewer bank branches per resident than any other D.C. suburb. One underserved neighborhood in the county has an average household income of $67,000. Overall, two-thirds of D.C.–area African-Americans versus 26 percent of whites have poor bank access. In addition, banks in black neighborhoods tend to be in worse physical shape and give worse service. The *Washington Post* asked the head of Signet Bank why the branches in white neighborhoods were so much nicer. He replied: "People in those neighborhoods [black neighborhoods] wouldn't go into a plush office. That's an intimidating environment."[14]

Despite the sometimes condescending or discriminatory attitudes of banks and lenders, African-American families continue to do their best to build nest eggs for the future. In fact, the net worth of the black middle class alone totals well over 40 billion dollars. That is the success story behind the strivings of the African-American family. Unfortunately, the best efforts of most African-Americans to build on their lifetimes in the workplace don't usually bring them the same financial security that other Americans obtain.

Notes to Chapter Ten

1. Michel Marriott, "Out of the Woods," *New York Times* (11/7/93).
2. Ibid.
3. Violet E. Gill, "Letters to the Editor; Timberland Message," *New York Times* (12/5/93).
4. Chuck Hawkins, "Denny's: The Stain That Isn't Coming Out," *Business Week* (6/28/93).
5. Walter L. Updegrave, "Race and Money," *Money* (December 1989): 152–172.
6. Sylvia Nasar, "Fed Gives New Evidence of Eighties Gain by Richest," *New York Times* (4/21/92).
7. Audrey Edwards, "The Black-White Money Gap," *Essence* (April 1993).
8. William D. Bradford, "Wealth, Assets, and Income of Black Households," (College Park, MD: Department of Finance, University of Maryland College Park, September 1990).
9. Updegrave, "Race and Money."
10. Ibid.
11. Llewellyn H. Rockwell, Jr., "Discreditable Reports," *National Review* (7/19/93): 45–48.
12. Liz Spayd and Joel Glenn Brenner, "Area Blacks Have Worst Bank Access," *Washington Post* (6/7/93).
13. Steve Bates, "Virginia Suing Firms with Fast Money," *Washington Post* (7/6/93).
14. Spayd and Brenner, "Area Blacks Have Worst Bank Access."

Culture Clash:

African-Americans
in the Arts

Is it accidental that rap has erupted precisely at an historical moment when African-American unemployment is massive, when crack has become a crippling epidemic, and as prisons and the criminal justice system have become a means for the institutional regulation of hundreds of thousands of black people?

—From an article in *The Black Scholar,* responding to
the disproportionate criticism of rap music.[1]

THE arts, like sports, are an area in which white America regularly recognizes the contributions of African-Americans. But, just as with athletics, there is often a catch. Although African-Americans have been stereotyped as natural singers, dancers, and entertainers, they too-often have been out in front as talent but kept from full control over what they produce.

Critics, white and sometimes black, have also painted black entertainment as debased and immoral. In this context, rap music is the most misunderstood and besieged black art form, demonized by countless articles as the symbol of urban "pathology." This chapter explores the culture clash between black artists and the mostly white power structure, in genres ranging from rap to visual art.

African-Americans in Film and Television

Although the late 1980s and early 1990s brought a resurgence of black cinema, the film and television industry is still very difficult for African-Americans to break into. Part of the problem is that the industry is small and exceedingly reliant on in-house reputation and word of mouth. But the statistics on minority employment are often grim. Or as Spike Lee put it: "You really get the feeling that white people think [blacks] got sports, they got music. So they say, 'You got that but you can't have the film business, too. We got that, Jack!' "[2]

A report by the Writer's Guild of America (WGA), the professional organization of film and television writers, shows just how few minority television and film writers there are. In 1993, only 4.4 percent of the writers at the major TV studios were blacks or other minorities. In film, black writers make up only 2.6 percent of the total—a mere 39 individuals. Minority writers are also typecast. The vast majority work on sitcoms, specifically black sitcoms, which limits their potential for advancement. And, predictably, minority writers earn less than white ones: working minority writers earned 79 cents for every dollar earned by white males. In addition, because of the seasonal nature of film and TV work, the majority of WGA members are not even employed during a given year.[3]

At the same time there is bias, there are a significant number of African-Americans making contributions in the film and television industry. Here is a sample of some of the African-Americans who are power players in today's film and television industry:

- Actors Denzel Washington, Whoopi Goldberg, Laurence Fishburne, Angela Bassett, Eddie Murphy, Wesley Snipes, Danny Glover, Morgan Freeman, Mario Van Peebles, Forest Whitaker, Debbie Allen, Lonnette McKee.

- Film directors Spike Lee *(Do the Right Thing, Malcolm X)*, John Singleton *(Boyz N the Hood, Poetic Justice)*, Julie Dash *(Daughters of the Dust)*, Mario Van Peebles *(New Jack City, Posse)*, Robert Townsend *(Hollywood Shuffle, Meteor Man)*, Joseph Vasquez *(Hangin' with the Homeboys)*, Matty Rich *(Straight Out of Brooklyn)*, Bill Duke *(A Rage in Harlem)*, Albert and Allen Hughes *(Menace II Society);* television director Thomas Carter *(Equal Justice).*

- Film executives Stephanie Allain at Columbia and Cheryl Hill at Hollywood Pictures. Television executives Karen Barnes, Fox vice president of children's programming, Kim Fleary, ABC vice president of comedy development, Richard Hull, ABC director of dramatic programming, and Jennifer Lawson, executive vice president for national programming at PBS.

- Producers Quincy Jones *(The Color Purple,* "The Fresh Prince of Bel Air"), Keenan Ivory Wayans ("In Living Color"), and Suzanne Des Passes ("Lonesome Dove").

- And in a category by themselves are actor/producer/director/hosts Bill Cosby and Oprah Winfrey. Cosby has acted in, directed, and executive-produced "The Cosby Show" and "The Cosby Murder Mysteries" among others, and hosted the game show "You Bet Your Life." Oprah Winfrey hosts and produces her eponymous talk show, and has drawn large salaries for her acting work, half a million dollars just for her appearance in the television movie "There Are No Children Here." Winfrey donated her entire earnings from the movie to charity.[4]

Five Key Issues:
African-Americans in Film
and Television

African-Americans disappear from "black" movies. In several notable instances, movies about "black" events in American and international history have been told through the eyes of white characters. Not only does the retelling distort the historical accuracy, it makes blacks seem passive and powerless in the face of racism and whites seem omnipotent. The film *Glory*, starring Denzel Washington, highlighted the role of a white commander played by Matthew Broderick in the story of a black army regiment in the Civil War. *Mississippi Burning* cast Gene Hackman and Willem Dafoe in the center of a movie about the civil rights movement. And *Cry Freedom* cast Kevin Kline in the central role of a film about slain South African activist Stephen Biko (also played by Denzel Washington). In a 1989 article, Denzel Washington criticized *Mississippi Burning*, stating the film " 'is not our history. There were not two white FBI men who came in and made everything better.' . . . Yet," the article continued, "he acknowledges that *Cry Freedom* can be criticized on the same grounds as *Mississippi Burning*—that is, telling a black story through white characters." Blacks aren't the only ones hurt by Hollywood stereotyping, of course; Willem Dafoe's key role in the Vietnam movie *Platoon* was written for an Apache.[5]

Black films are labeled controversial, and have trouble being released. Many black films have had trouble being distributed to theaters because of the fear of violence. Universal City's theater complex put an opening weekend ban on John Singleton's *Poetic Justice* and Mario Van Peebles's *Posse*.[6] Rappers Ice-T and Ice Cube starred in *New Jack City* and

Boyz N the Hood respectively. Spike Lee's *Do the Right Thing* had a hip-hop sensibility—no doubt a key point in the troubles it ran into.[7]

Lee's *Do the Right Thing* may be the best example of media paranoia over black films. In a June 26, 1989 column for *New York* magazine, columnist Joe Klein raised the specter of violence—and then hung a weight of responsibility on the neck of then-mayoral candidate David Dinkins. "If Lee does hook large black audiences ... [and] they react violently—which can't be ruled out—the candidate with the most to lose will be David Dinkins."[8] There was no violence as a result of the film, a fact that doubtless disappointed some media observers.

Some reporters also criticized *Do the Right Thing* for not containing enough black "pathology." A *Village Voice* article claims a white reporter for *USA Today* attending the press conference for the showing of *Do the Right Thing* at the Cannes Film Festival criticized the movie as "too clean, there's no garbage, no drugs, where's the rape, where's the crack?"[9]

"Atypical" black films have trouble being marketed, which often hurts black women filmmakers. As of January 1994, only three African-American women had seen their films released nationally. Julie Dash was first, with her hauntingly beautiful tale of the disappearing culture of the Gullah Islands, *Daughters of the Dust.* Ruby Oliver's film *Love Your Mama* made it to the big screen because the director, who runs a chain of day-care centers, invested $1.2 million of her own money in her film. Leslie Harris *(Just Another Girl on the IRT)* saved, begged, and borrowed $130,000 to complete her film and then convinced Miramax to market it to the tune of half a million dollars. Harris won the special award for first-time filmmaker at the prestigious Sundance Film Festival. Dash had to scour the industry before she found anyone willing to distribute her film. When Kino International circulated just thirteen prints (typical features have *1,500* prints

in circulation), the film took in $1.8 million. Although Dash has won several awards, she still does not have a deal for a second picture.

The black female director who has had the most success in the industry is not American. Euzhan Palcy, from Martinique, directed the film *A Dry White Season*. In contrast to the situation of black women, in 1991 and 1992, nearly thirty films directed by black males were released.[10] In 1994, director Darnell Martin became the first African-American woman to direct a feature film for a major studio. *I Like It Like That* was released in October by Columbia Pictures.

On television, African-Americans are relegated to the "sitcom ghetto." Nearly all of the portrayals of blacks on television are comic, and the inability of sitcoms to adequately represent the black experience sometimes becomes painfully clear. The Fox sitcom "True Colors," about a black husband and white wife and their children from previous marriages, addressed the legacy of Malcolm X in one episode. Said a review: "The younger son, Lester (Adam Jeffries), feeling neglected by the family, suddenly withdrew to read *The Autobiography of Malcolm X*. In no time at all, Lester was badmouthing racially mixed marriages, calling his brother a clown in blackface and his sister a bleeding-heart liberal. But also in no time at all, Lester realized the error of his ways, especially after missing his own birthday party. Cake and ice cream, evidently, beat Malcolm X any day—on a television sitcom."[11]

African-Americans aren't shown in the course of typical television movies on subjects like divorce and medical drama. The ideas presented by black producers and directors often get turned down by studios. Actor Tim Reid proposed the true story of a single black man in Columbus, Ohio, who adopted thirty-six children. "They looked at me and said, 'What's the story?'" Reid recalls of his pitch.[12]

Finally, the lack of adequate representation on-screen is particularly harmful given the fact that African-Americans watch significantly more television on average than whites.

An analysis of November 1990 viewing patterns by Nielsen Media Research found that African-Americans watched 70 hours of television per week, almost 50 percent more than "all other" households. Black children (2 to 17) watched fully 64 percent more television than children of other races.

Current Black Popular Music: Focus on the Top Five Myths About Rap

Although black artists regularly hit the peaks of the Top 40 charts today, the path of black pop music to mainstream acceptance has been difficult. Initially, the pop- and rock-music press ignored black artists. Between 1978 and 1982, *Rolling Stone* featured only one black musician, Donna Summer, on its cover. When the magazine later ran a cover on Prince, publisher Jan Wenner said: "My circulation department certainly wasn't asking me to put Prince on the cover. They know the issue of color works against [all artists of color, including Prince]. It's a fact of life that the stars of 'The Jeffersons' aren't going to sell as well as Tom Selleck." MTV (the cable channel Music Television) also began by excluding blacks. In 1983, for example, only sixteen of the 800 bands on the current video playlist were black.[13]

At the same time as this media white-out, rap music was beginning to grow. In 1979 the group Sugarhill Gang recorded the seminal "Rapper's Delight." Two other ground-breaking songs, "The Message" by Grandmaster Flash and the Furious Five and "Planet Rock" by Afrika Bambaataa, were recorded in 1982. By 1984, America had its first gold rap album: Run-DMC's self-titled debut. Public Enemy, with its samples of black leaders like Martin Luther King, Jr., and Malcolm X, hit new heights of popularity with its blending of music and black consciousness. Today rap music is in heavy rotation on MTV's video playlist.[14] But that far from ends the controversy. Following are five of the biggest myths about rap music:

Myth #1: *Rap is all the same.*

In the month of August 1993, the *New York Times* ran no less than four substantial articles on rap music, including a front page story and an editorial, each of them criticizing the genre "gangsta rap." For example, on August 27, a *Times* editorial by African-American journalist Brent Staples labeled gangsta rap "that wildly successful music in which all women are 'bitches' and 'whores' and young men kill each other for sport."[15]

Reality: The problem here is not so much the individual articles, but the lack of context of the pieces. Many of the individual articles made excellent points, particularly the August 15 piece "Hard Core Rap Lyrics Stir Black Backlash," which examined the black community's reaction.[16] But taken together, these stories paint a narrow, unrepresentative portrait of rap music, a form most of their readers probably are not overly familiar with. Rap is a diverse and constantly evolving art form that encompasses musical styles and artists of all descriptions.

Even "gangsta rap," a genre whose lyrics sometimes stoop to ethical and sexual lows, does accurately represent the desperation of young black lives on America's toughest streets. Not only that, but the music has become phenomenally popular with white, suburban listeners as well, indicating that the themes of alienation are generational as well as racial. In 1993, rap albums (by Ice Cube and Cypress Hill) hit the landmark of debuting on the Top 40 charts in the number one position for the first time, indicating an extremely strong following. Much of this following is young, suburban, and white.[17] Beyond this, however, rap is much broader than one controversial type.

There are several well-known female rappers, including the three-woman group Salt 'N Pepa, whose debut album went platinum, and Queen Latifah, a rapper, actress, and entrepreneur whose management company handles other hot rap groups.

There are pop/crossover rappers including (M.C.) Hammer and DJ Jazzy Jeff and the Fresh Prince (whose series "The Fresh Prince of Bel Air," is a popular sitcom).

There are alternative, experimental, and jazz-influenced rappers like Arrested Development, fusions of rap music and heavy metal, and, of course, Latino and white rappers. It's clear that the term *rap* is an umbrella for many different styles and art forms.

Myth #2: *Most rap lyrics are irredeemable, with no elements of political commentary whatsoever.*

Reality: Mainstream publications from *Newsweek* to the *New York Times* praised rap artists as prophets when their lyrics about black anger at police brutality were made all too real by the L.A. riots. In a rap-related incident, Ice-T's 1992 song "Cop Killer," about police brutality, was condemned by public figures such as President George Bush. Although Ice-T was always identified in the media as a rapper, which he is, "Cop Killer" was from his heavy-metal album *Body Count*. Pointedly, the National Black Police Association stood up to the attacks of other law enforcement organizations when questioned on the song. "Cop Killer" "did not happen in a vacuum," the association stated. "People have always expressed their feelings and opinions through songs, and they were talking about how African-American people have been victimized by police brutality. And that is very real. Where were those organizations when Rodney King was beat up and when the verdict came in?"[18]

Rappers do not just document black rage, they have also been active in trying to diffuse it. In 1989, an alliance of well-known rappers recorded the anti-violence song "Self Destruction" under the umbrella of the Stop the Violence movement. In 1990, a group of rappers from the West Coast recorded a similarly aimed song titled: "We're All in the Same Gang." Positive messages in rap are not just reserved for special occasions. Said a *Billboard* article by David Nathan, "Any examination of rap's content reveals a very high percentage of anti-violent, anti-drug messages, many aimed at improving self-esteem, encouraging the youth of the '80s to continue their education and approach adulthood with a positive approach."[19] One recent example includes the 1993 release "U.N.I.T.Y." by Queen Latifah, referred to above, which urged women not to fall into the trap of violence and to get out of abusive relationships.

Myth #3: *African-Americans all feel the same way about rap.*

Reality: The community's reaction to rap music is diverse, and black radio stations are increasingly making value judgments about the music they play. In 1993, top black radio stations in New York and Los Angeles decided they would no longer play misogynistic or violent rap songs. Other professionals have personally dealt with the wrath of rappers. At the 1993 convention of the National Association of Black Journalists (NABJ), rapper Bushwick Bill came to a session on the hip hop industry. A black female writer asked him, in essence, if he'd call his mother a "bitch" or " 'ho" (whore). The rapper answered no, then added, "I'm not fucking my mother. If I was fucking you, you'd be a bitch." The vast majority of attendees walked out in protest.[20] There have also been protests against rap from the pulpit. In 1993 the Reverend Calvin O. Butts of the Abyssinian Baptist Church in Harlem ran a series of demonstrations against violent and misogynist lyrics.[21] And the National Political Congress of Black Women has held protests in front of record stores in Washington, D.C.[22]

One of the most strident critics of rap is African-American

Stanley Crouch. In a 1993 interview in the *New York Times*, Crouch called rap "either an infantile self-celebration or anarchic glamorization of criminal behavior."[23]

Myth #4: *African-American rap artists are the only violent ones in the industry.*

Reality: Black musicians are often held to a much more stringent standard than white musicians, who don't face race-based criticism for committing crimes, and often avoid hitting the front pages of newspapers. At the very least, white musicians are not made stand-ins for an entire race.

Axl Rose of rock supergroup Guns and Roses has been cited for inciting a riot and assaulting a neighbor, and covered a song written by mass murderer Charles Manson on the 1993 album "The Spaghetti Incident?"[24] In 1994, his ex-wife filed suit against him for assault.

Anthony Kiedis, lead singer of popular alternative group The Red Hot Chili Peppers, was convicted of sexual battery in the late 1980s. One of his band's songs includes lyrics about raping a policewoman who pulls them over for speeding—yet this did not inspire a media frenzy the way rap lyrics have.

Even such mainstream music stars as crooner Harry Connick, Jr., have been cited for gun violations. (He was eventually acquitted because he told airport security that the gun was in his suitcase.)

As a result of this selective musical castigation, even mainstream rappers have often had a difficult time finding places to perform. The 1993 Coca-Cola Summerfest was headlined by rapper LL Cool J in most locations, but not in Washington, D.C., where the promoter at the Convention Center wouldn't take rap acts. LL Cool J performed for president-elect Bill Clinton during inaugural week.[25]

Rap music is unique in how often and harshly it is criticized by the media. But critics play the race card with black visual artists and writers as well. Art pegged as "multicultural" is often slammed the harshest. The 1993 Whitney Biennial, a major art exhibit, addressed the issues of race, gender, and class. It was far from perfect, but its reviews were positively scathing. "Its single theme is Victim Chic," stated the *New York Times*.[26] A *New York Times* review of an unrelated sculpture exhibit stated, "Of the ten sculptures—which can hardly have been selected for visual reasons and seem to have been selected instead for either their political content or to achieve a racially and sexually correct mix of artists. . . ." With reviews like this, the question arises, have white men never made bad art?[27]

Although African-Americans have been stereotyped as "natural" entertainers, their path in the arts world is far from uncomplicated. While all of mainstream America is familiar with black artists and entertainers, there is still too often stereotyping in the way everything from television roles to opportunities to exhibit art are assigned. Those African-American artists who stray from the areas in which blacks are already accepted may find resistance to their accomplishments. Others who stay within forms where blacks are traditionally accepted, like television comedy, may be criticized from both outside and within the black community. Hopefully the worlds of art and entertainment will only become more inclusive of African-Americans at all levels and in all disciplines of film, television, music, and visual art.

Notes to Chapter Eleven

1. Darlene Clark Hine, "The Black Studies Movement: Afrocentric-Traditionalist-Feminist Paradigms for the Next Stage," *The Black Scholar*, vol. 22, no. 3.
2. Patrick Goldstein, "Lights, Camera—Any Action?" *Los Angeles Times* (4/19/89).
3. William T. Bielby and Denise D. Bielby, "The 1993 Hollywood Writer's Report," commissioned by the Writer's Guild of America, West (June 1993).

4. Edward Ball, "Hollywood's Shuffle," *The Voice Film Special*, publication of the *Village Voice* (June 1991): 86; David Kissinger, "Blacks' Gains on TV Aren't Reflected in Networks' Executive Suite," *Variety* (5/30/90): 1.

5. Patrick Goldstein, "Lights, Camera—Any Action?"

6. Carla Hall, "Theater Chain's Action Triggers Cries of Racism," *Los Angeles Times* (7/25/93).

7. Jannette L. Dates and William Barlow, eds., *Split Image: African-Americans in the Mass Media*, second edition, (Howard University Press, 1993): 118–120.

8. "Joe Klein, Media Spokesperson for White People," *Extra!* (July/August 1992).

9. Samir Hachem, "Journey Into Fear," *Village Voice* special film issue (6/20/89).

10. Bronwen Hruska and Graham Rayman, "On the Outside, Looking In," *New York Times* (2/21/93).

11. John J. O'Connor, "Blacks on TV: Scrambled Signals," *New York Times* (10/27/91).

12. Patrick Goldstein, "Lights, Camera—Any Action?"

13. Jannette L. Dates and William Barlow, eds., *Split Image: African-Americans in the Mass Media*, pp. 103–120.

14. Ibid.

15. Brent Staples, "The Politics of Gangster Rap," *New York Times* (8/27/93).

16. Michael Marriott, "Hard-Core Rap Lyrics Stir Black Backlash," *New York Times* (8/15/93); James Ledbetter, "Media Blitz" column, *Village Voice* (9/7/93).

17. John Leland, "Rap and Race," *Newsweek* (6/29/92): 47–52.

18. Jannette L. Dates and William Barlow, eds., *Split Image: African-Americans in the Mass Media*, pp. 120–121.

19. Ibid, pp. 116.

20. Alysia Tate, "Hip Hop Session Walkout," *NABJ Monitor* (7/22/93).

21. Clifford J. Levy, "Harlem Protest of Rap Lyrics Draws Debate and Steamroller," *New York Times* (6/6/93).

22. Gretchen Lacharite, "Insulted Women Put Heat on Rap," *Washington Times* (12/18/93).

23. Lynda Richardson, "Conversations/Stanley Crouch," *New York Times* (8/29/93).

24. Richard Harrington, "Axl Rose Can Tour, Court Says," *Washington Post* (7/15/92).

25. Richard Harrington, "Bum Rap? LL Cool J Joins the Banned," *Washington Post* (7/14/93).

26. Paul Richard, "Scrawling in the Margins: Disenfranchised is De Rigueur at New York's Whitney Biennial," *New York Times* (3/4/93).
27. Michael Kimmelman, "Outdoor Sculpture in Review," *New York Times* (8/6/93).

twelve

Superstars:

African-Americans in the World of Sports

[T]he slave owner would breed his big black with his big woman so that he could have a big black kid. . . . The black is a better athlete to begin with because he's been bred to be that way because of his thigh size and his big size. [Blacks can] jump higher and run faster. . . . [I]f blacks take over coaching like everybody wants them to, there's not going to be anything left for white people.

—Jimmy (the Greek) Snyder, CBS Sports odds-analyst in a 1988 televised interview with a local station. He was later fired.[1]

FOR better *and* for worse, athletes hold a place of honor in the African-American society. According to one survey, the black community holds athletes as a group in the highest regard—64 percent of African-Americans polled said they saw athletes as role models.[2] That said, most African-Americans would agree that too many young people pin their hopes on making the high salaries of professional football, basketball, or baseball players, salaries which only a handful of Americans receive each year. Even for those African-Americans who achieve the rank of professional athlete, the opportunities are often not on par with those offered to white players of similar skill.

Sports Commentary and Journalism: The Myth of the _____ "Natural" Black Athlete

As evidenced by Jimmy the Greek's statement among countless others, many people want to believe that the success of African-American athletes is somehow *natural* and physical, even genetic. They do not choose to take into account the perseverance, skill, training, constant practice, and dedication of so many black athletes, particularly given the appeal of professional sports as a dream route out of poverty.

Addressing the issue of Jimmy the Greek's statement directly, most historians, liberal and conservative, don't believe that slavemasters deliberately "bred" enslaved Africans for physical prowess. More important, the physical differences among the races pale in comparison to the differences within them—who hasn't seen a short, clumsy African-American and a tall, white hoops hotshot?

The idea that African-Americans would not succeed in athletics if they were not somehow physically superior—and mentally inferior—is not new. In 1941, the University of Southern California's track coach wrote a book which included the passage: "The Negro excels in the events he does because he is closer to the primitive than the white man. It was not that long ago that his ability to spring and jump was a life and death matter to him."[3]

African-American athletes receive much harsher press coverage than their white counterparts. One of the most thorough studies of how sports reporters bring racial bias into their coverage was done by Derek Jackson of the *Boston Globe*. Jackson analyzed the coverage of five NCAA basketball games and seven NFL playoff games which occurred in the 1988–89 season. These were his findings:

- Seventy-seven percent of the adjectives used to describe white football players referred to their brains while 65 percent of the adjectives used for black players referred to their brawn.

- In basketball, the ratio was 63 percent brains for white players, 77 percent brawn for black players.

- In both sports, more than 80 percent of the references to stupid plays were about black athletes.[4]

Sports stereotyping may also go hand in hand with other stereotypes about African-Americans, like those concerning crime. As Northeastern University professor Richard Lapchick writes in his analysis of race and athletics, *Five Minutes to Midnight*: "From 1988 through 1990, there were thirty newspaper accounts of athletes who were charged with some form of sexual assault on women. Twenty-one of the thirty were white athletes, yet the only cover story done by *Sports Illustrated* on this issue was about black athletes charged with these offenses while playing at Oklahoma and Colorado."[5]

Blacks in white-dominated sports are often covered sporadically or sensationally (for their racial novelty alone). One of the two sportscasters at a 1993 international ice-skating exhibition said of Olympian Surya Bonaly, a black figure skater from France, "Well, she certainly does create an exotic presence on the ice." More to the point, she's excellent. She came in second in the competition—and though the first and third place winners were interviewed, she was not.[6]

Not just African-Americans but other ethnic groups in sports have been stereotyped by the media. In the 1920s and 1930s, Jewish players dominated basketball, which like most facets of American life was racially segregated. A 1933 sports column in the *New York Daily News* by Ed Sullivan (later of broadcasting fame) stated: "Holman, Jewish star of the Celtics, is a marvelous player. He has always reminded me of Benny Leonard. Both are of the same alertness and general make-up. Jewish players seem to take naturally to the game. Perhaps this is because the Jew is a natural gambler and will take chances."[7] No matter what the time period or the group, some members of the media have read racial interpretations into whatever facet of American life they choose.

On the Field: Statistics on African-Americans in Pro Sports

According to the Bureau of Labor Statistics, 10 percent of the 71,000 people employed as athletes are black.[8] The three biggest sports—football, basketball, and baseball—draw overwhelming public support. Attendance at pro sports games over an entire season is 58 million for American League and National League baseball, 18 million for NBA basketball, and 18 million for NFL football.[9] African-American professional athletes are clustered in the three big sports. Sixty percent of NFL football players are African-American, 75 percent of NBA basketball players are African-American, and over 15 percent of major-league baseball players are black.[10] By contrast, in 1990 there had only been thirteen black hockey players in the entire history of the National Hockey League.[11] Even in the big three American sports, there are deep racial fault lines in the sports world, concerning everything from restricting what positions black athletes play to how much they earn relative to white players.

Because of the stereotype that African-Americans are not as intelligent as whites, black athletes are often steered away from the "thinking" positions on sports teams. Team leadership positions like football quarterback are overwhelmingly white. In 1990, for example, 93 percent of NFL quarterbacks were white, in a league where 60 percent of all players were black. That was an improvement from 1983, when the figure was an astonishing 99 percent.

The evidence that such a figure reflects racial stereotyping comes in part from a study by sociologist Jonathan Brower. Brower asked football coaches to describe the skills needed by players in the three positions which white football players dominated—quarterbacks, centers, and tackles—and the three positions black players dominated—running backs, wide receivers, and cornerbacks. For white players, the coaches chose terms like intelligence, leadership, and emotional control. For the positions dominated by blacks, the words were strength, quickness, and instinct. Not surprisingly, several African-Americans who proved themselves as college quarterbacks had a difficult or impossible time finding positions as quarterbacks in the pros. The situation is much the same with pitchers and catchers in baseball.[12]

There is still evidence that white basketball players in particular are given salaries and positions comparable to black players of higher skill and scoring abilities. In the 1990–91 NBA register, over 50 percent of all black players scored over 10 points per game, while less than 20 percent of all white players met the same standard. One possible reason whites are paid more for comparable scores: a poll by the *Philadelphia Daily News* revealed that 57 percent of respondents said white fans won't pay to see black players.[13]

Here are the 1991 average yearly salaries for professional athletes in the nation's three biggest sports:[14]

- Major-league baseball players: $851,000

- NBA basketball players: $989,000

- NFL football players: $415,000

There is evidence that African-American athletes are not as quickly recognized for their accomplishments as players by honorary sports organizations as well. In 1990, the NBA was 75 percent black. Yet the Basketball Hall of Fame was 88 percent *white*. The same year, the NFL was 60 percent black, while the Pro Football Hall of Fame was 79 percent white.[15] In addition, Andre Ware became the first African-American quarterback to win the top college football award, the Heisman trophy, in 1989.[16]

Behind the Scenes:
_____ Bias in the Sports Boardroom

The playing field isn't the only place where race plays a part in sports. The coaching, management, and ownership of major sports teams is as much a part of the big picture. The statement by Jimmy the Greek which opens this chapter mentions his paranoia that African-Americans could take over coaching as well as competing. Coaching and management are fields traditionally filled with ex-sportsmen—but not so for African-Americans:

- In 1994, there were four black head coaches at the 26 major-league baseball teams.

- The NBA has the best record on coaching. In 1993–94, almost a fifth of teams had black head coaches: 5 of 27.

- In the NFL, however, only 2 of 28 head pro-football coaches was black in 1994. There were no black coaches in the NFL at all until 1989.[17]

The issues of the lack of African-Americans in sports management came to abrupt prominence in 1987, when Al Campanis, the executive vice president of the Dod-gers, stated in an ABC "Nightline" interview that "blacks lack the necessities" to manage major-league baseball teams. Campanis was fired and major-league baseball claimed that it would make a serious effort to hire African-Americans in the administrative ranks. But little has changed. Between 1987 and 1990, there were twenty-three openings for general managers of major-league baseball teams. All of the jobs went to white Americans.[18] And in 1992, Marge Schott, owner of the Cincinnati Reds baseball team, was censured for open racism, including allegedly calling two former players "million dollar niggers," and saying, "I would rather have a trained monkey working for me than a nigger." Although she denied making these particular statements, she did admit to using the racial slur.[19]

There is positive news. In 1989, African-American businessmen Bertram Lee and Peter Bynoe purchased the Denver Nuggets, making the Nuggets the NBA's first African-American–owned team. The business offices of pro sports remain largely segregated, however. For example, in 1989, 93 percent of the front-office staff of the NFL were white.[20]

Some sports where African-American athletes are few and far between have only begun to deal with the racism inherent in their organizational structures. In 1990, for example, seventeen of thirty-nine sites for the Professional Golf Association (PGA) tour were scheduled at all-white clubs. A media uproar and $2 million in canceled advertisements by companies like IBM forced the PGA to insure that all sites were at racially integrated golf greens.[21]

College Athletics:
_____ An Academic Disgrace

Every year, the National Collegiate Athletics Association (NCAA) publishes statistics on the academic performance of players. The 1993 NCAA Division I Graduation-Rates Report found that a shockingly high percentage of black players never receive a degree. They are recruited, play, and fade from view without the benefit of an NBA career *or* a college education. Black athletes often find themselves isolated in college, expected to devote themselves to their playing first and their studies second, if at all. Less than 10 percent of students at predominately white colleges are African-American. Yet over half of all basketball players and nearly 40 percent of all football players of those same colleges are black.[22] Only one percent of college athletic directors, associate and assistant athletic directors are black.[23]

Young black athletes hoping to go pro are chasing a very distant dream.

- The chances of a black high school basketball player making the NBA are over 7,600 to 1.

- The odds of a black college senior basketball player making the NBA are 15 to 1.

- For football, the equivalent figures are over 3,800 to 1 for high school players, and 23 to 1 for college senior players.[24]

Sixty-four percent of NCAA Division I men's players are black. As a report in *Emerge* magazine pointed out, out of the over 200 NCAA Division I schools, "[m]ore than 40 major universities . . . have graduated, within a six year period, none of their black basketball players in freshman classes 1983–87. Three universities—Akron, Hawaii, and Texas at El Paso—failed to graduate any black players while graduating 100 percent of their white counterparts." For example, coach Bobby Knight led the USA basketball team to a gold medal in the 1984 Olympics. But his team at Indiana University graduated no blacks over the time period studied, versus 75 percent of whites. Other teams indicate that things don't have to be this way. Top-ranked North Carolina graduated 83 percent of black players and 88 percent of whites; University of Mississippi graduated all of its players, both black and white.

The reporter for *Emerge* asked Don Haskins, coach at University of Texas at El Paso, why none of his black players versus all of his white players graduated. " 'They're poor students to start off with, with poor habits. They're not good students, they're athletes.' When asked why he recruits poor students, Haskins hung up the telephone." The disregard for players can sometimes be startlingly transparent. Former Central Michigan University coach Keith Dambrot, who is white, told his players after a loss, "We need to have more niggers on this team."[25]

Black athletes can meet academic challenges as long as colleges put their academic success on par with their athletic success. A college basketball rule titled Proposition 48 mandated that to play in their first year of college, high school athletes had to have a "C" average and a minimum 700 score on the SAT test. At the time Proposition 48 passed, over 75 percent of the total number of black football and basketball players would have been ineligible to play in their first year of college. But by the year it was first implemented, less than 12 percent of the total black college freshman ballplayers had to sit out the 1989–90 season.[26]

One final irony: overall, African-Americans receive less than 10 percent of all college athletic scholarships, less than the percentage of blacks in the U.S. population. Basketball and football games usually earn money for colleges. Thus, as Richard Lapchick puts it, "[T]he black athlete, in addition to everything else, helps raise the money to carry the white sports like fencing, swimming, tennis, golf, and lacrosse."[27]

Notes to Chapter Twelve

1. Michael Goodwin, "CBS Dismisses Snyder," *New York Times* (1/17/88).
2. *USA Today*, "Race Relations in the '90s," no byline, (8/27/93).
3. Richard Lapchick, *Five Minutes to Midnight: Race and Sports in the 1990s* (Madison Books, 1991): 234.
4. Ibid, p. 249.
5. Ibid, p. 248.
6. ABC Sports coverage of the Sudafed Skate America International, (11/7/93).
7. Lapchick, *Five Minutes to Midnight*, p. 234.
8. Bureau of the Census, "Employed Civilians . . ."—table 644, *The Statistical Abstract of the United States: 1993* 113th edition (Washington, D.C.: 1993): 405.
9. Ibid.
10. Lapchick, *Five Minutes to Midnight*, pp. 294–297.
11. Ibid, p. 272.
12. Ibid, pp. 291–295.
13. Ibid, pp. 282–283, 287.
14. Bureau of the Census, "Selected Spectator Sports," table 410, *The Statistical Abstract of the United States: 1993*.
15. Ibid, p. 298.
16. Ibid, p. 240.
17. Per conversation with Jeff Benedict of the Center on Sports and Society (10/94).
18. Ross Newhan, "Minority Hiring is Still on Holiday," *Los Angeles Times* (11/23/90).
19. Lorraine Kee Montre, "Baseball Mum After Schott's Racial Slurs," *St. Louis Post-Dispatch* (11/29/92).
20. Lapchick, *Five Minutes to Midnight*, p. 312.
21. Ibid, p. 271.
22. Ibid, p. 229.
23. Ibid, p. 251.
24. Ibid, p. 260.
25. Jimmie Briggs, "A Net Loss," *Emerge* (December/January 1994): 49–52.
26. Lapchick, *Five Minutes to Midnight*, pp. 265–66.
27. Ibid, p. 262.

PART IV

The Structures of Society

thirteen

A Quick Look Back

THE history of race in America is one of great gains and equally great losses. The institution of slavery was followed by a period of relative racial equality called Reconstruction, which was followed by the segregation and repression of Jim Crow. Today, America finds itself faced with new problems: the violence of the inner city, the imperfect status of integration in schools and housing. Between the earliest moments of black life in America and the present day, however, the veil of time seems thick—for all that we have accomplished and all we have yet to accomplish, how did we get here?

This chapter attempts to put the events of black history back into perspective with a timeline that illustrates the length of black experiences in America and the depth of the struggle. Following the timeline is a discussion of several controversies about African-American history.

Timeline: African-Americans
_____ from the 1600s to the 1970s

Much of the information in this timeline is drawn from Lerone Bennett, Jr.'s, _Before the Mayflower: A History of Black America._[1]

August 1619: The first people of African descent in America land at Jamestown, Virginia. They are not slaves but indentured servants—people who must work off debts—just as many of the white settlers are.

December 1641: Massachusetts becomes the first colony to legally recognize the institution of slavery. Other states follow haphazardly; Georgia did not give official recognition to slavery until 1750 (though of course, slavery existed there far before that date).

The American Revolution

March 5, 1770: Crispus Attucks, a free black who had escaped from slavery twenty years before, becomes the first martyr of the American Revolution. He is the first person killed in the Boston massacre.

_1775–1776:_ The revolutionary war. Many blacks fight on the side of America during revolutionary war battles; some fight on the side of the British, who offer blacks their freedom in exchange for enlisting. George Washington issues an order forbidding blacks from enlisting in the revolutionary army, then reverses himself after being alarmed by the British inducement. Among the battles for American independence in which blacks fight are the battle of Bunker Hill, and Lexington and Concord.

July 4, 1776: The Declaration of Independence is adopted. It originally contained a section decrying the slave trade, but that was deleted.

1777: Vermont becomes the first American colony to abolish slavery. By the turn of the century, all New England colonies have abolished slavery.

September 4, 1781: Los Angeles is founded by 44 settlers, 26 of whom are black or of mixed race.

September 17, 1787: The U.S. Constitution is ratified, explicitly protecting slavery.

August 1, 1834: Slavery is abolished in England.

1850: The Supreme Court rejects a school integration argument by a black Boston father on behalf of his daughter, codifying in law the "separate-but-equal" rationale for segregated American schools.

1857: The Supreme Court's Dred Scott decision (named for an enslaved man who unsuccessfully argued for his freedom before the court) makes slavery legal in the Northern Territory, which includes what is now Kansas and Missouri. The decision also denies citizenship and the protections of the law to blacks in America.

1859: The last slave ship, the *Clothilde*, lands in Alabama.

The Civil War

December 18, 1860: South Carolina's declaration that it is an "independent commonwealth" is the opening volley of the Civil War. Over the next five years, 2.2 million Americans will fight and 140,000 will die in the clash between the Union and the Confederacy.[2] Among them are over 200,000 black soldiers and sailors (a very few on the Confederate side), who for most of the war are paid a pittance compared to their white counterparts, given shoddy equipment, and placed in some of the most dangerous engagements. Unlike captured white soldiers, captured black soldiers of the "USCT"—or United States Colored Troops—are frequently murdered. Over 37,000 black fighters lose their lives in the war; at least

20 black soldiers and sailors receive the Congressional Medal of Honor.

January 1, 1863: Abraham Lincoln issues the Emancipation Proclamation ordering the freedom of enslaved blacks (with the exception of those in some areas of Louisiana and the Virginias). There are an estimated four million enslaved African-Americans.[3] Despite the proclamation, the war will continue for two more years.

April 14, 1865: Abraham Lincoln is shot; he dies the following day. Due to Lincoln's actions, most blacks are loyal to his party, the Republicans, for decades.

May 26, 1865: The last Confederate troops surrender, ending the Civil War.

Although in theory black Americans are now free, several southern states quickly move to pass codes which all but reenslave them. Mississippi bars African-Americans from owning farms. South Carolina requires all blacks besides farmworkers and domestics to get a special license. Overall, white America moves quickly to consolidate its hold over land and power—political, economic, and the psychological power of intimidation.

1855–1867: Several prominent black colleges are founded, including Virginia Union, Fisk, Morgan State, and Howard Universities, and Morehouse College.

April 1867: The Ku Klux Klan holds its first national meeting in Nashville, TN.

Reconstruction

1867–77: A period of remarkable—and short-lived—racial progress called Reconstruction. During this time, black political figures achieve prominence in state and national arenas, many blacks and whites attend integrated schools, and African-Americans are able to hold desirable and respectable jobs (police officer, postman) in the community. At the same time, however, the Ku Klux Klan is beginning to step up their lynchings of blacks, setting the scene for dramatic reversals in racial progress.

1868: The South Carolina General Assembly becomes the first, and last, state legislature with a black majority: eighty-five African-Americans to seventy whites. The legislatures of North Carolina, Georgia, and Alabama all have significant black minorities the same year. Also, southern black voters provide the margin of victory for Ulysses S. Grant in the U.S. presidential race (only a minority of whites vote for him).

1870: Mississippi's Hiram Revels is sworn in as the first black U.S. Senator. Later in the year, several black Congressmen win offices. Two years earlier, a black Louisianian, John W. Menard, won a congressional race but was barred from taking office.

1872: Blacks are elected lieutenant governor in both South Carolina and Louisiana. For a brief period at the end of 1872 and beginning of 1873, following the impeachment of the governor, African-American P.B.S. Pinchback is acting governor of Louisiana.

July 31, 1874: Patrick Francis Healey is inaugurated as president of Georgetown University, becoming the first black head of a white institution of higher learning. The next year his brother James A. Healey becomes the first black Roman Catholic bishop.

1875: The 44th Congress (1875–77) includes seven black Congressmen and one black Senator, all from southern states.

1881: Reconstruction can officially be declared dead as modern segregation begins with Tennessee's institution of the Jim Crow railroad car. Thirteen other states follow suit by 1907.

1880s–1920s: Lynchings. During the post-Reconstruction period, lynchings increase and the fear of death at the hands of white mobs becomes an all too regular part of life for American blacks. In the ten year period of 1885 to 1894, over 1,700 African-Americans are lynched—some hung, some beaten, some burned to death, some castrated. The racial warfare is so accepted that white women and children sometimes keep the bones left from the charred bodies as souvenirs. Although white vigilantes usually claim that lynched blacks had committed crimes or made sexual advances to white women, the most common reason for lynching is the economic threat that skilled blacks (like cabinetmakers and blacksmiths) pose. During the same period, scores of race riots occur in major cities. Although the bulk of lynchings occurs from the 1880s to the 1920s, African-Americans are lynched as late as 1955, when fourteen-year-old Emmett Till is kidnapped and murdered.

1901: Alabama adopts a voter "grandfather clause"—to vote, a citizen's grandfather must have been registered—designed to keep blacks from participating in the political process. (The grandfathers of most African-Americans were slaves, and they, of course, were barred from voting.) The "grandfather clause" is upheld by the Supreme Court the next year.

1909: The National Association for the Advancement of Colored People (NAACP) holds its first conference in New York City. The following year historian W.E.B. DuBois, the first African-American to graduate from Harvard University, begins publishing the NAACP's magazine *Crisis.*

1918: World War I ends. Over 370,000 black soldiers enlisted, over half of them fighting in Europe. The same year, sixty blacks are lynched.

1920s: The Harlem Renaissance. Black artists and writers produce some of the best works of the twentieth century and find a broad audience among both blacks and whites. Among works produced during this time are *The Weary Blues* by Langston Hughes and *Cane* by Jean Toomer. Louis Armstrong produces his earliest influential recordings.

October 29, 1929: The stock market crashes, beginning the Great Depression. By 1937, 26 percent of black men are unemployed.

September 2, 1945: The Japanese surrender ends World War II. Over one million black troops enrolled or had been

drafted into the armed services. But instead of a hero's wel-
come, black veterans returned home to scorn and a resurgence
in lynchings designed to remind black men of their "place."

The Civil Rights Movement

1950s–1960s: For white America the decade of the 1950s is
characterized by unprecedented prosperity and burgeoning
suburbanization. But for African-Americans, the 1950s begin a
daring and decisive push for equal treatment, both in law and
in social reality. The struggle is far from easy. In 1951, a
Florida NAACP official is assassinated in the bombing of his
house. In 1955, Rosa Parks is arrested after refusing to give
her seat on a Montgomery, Alabama, bus to a white man,
spurring a boycott which eventually results in an integrated
bus system. College students stage sit-ins at segregated
southern lunch counters throughout the fifties and early sixties. In 1960, four national chain stores give in to pressure and
integrate their counters. By the start of 1962, over 70,000 students have participated in sit-ins.[4] In the summer of 1961, civil
rights freedom riders begin a bus trip through the South. The
freedom riders are repeatedly attacked, one of their buses is
bombed, and they are arrested.

School desegregation. On September 24, 1957, President
Eisenhower orders federal troops to aid in the desegregation
of Central High School in Little Rock, Arkansas. The following day, soldiers escort nine black students to the school. In
1958, the first black student, Ernest Green, graduates with
600 white classmates. Later that year, ten thousand black students participate in the Youth March for Integrated Schools in
Washington, D.C. By 1962, less than eight percent of black
students in southern states attend integrated classes.

The same struggles occur on the college level. In 1962, one of
the biggest desegregation crises comes to a head. The Supreme
Court orders the University of Mississippi to admit black stu-

dent James H. Meredith. But Meredith is personally denied admission by Governor Ross R. Burnett, who states that, "There is no case in history where the Caucasian race has survived social integration." In October, following campus rioting, Meredith registers under the protection of federal marshals. The next year, blacks enroll at the University of Alabama.

September 15, 1963: Four black girls are killed in the bombing of the Sixteenth Street Baptist Church in Birmingham, Alabama.

November 22, 1963: President John Fitzgerald Kennedy is assassinated in Dallas, a death deeply mourned by the African-American community.

December 1964: Martin Luther King, Jr., is awarded the Nobel Peace Prize.

January 21, 1965: Malcolm X is assassinated at the age of 39 in New York's Audubon Ballroom, less than a year after his resignation from the Nation of Islam.

March 21-25, 1965: Reverend Martin Luther King, Jr., leads thousands on a march from Selma to Montgomery, Alabama, which culminates in a rally of 50,000 at the state capitol. One of the marchers, white civil rights worker Viola Liuzzo, is shot to death by three Klansmen after the rally.

August 1965: Rioting in the Watts section of Los Angeles. Thirty-four people are killed; the riots cause $35 million worth of property damage.

June 1966: James Meredith is wounded by a sniper during a Mississippi voter registration drive.

January 1967: The Georgia legislature capitulates and seats Republican Julian Bond, head of the Student Nonviolent Coordinating Committee (SNCC). They had previously refused to seat him, though he was duly elected, because of his opposition to the Vietnam War.

June 1967: At this late date, there is still a law on the books in Virginia making marriage between blacks and whites a crime. The Supreme Court overturns it. As late as the 1950s, the law had been used to ban a couple from the state.

November 1967: Carl B. Stokes is elected the first black mayor of a major U.S. city, Cleveland, Ohio.

February 1968: The National Advisory Commission on Civil Disorders, also known as the Kerner Commission, pinpoints racism and racially polarized news coverage as a cause of recent riots in several U.S. cities. All told, there were seventy-five major riots in 1967 and twenty-one in 1966. The Kerner Commission's report states that America is "moving towards two societies, one black, one white—separate and unequal."

April 4, 1968: The Reverend Martin Luther King, Jr., is assassinated in Memphis, Tennessee. His death sets off riots in forty-six cities. President Lyndon B. Johnson declares April 6 a national day of mourning. The following day, the Reverend King is buried; 300,000 mourners march behind his coffin. In March 1969, James Earl Ray pleads guilty to the slaying and is sentenced to ninety-nine years in prison.

June 19, 1968: 50,000 people participate in the Solidarity Day March of the Poor People's Campaign, a protest which the Reverend King had announced one month before his death. Civil rights leader Ralph Abernathy, Coretta Scott King, and Vice President Hubert Humphrey address the crowd at the Lincoln Memorial.

September 9, 1968: Arthur Ashe becomes the first black winner of the U.S. Open tennis tournament.

November 5, 1968: Shirley Chisolm of New York becomes the first black woman elected to Congress. Nine black men (eight Representatives and one Senator) are elected to Congress.

The Black Power Movement

The movement begins in 1966, founded by Stokely Carmichael. The Black Panther Party is founded the following year by Huey Newton and Bobby Seale.

October 16, 1968: John Carlos and Tommie Smith, Olympic

medalists in the 200-meter run, give the black power salute while standing on the winner's podium in Mexico City. The photograph of the two African-American men raising their fists to the sky remains famous to this day.

April 19, 1969: One hundred black students, many of them armed, seize the administration building at Cornell University.

August 1970: A white policeman is killed in a shootout with Black Panthers. Panther Lonnie McLucas is convicted of conspiracy to murder an FBI informant.

Four people including a judge are killed in a Marin County, California, courthouse. A warrant is issued for the arrest of Angela Davis, who is accused of having provided weapons to the convicts. She is arrested in October in New York City. In 1972, she is acquitted by an all-white jury.

Vietnam and Beyond

1971: African-Americans are again fighting for their country—and disproportionately dying for it. A Pentagon report reveals that while blacks make up 11 percent of the U.S. forces in Vietnam, they comprise 12.5 percent of the dead.

December 1971: The Reverend Jesse Jackson founds Operation PUSH (People United to Save Humanity).

May 1973: Tom Bradley is elected mayor of Los Angeles.

1976: FBI documents released after a Freedom of Information Act suit reveal the existence of COINTELPRO, an intensive surveillance and misinformation campaign mounted by the U.S. government. The target: civil rights organizations including SNCC and the Southern Christian Leadership Conference. A 1967 document described the mission of COINTELPRO thus: "to expose, disrupt, misdirect, discredit, or otherwise neutralize the activities of black nationalists, hate-group types, their leadership, spokesmen, membership, and supporters, and to counter their propensity for violence and civil disorders."

January 23–30, 1977: The ground-breaking television mini-series of Alex Haley's *Roots* becomes the most watched television event of all time, with 130 million viewers.

June 28, 1978: The U.S. Supreme Court orders University of California, Davis Medical School to admit white American Allan P. Bakke in a "reverse discrimination" suit.

August 15, 1979: Andrew Young resigns as UN ambassador, under criticism for meeting with members of the Palestine Liberation Organization.

Q & A: The African-American Experience

Q: *If enslaved blacks in America hated being slaves so much, why didn't they rebel?*

A: They did rebel. On numerous occasions, enslaved blacks tried to, and occasionally succeeded in, mounting rebellions. In 1822, Denmark Vesey devised one of the biggest planned slave insurrections, involving thousands of blacks in South Carolina. The plan was foiled, and Vesey and over thirty others were hanged. In the Nat Turner rebellion in 1831, sixty whites were killed before the plot was foiled and Turner was captured. In 1839 and 1841, blacks on slave ships overpowered the crews. The first ship, the *Amistad,* was captured off of Long Island, but some of the captives were later returned to Africa. Would-be slaves on the second ship, the *Creole,* managed to sail to the Bahamas, where they were granted freedom.

In 1849, Harriet Tubman escaped from Maryland. Eventually she would return to the South nineteen times and bring out 300 enslaved blacks via the underground railroad, a system of routes and safe houses. There were also many daring individual escapes. In 1848, the couple of William and Ellen Craft escaped from Georgia: she impersonated a sickly male slave owner wrapped in bandages, he her slave.[5]

Q: *Other immigrants came to America and succeeded. Why haven't African-Americans succeeded? They've been here for hundreds of years.*

One *Wall Street Journal* editorial clucks: "Ironically, and sadly, [assimilation] has not worked so well for American blacks, among the earliest arrivals."[6]

A: This kind of argument represents historical amnesia at its worst. African-Americans did not simply "arrive"; they were captured, transported—as economic chattel, "imported." They certainly were not given the choice to assimilate, and in many cases still are not today. In fact, blacks in America have been enslaved (more than 200 years from the 1600s to 1865) longer than they have been free (a mere 130 years). The African-American community did not begin to enjoy anything close to the full advantages of citizenship until the push for civil rights.

In addition, it is a myth that all Europeans who came to America "made it." Fully *one-third* of voluntary immigrants to America failed in their quest to make this country their new home and moved back to their country of origin—a luxury not available to African-Americans.[7]

Q: *Why do African-Americans keep harping on the issue of slavery? It's so far in the past as to be insignificant.*

A: Family history and genealogy is just as important to African-Americans as it is to other peoples. For example, Dorothy Spruill Redford of Portsmouth, Virginia, performed

ten years of genealogical research in order to host a plantation "reunion"—a gathering of the descendants of slaves
from the plantation her forbears had worked on. Stated in an
article on the reunion, " 'I'm the third generation in my family born free and I learned that I wasn't talking about something ancient' in speaking about slavery, [Redford] said. 'It
makes you think of the monumental accomplishments in two
generations.' "[8]

While the destruction of records during and after the
Civil War makes genealogical research difficult for African-
Americans, many have traced their family histories. Redford's 1986 reunion brought together 1,500 descendants of
twenty-one enslaved families at Somerset Place, once North
Carolina's largest plantation. Among those attending were
descendants of slaves including Clarence Blount of the
Maryland State Senate, a descendant of the plantation's
founder, and author Alex Haley. Redford was lucky in that
the records of the family that owned the plantation had been
donated to a local archives.

Some African-Americans have even asked that the U.S.
government investigate setting aside funds for the development of the black community, reparations for the years of un-
paid backbreaking labor which enslaved blacks performed.
The Detroit City Council passed a resolution asking the federal government for a $40 billion educational trust fund for the
descendants of slaves. The idea of reparations, while unlikely
to ever succeed, is not without precedent. In 1988, Congress
awarded $20,000 each to all surviving Japanese-Americans
who were put in internment camps during World War II.[9]

Myth: *Blacks were on the sidelines of American history.*

Reality: African-Americans have played a role in every
major accomplishment of this country. Lerone Bennett, Jr.,
who wrote the best-selling chronicle of black history *Before*

the Mayflower, told one reporter: "[W]hat is hard for white people to understand . . . is that while black Americans have been part and parcel of this country virtually from its inception, their history is not part of the everyday texture of life in this country." For example, Chicago was founded by Jean Baptiste DuSable, a free black man who formed a settlement where the *Chicago Tribune* building is today. But, says Bennett, there is not a single street or building in the city named for DuSable, one of the many times when black contributions have been erased and largely forgotten.[10]

Blacks in the American West

African-Americans also helped claim the American West as U.S. Army "Buffalo Soldiers." As an article in the *Washington Post* puts it: "There is scant notice that thousands of Buffalo Soldiers scouted 34,420 miles of western desert and plain, laid hundreds of miles of new roads and telegraph lines, protected the mail coaches, were instrumental in the military actions against the great Apache chiefs Victorio and Geronimo, fought valiantly at the side of Teddy Roosevelt's Rough Riders in Cuba during the Spanish-American War and then returned to the West—all with inferior horses, miserable rations, and third-rate equipment discarded by white regiments." Buffalo Soldiers won nineteen medals of honor and had a desertion rate one-third that of their white counterparts.

One of the leaders of the Buffalo Soldiers was Henry Ossian Flipper, a former slave who became the first black graduate of West Point in 1877. He was court-martialed for embezzlement after being set up by jealous white officers. Afterward, he became a mining engineer, legal author, and the first black editor of a white paper, the *Nogales Sunday Herald*. In 1976, the military posthumously exonerated Flipper, ninety-four years too late.[11]

_____ A Word from the Past

Finally, history teaches us we must have hope. From the grave of a former slave who saw the world change around him and, more important, changed his own world:

> SACRED, to the memory of Amos Fortune, who was born free in Africa, a slave in America; he purchased liberty, professed Christianity, lived reputably, and died hopefully, November 17, 1801.[12]

Notes to Chapter Thirteen

1. Lerone Bennett, Jr., *Before the Mayflower: A History of Black America* (Johnson Publishing Company, 1986): 441–611.
2. Mark S. Hoffman, ed., *The World Almanac and Book of Facts 1992* (New York: Pharos Books, 1991): 702.
3. DeNeen L. Brown, "Celebrating Freedom Together," *Washington Post* (9/23/93).
4. *The World Almanac*, p. 448.
5. Bennett, *Before the Mayflower: A History of Black America.*
6. Irving Kristol, "The Tragedy of Multiculturalism," *Wall Street Journal* editorial (7/31/91).
7. Tom Morganthau, "America: Still a Melting Pot?" *Newsweek* (8/9/93).
8. *New York Times*, "1,500 Slave Descendants Attend Plantation Reunion" (8/31/86).
9. Eloise Salholz, "Paying for Sins of the Past," *Newsweek* (5/22/89).
10. Ken Ringle, "Against the Drift of History," *Washington Post* (8/27/93).
11. David Maraniss, "Due Recognition and Reward," *Washington Post* magazine (1/20/91): 15–26.
12. Andrew Billingsley, *Climbing Jacob's Ladder* (New York: Simon and Schuster, 1992): 99–101.

fourteen

The New Old Racism

I have no more objection to the use of the word 'nigger' than I do to 'white dude.' . . . I find all of these words [i.e., ethnic slurs] to be vaguely amusing.

—"60 Minutes" humorist Andy Rooney, speaking at a 1991 video-taped forum on "politically correct" at Stanford University.[1]

NEEDLESS to say, most African-Americans don't agree with Andy Rooney.

Statements like the one above indicate the deep rift between blacks and whites concerning what exactly constitutes "racism"—bold, overt discrimination based on the color of one's skin. As evidenced by polls and studies, Americans overall are becoming increasingly pessimistic about the ability of blacks and whites to live together harmoniously. The media's insistence that racism doesn't exist anymore (at least according to the ceaseless articles which chastise civil rights leaders for being obsessed with the social ill) do not help. Unfortunately, the belief that African-Americans are inferior, and the corresponding mistreatment that goes with these beliefs, are still both widespread and widely accepted. Some black leaders believe the clock is even turning back.

A report on white Michigan voters revealed the depth of racial animosity. Working-class whites, it found, "express a profound distaste for blacks, a sentiment that pervades almost everything they think about government and politics ... Blacks constitute the explanation for their vulnerability and for almost everything that has gone wrong in their lives; not being black is what constitutes being middle class; not living with blacks is what makes a neighborhood a decent place to live."[2] African-Americans are half saddened, half vindicated by reports like this one. The studies provide a depressing commentary on race relations; at the same time they verify what African-Americans see and experience in their own lives every day.

This chapter uses some of the latest studies and surveys to explore the present state of racial attitudes in this country, the ramifications of those attitudes, and the existence of white supremacist and hate groups.

Q & A: Racism in the '90s

Q: *Hasn't racism all but disappeared from today's society?*

A: An August 1993 editorial in the *Wall Street Journal* chided civil rights leaders for continuing to talk about racism: "Perhaps, as the [former NAACP chair] Ben Chavises and Lani Guiniers of the world believe, there are still pockets of bigotry and resistance residing in the psyches of some Americans."[3]

The *Journal*'s editorial board hasn't been paying much attention to the evidence to the contrary. A 1990 study by the University of Chicago's National Opinion Research Center found that the majority of whites still believe blacks to be inferior. Among the results: 53 percent of non-black respondents said they thought blacks were less intelligent than whites, 51 percent agreed blacks were less patriotic, 62 percent thought blacks were lazier, and 78 percent said that blacks "prefer to live off welfare." To a lesser degree Hispanics and southern whites were pegged with the same stereotypes.[4]

According to young Americans, this country is getting more racist, not less. A 1992 poll of over 1,000 Americans aged 15 to 24 conducted by People for the American Way revealed that half described the state of race relations as "generally bad." Black youths were more pessimistic (57 percent responding "generally bad") than whites (48 percent). Other findings of the survey:

Young whites now believe that they're hurt more by "reverse discrimination" than blacks and Hispanics are by racism. Participants were asked which was more likely: qualified minorities losing out on scholarships, jobs, and promotions because of prejudice, or qualified whites losing out on opportunities because minorities get special preference. Forty-nine percent of whites surveyed thought they lost out, versus 34 percent who thought minorities did. Although the vast majority of blacks thought minorities were more likely to have their opportunities cut short by racism, 19 percent believed whites were discriminated against more. At the same time, however, 82 percent of whites agreed that "racial and ethnic minorities still face a lot of discrimination in our society."

Despite these rifts, blacks and whites tend to hold very much the same values. Eighty percent of whites and 87 percent of blacks said that family was "extremely important"; 77 percent of whites and 86 percent of blacks said the same for "fair treatment for all"; and 73 percent of whites and 84 percent of blacks said that "emphasis on self-reliance and taking care of yourself" was extremely important.

Over 70 percent of all youths said they have at least one good friend of another race. But, like the halfhearted social apology, "Oh, I have a friend who's black," friendships do not eliminate underlying bias. States the report: "Personal friendships may contribute to better understanding, but do not bridge the gap between groups created by stereotypes or myths. Young white focus group participants told moving stories about friendships with individual blacks, while repeating or assenting to negative clichés pinned on blacks as a group, such as 'lazy' or 'waiting for a handout.' "

The poll also revealed an overall pessimism about the country. Forty-eight percent of whites think the best years are behind America; 68 percent of blacks believe that is the case.[5]

Another poll revealed that younger African-Americans are less optimistic about the future than older ones. For example, 52 percent of African-Americans over forty believe there could be a black president in the next twenty years, but only 35 percent of those younger believe it could happen. Interestingly, younger African-Americans are less likely to believe discrimination is the major reason for problems in the black community: 53 percent of those over 40 believe discrimination is the primary cause, versus 37 percent of those younger.[6]

Q: *Aren't middle-class blacks able to insulate themselves from racism? Any African-Americans who have good jobs and enough money not to live in the ghetto ought to be just fine.*

A: As the examples in this book demonstrate, racism affects African-Americans of all social and economic classes. An article in *Essence* magazine detailed the stories of successful black men who were faced with blatant ignorance. The article's author, Charles N. Jamison, Jr., relates the time, less than five years ago, that a realtor flat out told him he wouldn't be welcomed in a New York luxury apartment building, despite the fact that he was a vice president at one of the top five advertising agencies in the country. Other black men recounted how they were stopped and searched for crimes they did not commit (one was forced to lead police through his house while they searched for his "accomplice" in a burglary he did not commit). A less dangerous but just as personally devastating tale came from a photographer who, sailing with a white friend off the Virginia coast, docked during bad weather, and went into a club for food. The article recounts: "[T]he waitress came over and told us that the members had told her to tell me that they would prefer it if I ate my food outside. I was numb." Old-style racism is alive and well, and it creates an on-going legacy of pain.[7]

The television news program "20/20" illustrated that racism knows no socioeconomic bounds in a segment that paired two well-dressed, -spoken, -groomed, and -educated young men to illustrate the real cost of racism to African-American individuals. At every step, the white young man received better treatment or opportunities than the African-American. When they went to the same employment agency, the white man was pleasantly helped and the black one was grudgingly lectured. When inquiring about a Help Wanted sign at a drycleaner, the black man was told the position was filled, and later the white man was urged to apply. When looking at cars, a salesman gave the black man a higher price and stiffer terms; and finally, in a now-classic example of racism, a taxicab passed the black man by to pick up the white one. In instances like the car shopping and drycleaner's job application, the black man would have no definitive way of knowing he was being treated unfairly.[8]

The NAACP has been instrumental in developing economic solutions to discrimination. After several African-Americans filed suit against the Denny's restaurant chain, the NAACP negotiated an agreement with Flagstar Corporation, owner of Denny's, Hardees, El Pollo Loco, and other restaurants. The pact sets up minority recruitment and training programs designed to raise the percentage of African-American employees to 12 percent in the managerial ranks and 20 percent in non-manager's jobs; to develop franchise opportunities; and to have the company buy 12 percent of supplies from minority firms. The agreement has teeth: the NAACP will coordinate an on-going random testing program at the 2,000 Flagstar restaurants.[9]

Q: *Hasn't at least one factor in racism changed, that white supremacist groups like the KKK are no longer powerful?*

A: There are several strong white supremacist groups in America, and by some estimates their influence is growing. There are an estimated 250 to 300 white supremacist groups with a total of 10,000 to 30,000 hard-core members. There may be hundreds of thousands of other Americans who support the ideology.

By some estimates, the number of hate crimes is rising. According to the Southern Poverty Law Center's project Klan-Watch, in 1989 there were 7 cross burnings, 34 instances of vandalism, and 125 hate-crime related murders. By 1992, those numbers had risen to 31 cross burnings, 117 instances of vandalism, and 322 murders. And in 1991, the FBI counted a total of over 4,500 hate crimes in the United States.

In the summer of 1993, eight people were arrested on suspicion of trying to start a race war by planning to bomb Los Angeles churches and synagogues. Among their alleged targets was the First African Episcopal Church in South Central Los Angeles. The white supremacists arrested told investigators they had already committed other racial attacks. Interestingly, papers did not print the names of two juveniles involved in the case. Black juveniles charged with serious crimes are often charged as adults, and thus their names are printed, even if they are later found innocent.[10]

California is headquarters to the largest white supremacist group in the nation. The group White Aryan Resistance (WAR) is headed by Tom Metzger, a former Ku Klux Klan leader who lives in San Diego County. In 1990, a Portland, Oregon, jury ordered Metzger and his son to pay $12.5 million for inciting followers to beat to death an Ethiopian man. In 1991, he was jailed for forty-six days for charges stemming from a 1983 cross burning. Despite those legal losses, Metzger still has an estimated 3,000 paying subscribers to his $30 per year newsletter and runs a telephone line with recorded hate messages. Members of another hate group, the Order, murdered Denver radio host Alan Berg in 1984.[11]

_____ **Toward the Future**

One of the main reasons for miscommunication between non-black Americans and African-Americans is a disagreement over the existence and impact of modern-day racism. As this chapter demonstrates, race is far from a neutral factor in determining how individuals are treated, from applying for jobs to finding housing. What these statistics and studies ≈can't illustrate, however, is the pain experienced by African-Americans who are discriminated against. Conversely, statistics alone do not get to the heart of why many non-black Americans hold stereotypic views about African-Americans. The first step in resolving some of the tension between the races in this country is to talk about these issues honestly. Racism unexamined will always be racism unresolved.

Notes to Chapter Fourteen

1. "Safe Speech, Free Speech, and the University," transcript of the 4/10/91 videotaping for PBS at Stanford University, p. 13.
2. Stanley B. Greenberg, *Report on Democratic Defection* (Washington, D.C.: Analysis Group): 13–18, 28.
3. *Wall Street Journal* editorial, "Civil Rights: The Next Generation," (8/31/93).
4. Tom W. Smith, *Ethnic Images* (National Opinion Research Center: University of Chicago, December 1990).
5. People for the American Way and Peter D. Hart Research Associates, *Democracy's Next Generation II: A Study of American Youth on Race* (People for the American Way: Washington, D.C., 1992).

6. Patricia Edmonds, "Civil Rights Issues, by Age and Race," findings of a USA Today/Gallup Poll in *USA Today* (8/30/93).

7. Charles N. Jamison, Jr., "Racism: The Hurt That Men Won't Name," *Essence* (November 1992).

8. Russ W. Baker, "Truth, Lies and Videotape," *Columbia Journalism Review* (July/August 1993): 25–28.

9. NAACP press release, "NAACP and Flagstar Reach $1 Billion Historic Accord to Expand Opportunities for Minorities."

10. *New York Times*, no byline, "Papers Tie Three Held in Racial Plot to Other Attacks," (9/9/93); Veronica T. Jennings and Stephen Buckley, "Montgomery Rape Case Inquiry Faults Both Police, Prosecutors," *Washington Post* (5/24/94).

11. David Freed, "Southland Is Ripe Turf for White Hate Groups," *Los Angeles Times* (7/25/93).

fifteen

Whose Justice?

The vast majority of the people blacks kill are other than [i.e., are not] blacks.

—Conservative standard-bearer and *National Review* editor William F. Buckley, Jr., writing about "the black problem" in a January, 1993 syndicated column.[1]

WILLIAM F. BUCKLEY could have chosen any number of statistics to illustrate a story, no matter how unobjective and preconceived, on race and crime. For example, one-quarter of young black men are in prison, on parole, or on probation—a staggering, and true, figure. But Buckley chose to assert that black murderers are overwhelmingly slaughtering white Americans.

That is an outright lie. Criminals tend to stick to their own race; three-quarters of white victims of violent crime say their attacker was white; well over 85 percent of African-American victims say their attacker was black. The same is true for murder—fully 80 percent of murdered whites were killed by other white Americans.[2] Unfortunately, this doesn't fit Buckley's thesis—nor do these statistics fit the pattern of race-based crime reporting in America today.

An example from my own experience as a journalist illustrates how deep the focus on blacks as criminals is. At one point, I was talking to a *Newsweek* editor about doing a story on the disproportionate arrest and incarceration rates for young black men. He shook his head, "Something is missing. Even if more blacks are being arrested, if they're criminals, you should want them off the street." I discussed how African-Americans are sentenced more harshly, sometimes receive felony records when whites receive misdemeanors, which hurts the future job prospects for these black men. And some prisoners, black and white, have been wrongly convicted. One celebrated case is that of Randall Dale Adams, an Ohio man whose wrongful conviction for killing a police officer was documented in Errol Morris's film *The Thin Blue Line*. At one point, Adams, who is white, came within seventy-two hours of execution; he spent over fifteen years in prison for a murder he did not commit. In another case, African-American Clarence Lee Bradley was sentenced to death after he was wrongly convicted of murdering a sixteen-year-old white female. The investigators who helped free him after eight years in prison found that the police had conducted a racially biased investigation. In many cases, says an article on death row appeals, a prisoner's "freedom was often discovered by luck, and . . . unscrupulous investigators and law-enforcement officials, con-man informants, or neglectful defense counsel often thwarted their efforts to establish their innocence."[3]

Perhaps this editor and I were circling around a more subtle issue. The problem, after all, is not just the 25 percent but the 75 percent: the 75 percent of young black men who aren't involved with the criminal justice system, but who are still viewed with suspicion by potential employers, store clerks, passers-by. The problem with the criminal justice system's intense scrutiny of African-Americans and the incessant media coverage of black crime is that it ultimately has ramifications on the marriage, job prospects, and daily life of law-abiding black Americans.

_____ The Violence "Gene"

Myth: _African-Americans are born violent._

"If you look, for example, at male monkeys, especially in the wild, roughly half of them survive to adulthood. The other half die by violence. That is the natural way of it for males, to knock each other off, and, in fact, there are some interesting evolutionary implications of that because the same hyper-aggressive monkeys who kill each other are also hyper-sexual, so they copulate more. . . . Maybe it isn't just the careless use of the word when people call certain areas of certain cities 'jungles.'. . ."

—Dr. Fredrick K. Goodwin, Director, Alcohol Drug Abuse and Mental Health Administration (ADAMHA), in referring to the "Violence Initiative," February 11, 1992

Reality: The "Violence Initiative" was a program proposed by Dr. Goodwin, one that was prevented from becoming reality only due to the efforts of black politicians and social scientists. This program would have identified up to 100,000 inner-city (read: black) children each year as potentially violent. Then these children as young as five would be given powerful psychoactive drugs to combat their "tendencies." In 1991, Representative John Conyers, head of the Congressional Black Caucus, began to ask serious questions about the "Violence Initiative." In February of the next year, after Dr. Goodwin made his outrageous statement, Conyers asked for Goodwin's resignation as director of the $2.7 billion-per-year ADAMHA. The Violence Initiative incident did not destroy Goodwin's credibility. He did resign—but was promptly appointed head of the National Institutes of Mental Health. We may not have heard the last of the Violence Initiative yet.

The idea that the so-called "urban jungle" is a result of genetics is patently false. What is true is that the neighborhood that an American lives in has a lot to do with how likely he is to commit a crime. But what's not true is that this neighborhood has to be black. A study by the Massachusetts Department of Public Health found that poverty, not race, is the biggest factor in who turns to violence. "South Boston, the most exclusively white neighborhood in Boston, has a homicide rate equal to that of South Dorchester/Mattapan, a poor community that is nearly 50 percent black," the report read. But of course it is Mattapan and Roxbury, another black Boston neighborhood, that are constantly written up in the pages of Boston's homicide news.[4] According to the Bureau of Justice Statistics, both black and white crime rates drop precipitously the more income a person has.[5]

Finally, the idea of a "violence gene" simply runs counter to common sense. If we look at world conflicts, from the wars between Asians in Korea and Vietnam, to the on-going wars between blacks in Rwanda and whites in Bosnia, it's easy to see that no *one* race is born into—or born free from—violence.

Overview: African-Americans and Criminal Justice

Unfortunately, Goodwin is far from alone in his views: the National Opinion Research Center's 1990 poll on racial views found that 56 percent of non-blacks believe blacks are more violent. The conventional wisdom is that the disproportionate number of blacks in prison simply reflects an African-American tendency to commit crime. While it is true that black Americans are more likely to commit crimes than whites, the statistics are too often left unanalyzed. Poverty and social class deeply affect black commission of crimes; just as important, the numbers are skewed by a pattern of race-based treatment in the judicial system.

Even criminal justice officials recognize a pattern of bias in arrests and prosecutions. A survey of New Jersey judges found that significant numbers of them perceived the courts to be easier on white criminals. The findings[6]:

Twenty-six percent of judges answered "usually" or "sometimes" to the statement: "Prosecutors are more likely to insist on more serious charges against minority defendants than white defendants."

Twenty percent gave the same response to the statement: "In your county, sentences for minority offenders are more severe than for similarly situated white offenders."

And 40 percent agreed that: "There are small increments of discrimination against minorities at each step of the criminal justice process (e.g., arrest, indictment, sentencing, etc.).

If judges who responded that these events occurred "rarely" are added in, for each question a majority of judges agreed with the statements above. Only a minority say racial discrimination "never" occurs in the courts.

African-Americans are arrested at rates disproportionate to their commission of crimes. The U.S. government records crime victims' descriptions of their attackers, including race, even in instances when the cases are not solved. For virtually every type of crime, African-American criminals are arrested at rates above their commission of the acts. For example, victimization reports indicated that 33 percent of women who were raped said that their attacker was black; however, black rape suspects made up fully 43 percent of those arrested.[7] The disproportionate arrest rate adds to the public perception that rape is a "black" crime.

It can't help that only 6.5 percent of America's police officers are black. The numbers vary greatly in America's cities: for example, only 11 percent of officers in New York are black, while 67 percent of officers in the District of Columbia are black, matching the city's 66 percent black population.[8]

Too often, "black" is a sufficient physical description of suspects. After a British tourist was killed in Florida in 1993, officials rounded up black males between the ages of 15 and 21 in Jefferson County, even pulling them out of school for questioning. Residents did not object to the vigorous search for the killer, but they were livid over the "dragnet" for young black men.[9]

In a similar incident in 1992, all black men at the State University of New York's Oneonta College were questioned as suspects simply because of their race. Local police, looking for a black suspect, asked college officials for the names and locations of all black male students—and the school obliged.

Being a student or professor on a university campus is little protection. In a *Wall Street Journal* editorial on police harassment, Yale law professor and author Stephen L. Carter wrote about a professor at Washington University in St. Louis who was detained because of his "suspicious" behavior—looking at jewelry in a shop window.[10] Yet another incident occurred in Harvard Square in 1990. Two black students running for a school shuttle bus were grabbed and handcuffed by police in front of their classmates after the description of a robbery suspect went out over police radio. The suspect's description? A single, tall, *white* man.[11]

African-Americans fare even worse when it comes to conviction and sentencing. For example, while 29 percent of those arrested are African-American, the United States prison population is nearly half black.[12] Blacks are disproportionately convicted for the crimes they are arrested for, and often given longer prison terms than whites convicted for the same crimes. According to the Federal Judicial Center, in 1990 the average sentences for blacks on weapons and drug charges were 49 percent longer than those for whites who had committed and been convicted of the same crimes—and that disparity has been rising over time.[13]

U.S. drug sentencing policies disproportionately affect African-Americans. The same penalty—five years—is provided for possession of five grams of crack cocaine as it is for *five hundred* grams of powder cocaine.[14] Not only is powder cocaine actually purer than crack, it's used primarily by whites, while crack is used primarily by blacks. And compare the street value: in 1994, 500 grams of powder cocaine were worth $40,000; five grams of crack were worth only $250.[15]

We're only catching the small-fry: the national arrest rate for possession of drugs is twice as high as the rate for sale and/or manufacturing.

Ninety-one percent of prisoners sentenced under the mandatory minimum guidelines are non-violent, first-time offenders—usually for small sales or even simple possession of drugs. And at the same time America is putting more drug users behind bars, it has let the funding for drug rehabilitation centers dry up.

The Judicial Conference, an organization representing federal judges, has come out against mandatory minimum sentences. Several judges have defied U.S. sentencing guidelines in sentencing first offenders.[16]

The link between poverty and crime goes unexplored. Given that poverty is a key indicator of crime, it can only come as doubly bad news that it's becoming more difficult for black men in particular to rise into the working and middle classes. With a sharp and continuing decline in industrial jobs, the proportion of black men aged 25 to 34 who were unemployed or earned wages below the poverty level rose from 37 percent to a staggering 45 percent over the decade of the 1980s.

In his book *Two Nations*, Andrew Hacker points out that people of higher socioeconomic classes are not innately less prone to crime: but first, they have less of a reason to turn to crime for sustenance, and, second, they can hide their actions more easily. "For reasons we only dimly understand, some individuals are prone to steal," he writes. "Among the middle and upper classes, thieves are in less danger of getting caught, since the kind of crimes they commit may be difficult to detect. (In many cases, victims never realize they have been swindled.) . . . Department stores suffer more from thefts by their employees than they do from shoplifters."[17]

Public defenders, who have huge case loads, often do not provide the best legal advice to defendants. Because African-Americans on average are poorer than whites, black defendants rely more often on public lawyers. One egregious example: in 1993, a seventeen-year-old black male with no previous criminal record was sentenced to three years without parole for stealing a box of ice-cream bars from a school cafeteria. There wasn't even any conclusive evidence in the case, and yet his court-appointed lawyer did not advise him against pleading guilty to "burglary." Although he's been freed, the felony conviction may stay on his permanent record and make it more difficult for him to get a job.[18]

The media and criminal justice focus on crime as an African-American "pathology" creates a Catch 22. To law enforcement officials, the disproportionate number of African-Americans in prison justifies their use of skin color as "probable cause"; in turn, the equating of "criminal" with "black" feeds the frenzy of monitoring, arresting, prosecuting, and sentencing African-Americans at ever greater rates.

The Complicity of the Media: Overreporting of Black Crime, Underreporting of Black Victims

Q: *Aren't there more black men in prison than in college? I've seen that statistic quoted by people ranging from the criminal justice organization The Sentencing Group to Jesse Jackson.*[19]

A: In 1991, there were 136,000 black males aged 18 to 24 in prison, and fully 378,000 black males the same age in college. The Sentencing Group's statement is misleading: comparing black male prisoners of all ages to the overwhelmingly young college population gives a very false perception.[20] Although The Sentencing Group has the best of intentions, it shouldn't be necessary to resort to misleading statements to get across the idea that black men are being locked up at disproportionate rates.

Q: *There* are *an awful lot of black criminals on television news and in the papers. But doesn't that just accurately reflect how many of America's criminals are black?*

A: It may be the media's best-kept secret: the majority of violent criminals are white. According to arrest, conviction, and incarceration data from the Bureau of Justice Statistics, over half of violent crimes are committed by whites. But numbers from the bureau's victimization surveys indicate that an even greater percentage may have been committed by whites. The victimization statistics say that only 28 percent of victims attacked by a single person pinpointed their attacker as black; fully 64 percent pinpointed their attacker as white.[21] In addition 41 percent of violent crime is committed by offenders known to the victims, including 4 percent by a current or former spouse and one percent by a child.[22] Given those statistics, coverage of violent crime ought to at least reflect an equal number of blacks and whites. Unfortunately, that is far from the case.

A study of local television news found that black criminals are portrayed less evenhandedly than whites (for example, as more menacing) based on several criteria. Accused blacks were:

- Significantly less likely to be shown in live footage and more likely to be shown in a still photo

- Less likely to be named

- More likely to be shown in the grip of an officer

- More likely to be shown in street or jail clothing rather than a jacket and tie (a function of income and class, where wealthier defendants can afford bail and lawyers to coach them on appearance).

All of these differences in the way that black and white criminals were portrayed make it easier to stereotype the black defendants as "a statistic" rather than identifying each of them as (potentially innocent) individuals. The portrayal of black criminals as an undifferentiated menace exacerbates racial stereotyping.[23]

Q: *Aren't white Americans the target victims of black violence?*

In an apparent attempt to justify white bias, columnist Joe Klein wrote in the May 7, 1990, issue of *New York* magazine that: "White racism is on the rise, largely in reaction to the horrendous, crack-driven city crime wave of recent years."

Q: African-Americans have the most to fear from crime, especially from crime in black neighborhoods. In fact, African-Americans are twice as likely to be victims of violent crime as whites. What is true about Joe Klein's assessment is that white Americans *have* deeply absorbed the stereotype of blacks as criminals. In one study, subjects were shown a picture of a white man holding a razor in an argument with a black man. When the subjects were questioned, whites remembered the black man holding the razor.[24]

Stereotypes of black crime affect judicial outcomes as well. For example, *Two Nations* author Andrew Hacker stated that the overwhelming and overblown white fear of black criminals may have had a hand in the Simi Valley jury's acquittal of the officers who beat Rodney King. Suburbanites are half as likely to be victims of crime as city dwellers.[25] But, said Hacker, suburban fear of black crime may have spurred the Simi Valley jury to give the police carte blanche in keeping black suspects down—by any means necessary, if you will.[26]

Q: *Is the coverage of black crime overly sensationalistic, or is it just that the crimes blacks commit are worse?*

A: News organizations consistently characterize African-American criminals in ways whites are not, specifically when it comes to animalistic terms such as "pack" and "savage." "A Predator's Struggle to Tame Himself" was the sensationalistic cover line on a June 1993 *New York Times* magazine story about a black criminal trying to reform himself.[27] A 1981 front-page *Los Angeles Times* article was titled "Marauders from Inner-City Prey on L.A.'s Suburbs."[28] Both the *New York Times* and the *Washington Post* called the black suspects in the brutal rape of a jogger in Central Park a "wolf pack"; they did not do the same for the racist white mobs which caused the deaths of black men in the New York neighborhoods Howard Beach and Bensonhurst.[29]

The many types of crime that white Americans are more likely to commit, however, are not thought of as "white" crimes. It's not just white-collar crimes like embezzlement, but also some of the most shocking violent crimes like serial killings.

Q: *Does the criminal justice system treat black and white victims differently?*

A: In both the reporting of and penalties for crime, this country's media and criminal justice system place a greater value on white life than black. White victims are much more likely to be the beneficiaries of profiles and "follow-ups" with their friends and families, humanizing their pain. Black victims are quick statistics.

In 1989, the murder of pregnant white Bostonian Carol Stuart by a black man as she and her husband drove home from childbirth classes was splashed on the front pages of newspapers across the country. Article after article profiled her grieving family and detailed her short life; a front-page *Boston Globe* headline eulogized "The Passing of a Shining Life."[30] Unfortunately for the press, Stuart wasn't killed by a black man at all. That scenario was a hoax by her husband—her murderer—who stood to gain over $600,000 in insurance payments.[31]

Though the fact that her husband killed her does not, of course, lessen her nobility, what made her story so attractive to the media in the first place was the element of trans-racial crime. The white jogger who was raped in Central Park received similar media attention—the *Los Angeles Times*, clear across the country, put the story on the front page six times. But no one was around for follow-ups when, less than a month later, a black mother of four was raped and sodomized at knifepoint and thrown from the roof of a building, nearly to her death. Too often, the opposite of a "shining life" is, literally, a dark life.[32]

While whites are cast as martyrs of crime, blacks are often cast as "deserving" victims. When California physicians, who see the parade of killed and maimed go through their operating rooms every day, began lobbying for gun control, the National Rifle Association (NRA) reacted cynically. Said (NRA) research coordinator Paul Blackman, "They [the doctors] are weeping crocodile tears about hoodlums who shot, stab, and beat for fun"—as if, as is not the case, even the simple majority of black gun victims are criminals.[33]

Most disturbing is the Supreme Court's stance on racial injustice in the death penalty. A murderer is ten times as likely to be sentenced to death for killing a white American as for killing an African-American. Even when factors such as the brutality of the crime are taken into account, murderers are four times as likely to be sentenced to death if the victim is white. Although the justices did not dispute those figures, they ruled that this racism is "an inevitable part of our criminal justice system." And at the same time the court has decided not to value the lives of African-American victims, black criminals make up 40 percent of the death row population.[34]

Q: *Aren't African-Americans more interested in blaming white America for the crime problem than helping to take care of it themselves?*

"Instead of browbeating whites for being concerned about the epidemic of inner-city violent crime, African-American leaders could do everyone a favor by admitting that there is indeed a problem, and that blacks themselves have an interest in solving it."[35]

A: Major media outlets have consistently ignored the attention of black leaders to inner-city black-on-black crime. Apparently they're chagrined that African-Americans are still challenging white racism *as well as* trying to uplift their own communities. The former head of the NAACP, Dr. Benjamin Chavis, helped foster the "gang truce" movement, trying to get young black men to stop killing other African-Americans.[36] In May 1993, Dr. Chavis organized a "gang summit" which took place in Kansas City, Missouri. African-American efforts to stop crime have been consistently underreported in the press. For example, the few stories that have talked about the gang truce movement have been forced to admit that it has helped decrease fatalities, although it is no panacea.[37]

_____ "Old-style" Criminal Injustice

It would be nice to believe that the more blatant forms of criminal injustice were events of the past. Unfortunately, severe police misconduct and perhaps even lynchings are still a part of the judicial landscape.

In the South, several cases have come to light of black men being "railroaded" for crimes they did not commit, and in one case, even being killed, because they were dating white women. David Scott Campbell was just twenty-two years old when he died. In October 1990, officers at the same Mississippi jail where three civil rights workers were murdered in 1964 said he had committed suicide. Friends and family allege he was arrested on a trumped-up charge, hanged by jailers, and embalmed before an autopsy could be conducted. His is just one of forty-six suspicious suicides in the state, most of them black men, which civil rights leaders are asking be investigated by federal officials.[38]

In 1993, the murder conviction of Walter McMillan was overturned when prosecutors conceded that the testimony against him was perjured. McMillan spent six years on Alabama's death row, although at the time of the charge friends swore he had an alibi. McMillan was known in his town of Monroeville, Alabama, for dating a white woman.[39]

Police Brutality

Myth: *Police brutality is a rare occurrence.*

Reality: A study by Amnesty International of police conduct in Los Angeles found abuses too numerous to count. The Los Angeles Police Department and Sheriff's Department (LAPD and LASD), the two largest law enforcement agencies in the metropolitan area, committed numerous incidences of police brutality, police shootings, and cruel use of police dogs. The study was compiled from cases where damages have been paid in civil suits against the LAPD and LASD. Even in most of the cases where citizens won damages from the police, there was no criminal action taken against the officers.[40]

Myth: *Police brutality is a "black" problem.*

Reality: Police brutality, though it disproportionately targets African-Americans, is not a black problem. For example, whites, Latinos, and Asians have been beaten and killed by the LAPD and LASD. The cases include a white musician beaten until he sustained multiple fractures in his leg (resulting in an award of $225,000), a Korean-American shot during a car chase (his parents settled with the department for one million dollars), and a Latino man whose arm was torn by police dog bites (he received $65,000). Police brutality is a "luxury" taxpayers can't afford. The LAPD and LASD alone have paid out tens of millions of dollars to victims of brutality and surviving families.[41]

Myth: *The government is zealous about weeding out police offenders.*

Reality: Police procedure is rarely followed in investigating brutality cases. In March 1991, following a car chase, Rodney King was shocked twice with a Taser gun, kicked, punched, and beaten fifty-six times by batons wielded by Los Angeles police. After the beating, he was hog-tied and left lying on the roadway until an ambulance came. The next day, King's brother went to the station and tried to file a complaint. The station sergeant reported that no investigation was necessary. George Holliday, the man who filmed the police beating King, also tried to file a complaint, and was also rebuffed.[42]

Case Study:
The Rodney King Beating,
Verdicts and Aftermath

Most people reading the accounts of the violence following the April 30, 1992, acquittal of the four police officers who beat Rodney King thought that the reporting was fair, comprehensive, and objective. No doubt, watching the footage on television, they also thought that the unrest consisted mainly of black perpetrators and non-black victims. The reality:

The looting and violence was multi-ethnic. Sixty percent of arrests for "riot-related" violations were of Latinos, and over 10 percent were of non-Hispanic whites.

African-Americans were most likely to be victims. Of the fifty-four victims who died, twenty-five were African-American, nineteen Latino, ten white. Of the ten people shot to death by the police, six were black and four Latino; only one had a gun.[43]

During the riots, local television anchors gave up all pretense of objectivity. Bree Walker of KCBS spat out: "Savages." "They're not smart enough to recognize the damage they've done to themselves. By definition they're idiots," said Kent Shockneck of KNBC. John Beard, a reporter at the same station, said "This has nothing to do with the Rodney King verdict." And stated KABC anchor Paul Moyer: "The number one question here is law enforcement. . . . So what should we do? Warn them once and shoot them?"[44]

Blacks, at least initially, were not given credit for being "Good Samaritans" as well as perpetrators. An early *New York Times* account of the beating of Reginald Denny reads: "Mr. Denny, who is 33, managed to crawl back to his . . . truck and began driving away."[45] In fact, several African-Americans helped him to his truck and escorted him to the hospital.

Myth: *The punishment in the case of beating Reginald Denny was "softer" than the punishment in the beating of Rodney King.*

Another *Wall Street Journal* editorial read: "A rioter 'excited' by Reginald Denny walks; police 'excited' by Rodney King go to prison. . . . [A]ny notion we may once have had of commonly held justice has gone off the rails right now."[46]

Reality: In truth, for the *convictions* which came down in the cases, the officers who beat Rodney King got off easier. The defendants in the beating of Reginald Denny were being tried largely for attempted murder, a crime which required the jury to assess their state of mind and convict only if they thought the two were specifically trying to kill (as opposed to viciously injure) Denny. When the jury did not come to that conclusion, the two men received more minor convictions. One was sentenced to "time served" for the year and a quarter he spent behind bars between the 1992 arrest and the end of the trial in 1993; the other received a ten-year sentence. On the other hand, the judge in the "King II" case flagrantly disobeyed federal sentencing guidelines, which called for a seven- to-ten-year sentence. U.S. District Judge John G. Davies ruled, "The victim's wrongful conduct contributed significantly to provoking the offensive behavior." Sgt. Stacey C. Koon and Officer Laurence M. Powell could have been sentenced to up to ten years in prison and fined a quarter of a million dollars; instead, they received two-and-a-half-year sentences.[47]

If anything, both the first trial in the beating of Rodney King and the trial for the beating of Reginald Denny showed the weaknesses of the prosecution. The prosecutor in the first King case made no objections when the trial venue was moved to overwhelmingly white Simi Valley, and he did not mount a serious challenge to the successful "explanation" of the video by the defense. In the case of the Denny beating, the prosecutors were overreaching with their indictments. In addition, the media's constant focus on the Denny trial did not include enough of a focus on the successful defense arguments. Therefore, the acquittals on attempted murder came as a shock, and provoked outrage. We have a right to expect more from the criminal justice system, and more from the media, if we want both justice and peace in America.

Notes to Chapter Fifteen

1. William F. Buckley, Jr., "Black Crime: Is it Rooted in Racism? 'Racism' is Merely a Scapegoat," *San Diego Union Tribune* (1/6/93).

2. "Criminal Victimization in the United States, 1991" *Bureau of Justice Statistics* (December 1992); and author's interview with Alan Beck of the Bureau of Justice Statistics, October 1993.

3. *Legal Times*, "Former Death Row Inmates Speak Out" (10/3/94).

4. The Massachusetts Department of Public Health, *Violence in Massachusetts* (1987).

5. Author's interview with Alan Beck of the Bureau of Justice Statistics, October 1993.

6. E. F. Loftus and J. M. Doyle, "New Jersey Supreme Court Final Report of the Task Force on Minority Concerns," *New Jersey Law Journal* (8/10/93).

7. Andrew Hacker, *Two Nations Black and White, Separate, Hostile, Unequal* (New York: Scribners, 1992): 184.

8. *Sourcebook of Criminal Justice Statistics—1992*, The Bureau of Justice Statistics (1993): 46–47.

9. William Booth and Christina Sherry, "Civil Rights Leaders Decry Florida Dragnet," *Washington Post* (9/17/93).

10. Stephen L. Carter, "After L.A., How to Heal," *Wall Street Journal* (5/1/92).

11. Author's reporting for *Newsweek* in 1990.

12. "Persons Arrested, by Charge and Race," "Jail Inmates, by Race and Detention Status: 1978 to 1991," and "State Prison Inmates—Selected Characteristics: 1986 and 1991"; *Statistical Abstract of the United States: 1993:* 198 and 210. Totals include blacks of Hispanic origin.

13. Seth Mydans, "The Courts on Trial," *New York Times* (4/8/93).

14. U.S. Sentencing Commission, *Mandatory Minimum Penalties in the Federal Criminal Justice System.*

15. Author's conversation with John Dowd, information officer for the Drug Enforcement Administration, New York City office (10/31/94).

16. Don Edwards, "Congress Swamped the Courts," *New York Times* (7/7/93).

17. Hacker, *Two Nations*, p. 196.

18. Bob Herbert, "Injustice and Ice Cream," *New York Times* (9/15/93).

19. Mydans, "The Courts on Trial."

20. Calculations by Alan Beck of the U.S. Bureau of Justice Statistics, interviewed by author.

21. *Sourcebook of Criminal Justice Statistics—1992*, The Bureau of Justice Statistics (1993); *Criminal Victimization in the United States, 1991*, Bureau of Justice Statistics (December 1992): 60.

22. *Criminal Victimization in the United States, 1991:* 150.

23. Robert M. Entman, "Blacks in the News: Television, Modern Racism and Cultural Change," *Journalism Quarterly*, vol. 69, no. 2, (Summer 1992): 341–361.

24. Coramae Richley Mann, *Unequal Justice: A Question of Color* (Indiana University Press, 1993).
25. "Criminal Victimization in the United States, 1991": front cover chart.
26. Author's interview of Andrew Hacker, April 1992.
27. Peter Kerr, "A Predator's Struggle to Tame Himself," *New York Times* magazine (6/27/93).
28. David Shaw, "Newspapers Struggling to Raise Minority Coverage," *Los Angeles Times* (12/12/90).
29. David Shaw, "Despite Advances, Stereotypes Still Used by Media," *Los Angeles Times* (12/12/90).
30. Sally Jacobs, "The Passing of a Shining Life," *Boston Globe* (10/25/89).
31. Kevin Cullen and Mike Barnacle, "Probers Suspect Stuart Killed Wife to Collect Insurance, Start Restaurant," *Boston Globe* (1/10/90).
32. Shaw, "Newspapers Struggling to Raise Minority Coverage."
33. Jane Gross, "Joining War Over Guns, New Voices: Physicians," *New York Times* (11/16/93).
34. *McCleskey* v. *Kemp*, 481 U.S. 279, 312 (1987); *Sourcebook of Criminal Justice Statistics—1991:* 670.
35. Mark Thompson, "Violence and the Verdict," *Wall Street Journal* (4/19/93).
36. Author's interview with Dr. Benjamin Chavis, April 1993.
37. Alex Kotlowitz, "Urban Cease-Fire," *Wall Street Journal* (4/29/93).
38. Peter Applebome, "Series of Deaths in Mississippi Jails Prompt Call for Federal Investigation," *New York Times* (3/18/93).
39. Richard Cohen, "Death by 'Justice,'" *New York Times* (3/4/93).
40. Amnesty International U.S.A., *Police Brutality in Los Angeles, California, United States of America* (June 1992).
41. Ibid.
42. Ibid.
43. Mark Schubb, "Race, Lies & Videotape," *Extra! Focus on Racism in the Media* (July/August 1992).
44. Ibid.
45. Seth Mydans, "11 Dead in Los Angeles Rioting," *New York Times* (5/1/92).
46. *Wall Street Journal* editorial without byline, "Verdicts and Violence," (10/22/93).
47. *New York Times,* no byline, "Sympathetic Judge Gives Officers Two and a Half Years in King Beating," (8/5/93).

Drugs and Health

There is no point in my making a speech on crime control to a bunch of addicts.

—Boston University President John Silber, a contender in the Democratic primary of the 1990 Massachusetts governor's race, when asked why he didn't take his "get tough on crime" message to black neighborhoods.[1]

THIS dual-issue chapter focuses on the devastating but misunderstood issue of drugs and the black community, and on African-American health. From the television images of black youths arrested for street dealing to photographs of black men and women smoking crack, coverage of drug issues leads Americans to believe that this national problem is a black problem. News organizations do not show the other side—that over 70 percent of American drug users are white. In addition, the drug use which does occur in the black community often is linked simply to race, as if African-Americans are *inherently* drug abusers, when socioeconomics is a far more important factor.

The second part of this chapter focuses on African-American health issues, from the startlingly high black infant-mortality rate to the inferior treatment of black heart-attack victims. Again, the issue of socioeconomics comes to the fore. Fifteen percent of Americans, a total of 37.4 million people, don't have any health insurance.[2] That figure includes a disproportionate number of African-Americans, who are generally less wealthy and well employed than whites and thus are even less likely to have sufficient health coverage. There's also bad blood between the black community and the medical establishment. The most famous example, though far from the only one, is a syphilis study popularly called the "Tuskeegee Experiment" which ran from the 1930s to 1970. Researchers studied black men with syphilis. Even after penicillin was proven a cure, the researcher withheld treatment, causing the unnecessary death or disability of many of the men. There is evidence, with examples listed below in the chapter, that racism still affects the way some patients are treated in today's medical establishment.

Drugs and the
_____ African-American Community

Myth: *Drugs are a black, inner-city problem.*

When John Silber made the statement at the top of this chapter in a debate during the 1990 Massachusetts governor's race, some in the media supported Silber's rhetoric; the *Christian Science Monitor* praised him as "tough-talking" and "forthright."[3] Endorsements like this from the media allow statements like Silber's to go unchallenged.

Reality: Although drug use tends to be higher in inner-city neighborhoods than better-off ones[4], Silber's statement betrays a shocking ignorance of just who is consuming the majority of drugs in this country. The truth of the matter is that African-Americans account for just 12 percent of users, while over 70 percent of drug users are white. While the government's "War on Drugs" and the media's coverage of urban users target African-Americans, the truth behind the images is startlingly different. Until age thirty-five, African-Americans are significantly less likely to have ever used an illegal drug than whites. Among all age groups, 38 percent of whites and 39 percent of blacks have used illegal drugs.[5]

Socioeconomics and neighborhood type are a much better predictor of drug use than race. Poverty, despair, and drug use go hand in hand. For both blacks and whites, unemployed people are over twice as likely to be current drug users as individuals with jobs. Fully 28 percent of unemployed African-Americans and 23 percent of unemployed whites use drugs. Homeless people are the heaviest drug and alcohol users; 20 percent of homeless Americans consume an average of at least five drinks a day. And, finally, college graduates are less likely than Americans with less education to use drugs. In fact, the National Institutes on Drug Abuse determined, "race/ethnicity was not a significant determinant" of drug use.[6]

Even Bush administration "drug czar" William Bennett identified the nation's typical cocaine user as "white, male, a high-school graduate, employed full-time, and living in a small metropolitan area." White users are more likely to have the means to hide their abuse. Said Hubert Williams, head of law-enforcement think tank The Police Foundation, "people likely to be running around on the streets are likely to be those on a lower socioeconomic level."[7]

Analysis: Drug Use Numbers by Race

Following are statistics from the National Institutes on Drug Abuse which illustrate the true scope of the problem:[8]
An estimated 75 million Americans have used a drug ille-

gally in their lifetime. Of these individuals, only nine million were black, or 12 percent of the total.

Young whites are more likely to use drugs than young African-Americans. In addition, white high school seniors are almost three times as likely to be binge drinkers than blacks: 33 percent versus 12 percent. The age at which Americans first try drugs is startlingly low: fourteen is the average age at which both black and white users first tried marijuana and/or cocaine. Children in single-parent homes are more susceptible to drugs: 15 percent of white and 11 percent of black youths in two parent homes have tried drugs, versus 25 percent of white and 15 percent of black youths in single-parent homes.

Overall, whites and blacks are roughly as likely to have ever used drugs: 38 percent of whites have tried controlled substances, compared with 39 percent of blacks. Here are the breakdowns by age:

Ever Used Illicit Drugs:

	White	Black
all ages:	38%	39%
12–17:	21%	20%
18–25:	59%	46%
26–34:	66%	58%
35+ :	27%	34%

Blacks, however, are more likely to be current drug users (within the past month) than whites: 6 percent of whites and 9 percent of blacks have used illegal drugs within the past month. In most large cities, the percentage of blacks currently using drugs is higher than for whites; however, Los Angeles is a notable exception, with 11 percent current use for whites, and 9 percent for blacks. Almost one-third of Americans twelve and over have smoked marijuana at least once in their lives; 12 percent of whites and 11 percent of blacks have tried cocaine.

Myth: *Crack is by nature a "black" drug, and its use is rampant within the community.*

Reality: Again, the answer is socioeconomics. A study in the *Journal of the American Medical Association* (*JAMA*) found that "given similar social and environmental conditions, crack use does not strongly depend on race-specific (e.g., biologic) personal factors." The study matched crack use figures with neighborhoods, analyzing them by factors including population density, neighborhood unemployment, and residents' education. The researchers found that blacks and whites from similar neighborhoods are equally likely to smoke crack. However, African-Americans are more likely to live in drug-infested neighborhoods than whites.

Even given that fact, the vast majority of African-Americans have never used crack. The 1988 National Household Survey on Drug Abuse, compiled during the height of the crack wave, found that over 97 percent of African-Americans had never smoked crack. Only 2.4 percent of blacks, 2.1 percent of Hispanics, and 1.0 percent of whites had ever used the drug. Among those aged 18 to 25, whites were *more* likely to smoke crack than blacks: 3.3 percent of whites and 2.8 percent of blacks had used the drug. Said the *JAMA* article, these numbers strengthen "the evidence that, given similar social conditions, crack cocaine smoking does not depend strongly on race per se" but rather on factors like the quality of neighborhood life.[9]

Myth: *The problem is not the drugs but the crime that goes with it—and that crime is black.*

Reality: Joe Klein's statement (analyzed in the previous chapter) that, "White racism is on the rise, largely in reaction to the horrendous, crack-driven city crime wave of recent years," follows this reasoning. But although drug users commit crimes at a far higher rate than non-users, Klein couldn't be more wrong about the problem being a "black" one. In 1989, 5 percent of non-drug-using whites had committed a crime in the past year, versus 20 percent of white drug users. For blacks, the figures were 8 and 25 percent. Black inmates were more likely to have committed their offense for drug money: 16 percent of blacks versus 12 percent of whites did, a difference consistent with the greater poverty in the black community. With cocaine, for example, costing $90–120 per gram, desperate users will quickly turn to crime. Most prisoners have taken drugs, with whites being slightly more likely to have tried drugs than African-Americans: 81 percent versus 77 percent.[10]

Myth: *Blacks are more cavalier in their attitudes toward drugs.*

Reality: Blacks are actually more likely than whites to perceive great risk in trying cocaine, the occasional use of crack, smoking one or more packs of cigarettes a day, and having one or two drinks daily. Most people also find it easy to get illegal drugs. A majority of blacks and whites of all ages said it was easy to obtain marijuana. Significantly more blacks than whites said it was easy to obtain cocaine, which may help explain differences in use.[11]

Drugs As a Health Issue

Blacks are two and a half times as likely to die of alcohol-induced causes as whites, and twice as likely to die of drug-induced causes. (In all, alcohol kills twice as many African-Americans as drugs do.)[12] One reason is likely the quality of treatment. Although blacks are more likely to mention drugs as one of the causes for a visit to the emergency room, they are more likely to be treated and released, whereas whites are more likely to be admitted.[13]

Whites are nearly twice as likely to drive drunk as blacks: 16 percent of whites aged 18 to 49 versus 9 percent of blacks.[14]

The Clinton administration proposed focusing on drug treatment during the national health care debate. There are estimated to be over a million people who need drug treatment and aren't getting it. In 1992, there were a record number of drug-related medical emergencies: almost 200,000 for cocaine and 48,000 for heroin.[15]

___ African-American Health Issues

Blacks and Inadequate Health Care: Medical Racism and Poverty

According to an article in the *New England Journal of Medicine,* black patients tend to receive less intensive hospital services and are less likely to be satisfied with the care they receive than are white patients with similar health insurance coverage. It's clear that there are still deep problems with the medical attention African-Americans receive. Overall, blacks die an average of six years younger than whites. The average life expectancy for black men is 66 years, compared with 72 years for white men. For women, the numbers are 74 years versus 80.[16] Following are some of the indicators of the substandard care African-Americans receive:

Black infant mortality is twice as high as that for whites. While black infants' chances of surviving to their first birthday are getting better in pure numbers, they are actually getting worse in relation to whites. In 1950, a black infant was 1.6 times as likely to die as a white infant. By 1988, black infants were 2.1 times as likely to die as whites.[17] According to the National Center for Health Statistics, in 1987 a stunning 11,461 of the 38,408 babies who died before their first birthday were black. Poverty isn't the only cause for the high black rate. Even black middle-class families suffer higher mortality rates, according to a study of black and white families where both parents had attended college. Suspected causes behind the mortality gap include a lifetime of shoddy medical care, lack of prenatal care and—most telling—the chronic stress of being black in America.[18]

Black heart patients get less-advanced treatment than white ones. A study of heart treatment in veteran's hospitals, where the patient's finances don't influence the picture, made it clear that racism and not economics are at work. White patients were consistently more likely to receive advanced surgery for certain heart conditions. An article on the broader issue of medical racism said that for health problems where there is one standard treatment, whites and blacks tend to receive the same care. But in situations where the doctor has more choices in the different types of treatments, blacks get less-advanced treatment than whites. "(B)lack patients are less likely than white patients to receive treatments that can often relieve symptoms and sometimes prolong life," said the paper. "When racism results in segregated housing, inferior schools, and unemployment for blacks, the negative consequences for health, such as infant mortality, are clear."[19]

Another heart study found similar evidence. Although the survival rate for all Americans who suffer massive heart attacks is staggeringly low, it is even lower for blacks. Blacks who go into cardiac arrest are half as likely as whites to survive once they are admitted to a hospital. (In all, 97 percent of whites who go into cardiac arrest die, compared with 99 percent of blacks.)[20]

Blacks are more likely to suffer kidney failure, but less likely to get a transplant. White dialysis patients are twice as likely as blacks to receive a kidney transplant, in part because blacks are less likely to have a suitable living kidney donor, and are also less likely to be the candidate with the "best" match on the national transplant list. Some physicians charge that the standard of "best match" is flawed, and that many more African-Americans could be successful transplant recipients. In all, blacks make up 31 percent of patients on the kidney waiting list, but received only 22 percent of available kidneys in 1990. Those African-Americans who got kidneys were on the waiting list an average of fourteen months, versus eight months for whites.[21]

"Environmental racism" makes it disproportionately likely that African-Americans will live in toxin-tainted areas. Sixty percent of the total black population in the United States (and 60 percent of the total Hispanic population as well) live in communities with one or more uncontrolled toxic waste sites. A confidential memo by the Environmental Protection Agency revealed that even they considered environmental racism "one of the most politically explosive environmental issues yet to emerge." They planned to diffuse the issue by seeking good press in minority publications, until the memo revealing their plan was leaked to the press.[22]

Money and Health Care

Money, like race, is a good predictor of how long Americans will live and how healthy they will be. In 1986, Americans making less than $9,000 per year were at least three times as likely to die early as people making $25,000 or more per year. And in 1991, people with incomes under $10,000 were more than seven times as likely to describe themselves as being in poor health as those making more than $35,000. Poor people also tend to be hospitalized more often than rich ones, often for conditions like asthma and diabetes that are treatable at home with the proper care.[23]

The Most Prevalent Diseases and Conditions in _____ the Black Community

In 1985, the U.S. Department of Health and Human Services reported that in excess of 60,000 minority Americans die each year from preventable diseases.

Cancer and Smoking Deaths

Black men have the highest cancer rates in the nation. Black women have a rate higher than white women, but lower than white men.[24] Lung cancer, which kills 140,000 Americans each year, is the most preventable form of cancer—90 percent of deaths come from smoking. Eleven percent of blacks and 14 percent of whites are heavy smokers.[25] All told, smoking causes 390,000 deaths a year.[26]

The instruments for diagnosing cervical cancer are so rare in New York City public hospitals that women have to wait an average of four months for the procedure, called a colposcopy. Black women are two and a half times as likely as whites to die of cervical cancer, which is slow-growing and highly preventable if caught early.[27]

AIDS

AIDS is now the eighth leading cause of death in the country, and is particularly hard on the black community.[28] Blacks are only

12 percent of the U.S. population, but 30 percent of people with AIDS. Fully 54 percent of children under age 13 with AIDS are black. An estimated 1 million Americans are infected with HIV, the virus that causes AIDS. More than 400,000 Americans have full-blown AIDS.[29] And a study by the Department of Veteran's Affairs found that AZT, the primary anti-viral drug licensed by the government against AIDS, is less useful for blacks.[30]

Diabetes

Adult-onset diabetes, the more treatable of two kinds, occurs 33 percent more often in blacks, who are twice as likely to die from it as whites with the condition.[31]

Heart Disease

Heart disease is the leading killer of black men and women, and the leading killer nationwide. Black men have the highest incidence of heart disease; the rate for black women is much higher than for white women, and almost as high as the rate for white men.[32]

High Blood Pressure

Blacks are 33 percent more likely than whites to have high blood pressure, which can lead to kidney disease, stroke, heart failure, and blindness.[33]

Diet

According to the National Medical Association, black eating patterns still reflect some of the foods available during slavery, when blacks tended to eat pigs' feet, chitterlings, and other cuts of meat undesirable to whites. Today, African-Americans (and all Americans) don't do as much physical work as in the past. And the availability of food has made it easy to overeat high-fat foods.

Homicide and Suicide

Blacks are vastly more likely to be murdered than whites. The black male homicide rate, seventy-one deaths per 100,000 black men, is seven times the white male rate. On the other hand, black men and women are less likely to commit suicide than whites. Black women have the lowest suicide rate, less than half that of white women and one tenth that of white men.[34]

A Final Word: Media Coverage of African-American Drug and Health Issues

On the surface, the media's handling of drug and health issues as they impact African-Americans may seem very dissimilar. In fact, the media coverage on these two crucial topics is like two sides of the same coin. African-American drug use is highly scrutinized—and, unfortunately, this scrutiny is very often completely factually incorrect and stereotypic. Racial discrepancies in health care and life expectancy, on the other hand, have just as profound an impact on the lives of African-Americans, but, if anything, tend to remain beneath the media's radar, and out of the public eye. There's a lesson in how both of these issues are handled by the media, and in their ultimate impact on African-American lives. Lack of exposure and overexposure are equally damaging phenomena in news coverage. At the same time African-Americans are stigmatized for supposedly high rates of drug use (a widely held belief which is, of course, a fiction), other issues such as black infant mortality and quality of hospital care go unexplored. Both African-Americans and non-black Americans would be better served by news coverage that devotes equal time to less "sexy" issues, like health care, as well as to typical front-page topics like drug use. With the 1994 debate over national health care, medical issues have gained a relatively new prominence in the media, potentially providing a forum for the airing of questions about racial equality in health coverage. The hype about race and drug use, however, shows little signs of abating.

Notes to Chapter Sixteen

1. David S. Broder, " 'Bunch of Addicts' Remark Stirs Primary Race," *Washington Post* (11/14/90).
2. U.S. Department of Commerce, *Money Income of Households, Families, and Persons in the United States: 1992*, (October 1993): xi.
3. Elizabeth Ross, "Late Deciders Will Call Bay State Governor's Race," *Christian Science Monitor* (11/5/90).
4. U.S. Department of Census Press Release, CB91–66 (2/21/91).
5. National Institute on Drug Abuse, *National Household Survey on Drug Abuse: Population Estimates 1991* (1992).
6. National Institutes on Drug Abuse, *Drug Abuse Among Racial/Ethnic Groups* (January 1993); Clare Mundell, "Patterns and Trends in Drug Abuse in Washington, D.C." (The Center for Substance Abuse Research [CESAR], September 1993).
7. Sam Meddis, "Whites, Not Blacks, at the Core of Drug Crisis," *USA Today* (12/20/89).
8. National Institute on Drug Abuse, *National Household Survey on Drug Abuse: Population Estimates 1991*.
9. Marsha Lillie-Blanton, et al., "Probing the Meaning of Racial/

Ethnic Group Comparisons in Crack Cocaine Smoking," *The Journal of the American Medical Association*, vol. 269, no. 8. (2/24/93): 993–997.

10. Bureau of Justice Statistics, *Survey of Inmates in Local Jails* (1989).

11. National Institute on Drug Abuse, *National Household Survey on Drug Abuse: Population Estimates 1991*.

12. National Center for Health Statistics, *Age-Adjusted Death Rates, Selected Causes, by Race and Sex, U.S., 1989* (Washington, D.C., 1991).

13. National Institute on Drug Abuse, *National Household Survey on Drug Abuse: Population Estimates 1991*.

14. Ibid.

15. Ronald J. Osttrow, "White House Shifting Focus of War on Drugs to Hard-Core Addicts," *Washington Times* (10/20/93).

16. National Center for Health Statistics, *Annual Summary of Births, Marriages, Divorces and Deaths: United States, 1992* (Washington, D.C., 1993): 16.

17. Paul H. Wise and DeWayne M. Pursley, "Infant Mortality as a Social Mirror," *New England Journal of Medicine* 326, no. 23 (June 4, 1992): 1558–59.

18. Kenneth C. Schoendorf, et al., "Mortality Among Infants of Black as Compared to White College-Educated Parents," *New England Journal of Medicine* 326, no. 23 (June 4, 1992): 1522–26.

19. Jeff Whittle, et al., "Racial Differences in the Use of Cardiovascular Procedures in the Department of Veterans Affairs Medical System," *The New England Journal of Medicine* 329, no. 9 (Aug. 26, 1993): 621–26; and John A. Ayanian, "Heart Disease in Black and White," *The New England Journal of Medicine* 329, no. 9 (Aug 26, 1993): 656–57.

20. Lance B. Becker, "Racial Differences in the Incidence of Cardiac Arrest and Subsequent Survival," *The New England Journal of Medicine* 329, no. 9 (Aug. 26, 1993): 600–606.

21. Robert S. Gaston, et al., "Racial Equality in Renal Transplantation," *The Journal of the American Medical Association* 270, no. 11 (September 15, 1993): 1352–56.

22. Elizabeth Martinez, "Media White-Out of Environmental Racism," *Extra!* (July/August 1992).

23. Marcia Angell, "Privilege and Health—What is the Connection?" *New England Journal of Medicine* 329, no. 2 (July 8, 1993): 126–27.

24. National Medical Association, "National Medical Association Fact Sheet: Cancer and Blacks."

25. Ibid.
26. National Medical Association, "National Medical Association Fact Sheet: Smoking."
27. J. A. Lobbia, "Anti-Smear Campaign," *Village Voice* (7/20/93); National Medical Association, "National Medical Association Fact Sheet: Cancer and Blacks."
28. National Center for Health Statistics, *Annual Summary of Births, Marriages, Divorces and Deaths: United States, 1992* (Washington, D.C., 1993).
29. American Medical Association, "Will Attention Bring Action? Federal AIDS Spending, Part I," *American Medical News*, 329. no. 3 (1/17/94).
30. Reuter's, "AZT's Effectiveness for Minority Groups Will Be Studied," (4/16/91).
31. National Medical Association, "National Medical Association Fact Sheet: Diabetes and Blacks."
32. National Medical Association, "National Medical Association Fact Sheet: Blacks and Cardiovascular Disease."
33. National Medical Association, "National Medical Association Fact Sheet: Blacks and High Blood Pressure."
34. National Center for Health Statistics, *Annual Summary of Births, Marriages, Divorces and Deaths, 1992*, (Washington, D.C., 1993): 20–22.

seventeen

The Politics of
Blackness

The trouble with Lani Guinier is that she believes it is "us versus them." In her writings she extrapolates from anachronistic southern situations—and assumes, against the evidence of the past quarter century, that white racism is structural, unyielding and insuppurable.

—From a *Newsweek* column by Joe Klein.[1]

A FRICAN-Americans have made great strides in getting equal access in America's political system. Black Americans could not fully participate in the political system until the civil rights movement of the 1950s and 1960s. But some things have not changed. Again and again, white fears of African-Americans are manipulated for political gain. Not just blatant racists like David Duke but politicians like former President George Bush have played the race card successfully. At the same time, the number of African-Americans succeeding in gaining political office grows greater with every passing year. This chapter begins with a short statistical overview of African-American politicians, then continues with five trouble spots in media coverage of black political issues. The chapter concludes with two political case studies that typify the political waters of the 1990s: the 1991 David Duke campaign and the 1993 Lani Guinier incident.

Black Political Participation in the 1990s: Overview

Black political representation has risen exponentially. The number of black elected officials at all levels of government rose from fewer than 300 in 1965 to more than 8,000 by January 1993. That year's roster included forty Senators and Congressmen and 356 black mayors, thirty-eight of whom presided over cities of 50,000 or more and sixty-nine of whom were women. Over 2,300 of America's 8,000-plus black elected officials were women.[2]

As of January 1994, some of America's current black mayors included Bill Campbell of Atlanta, Mike White of Cleveland, Dennis Archer of Detroit, Norm Rice of Seattle, and Sharon Sayles Belton of Minneapolis.[3] Within the past decade, African-American leaders presided over Philadelphia, Los Angeles, New York, and Chicago (Wilson Goode, Tom Bradley, David Dinkins and Harold Washington, respectively). Virginia Governor Douglas Wilder was the first elected African-American governor, and served from 1991 to 1994.[4]

There are several African-Americans in the cabinet of President Bill Clinton and other high federal positions. Among them: Commerce Secretary Ron Brown, drug czar (director of the White House Office of Drug Control Policy) Lee P. Brown, Surgeon General Joycelyn Elders, Secretary of Veteran's Affairs Jesse Brown, and Secretary of Energy Hazel Rollins O'Leary.[5]

African-Americans hold positions on all but one of the twenty-two standing committees of the House of Representatives. Among the most powerful representatives are John Conyers (D-MI), chair of the Government Operations Committee, and Ronald Dellums (D-CA), chair of the Armed Services Committee. Representative Kweisi Mfume (D-MD) is head of the Congressional Black Caucus, the organization of blacks in the House and Senate.[6]

African-Americans were instrumental in the Clinton victory. George Bush won 41 percent of the white vote, while Clinton won 39 percent. African-Americans made up the margin of victory. The same was true in 1976, when 47 percent of whites voted for Jimmy Carter and 52 percent for Gerald Ford.[7]

The Supreme Court: African-Americans in Peril.

In 1993, the Supreme Court decided a case that would make it harder for Americans to prove racial discrimination and allowed challenges to black Congressional districts, calling them "bizarrely shaped." The challenge was granted even though no one claimed they'd been injured. By contrast, equally oddly shaped districts drawn to favor incumbents were allowed to stand.[8] The conservative Reagan–Bush legacy on the court has been only partially mitigated by President Clinton's appointment of two new justices. Many African-Americans have been disappointed by the voting patterns of Clarence Thomas (appointed by former President Bush), who took the seat on the Court vacated by legendary Justice Thurgood Marshall. Thomas has consistently taken conservative, sometimes ultra-conservative positions. During his confirmation hearings, he was accused of sexual harassment by African-American law professor Anita Hill.[9]

Will the Real Black Voter
Please Stand Up?

African-Americans are labeled "liberal," when in fact, black political opinion covers a broad spectrum. A 1992 poll

by the Joint Center for Political Studies and HBO found that
African-Americans are far from the political monolith they are
often assumed to be. Some of the results[10]:

- Seventy-three percent of African-Americans consider
  themselves Democrats; 4 percent said they were Republicans, 23 percent said they were independents. For
  African-Americans under 35, 62 percent said they were
  Democrats and 34 percent said they were independents.

- Fifty-eight percent said they'd limit the benefits of single
  mothers who "have additional children while on welfare."

- Seventy-three percent supported mandatory sentences
  for drug dealers.

- Ninety percent said they'd increase government efforts
  to enforce child-support laws.

- Ninety-five percent favored enhanced job training, education, and child care for poor people.

- Eighty-one percent said they would cut defense "dramatically" in order to free up money to help the nation's cities.

- Seventy-one percent blamed "twelve years of Reagan-
  Bush neglect" for America's troubled cities, versus 13
  percent who thought that the Great Society programs begun during the sixties are to blame.

- Eighty-three percent favored school-choice voucher programs.

Conservatives are realizing what liberals have sometimes
not: that blacks hold many "conservative" values. For example, the traditionally white Christian Coalition, a group
founded by televangelist Pat Robertson, has in recent years
begun recruiting African-Americans and Hispanics on issues
like school choice.[11]

Media Failings in the Coverage
_____ of Black Political Issues

ISSUE #1: Black politicians are either depicted as "too black" or "not black."

Black politicians are rarely quoted on anything except racial issues, even if their expertise is far broader. For example, news organizations quote minority legislators when it comes to civil rights, but not "mainstream" issues like the economy. A report by Harvard's Kennedy School of Government studied coverage of Congressman William Gray (D-PA) and former New York Mayor David Dinkins, and found that they were identified as black even when the stories had nothing to do with racial issues. "The practice of constant racial identification for blacks but not for whites seems likely only to reproduce in voters' minds . . . the racial division," the report concluded.[12]

In addition, "crossover" black politicians, like Virginia Governor L. Douglas Wilder, Atlanta Mayor Andrew Young, and William Gray are set up by the press as and lauded for being less "black."[13] Often, these politicians are described as a "new breed" and set in opposition to other black politicians. This both bolsters the old stereotype of the loud, angry, racially polarized black politician and creates a new one of the "nonblack" black leader. One case in point: the *Wall Street Journal's* coverage of Mayor Michael R. White of Cleveland. The multi-level headline included the phrases: "Cleveland's Mayor Shuns Black Themes to Court White Votes," "Crossover Politics Help Blur Many Racial Lines Drawn by Previous Generation," and "New Pragmatism." The body of the story continued the theme. "Replacing older leaders such as [mayoral rival and fellow African-American] Mr. Forbes, with his hot temper and racially confrontative style, they [the "new" black politicians] see themselves as builders of broad constituencies working within the system, not envoys of the black community opposing the system."

White politicians are not judged against some media-created standard of their race, and certainly are not constantly compared to other politicians based on racial categories. For example, the actions of white public servants with reputations for steering money toward their districts and constituencies, like "Senator Pothole" Alfonse D'Amato (R-NY), are not given a racial spin by the media.

ISSUE #2: Black politicians who've committed crimes or other transgressions receive the most media attention. Often race is inserted in stories where it has no place.

In general, political stories about blacks are much more likely than coverage of whites to depict them as criminal or grasping and racially self-interested. A 1990–91 study of black images in network television news by Northwestern professor Robert Entman found that Supreme Court Justice Clarence Thomas and former D.C. Mayor Marion Barry received by far the most attention. Thomas, of course, was accused of sexual harassment during his confirmation hearings, and Barry had smoked crack cocaine. General Colin Powell and Health and Human Services Secretary Louis Sullivan, who got the most neutral and positive coverage, received far less attention. In fact, *one-third* of the coverage of black politicians included accusations that the leader had committed a crime. Black leaders are also likely to be shown making demands on government for the black community, and are less likely to be shown praising government. Says Entman, "That the Barry stories comprised a high proportion of all ABC images of black politicians during the sample year is due to network standards that emphasize unusual controversy and drama, not to a reality that the typical black mayor is, like Barry, a corrupt drug user."

However, "the networks might have promoted inaccurate cognitions among white audiences who took Barry as representing a larger category."[14]

1993 coverage of the allegations that Commerce secretary Ron Brown took money to influence U.S. Vietnam policy are a good example of the press's eagerness to insert race into unrelated controversies. *Newsweek*'s story on the controversy hinged on the conceit that Brown used his race to pull a fast one in Washington. The article described him as "a go-between whose ease and savvy in the white world. . . . has left Brown free to maneuver with a minimum of accountability." It also derides one of Brown's supporters with the phrase: "he knew another soul brother when he saw one."[15] Other publications, even ones with questionable records on racial issues, framed this story quite differently. A critical piece in the *Wall Street Journal* titled "Ron Brown, His Own Worst Enemy" described Brown as a consummate Washington insider and focused on his role as lobbyist with the law firm Patton, Boggs & Blow. Their coverage was critical without resorting to race baiting.[16]

ISSUE #3: *Many African-American candidates are not taken seriously by the media.*

One of the clearest examples is the 1983 race for mayor of Chicago. The candidacy of Harold Washington, who would win and become the city's first black mayor, was barely acknowledged by the local media, which preferred to see it as a two-way race between white politicians Jane Byrne and Rich Daley. In fact, editors were so sure of the outcome that a column by a black *Chicago Tribune* writer saying Washington had a chance was never run. (No African-American reporters even covered the campaign). And a *Chicago Sun-Times* poll which showed Washington in second place and Daley in third ran under the headline: "Daley Gaining on Byrne."[17]

1988 presidential candidate Jesse Jackson did not neatly fit the media's conception of a president, and thus was plagued with headlines like *Newsweek*'s cover line "The Power Broker: What Jesse Jackson Wants."[18] An analysis of the coverage Jackson's candidacy received points out that many journalists "were offering the profoundly racist notion that since it was obviously out of the question for a black man to try and be president—Mr. Jackson's proclaimed goal—he must have some secret agenda. No one asks, 'What Does Al Gore Really Want?' " But this was no protest run for the presidency. Jesse Jackson came in first in five states on Super Tuesday, and second in ten more. The media simply could not believe there was a broad-based white Jackson constituency. Said an article in the *Chicago Tribune*: Jackson's "white voters appear to be from both very identifiable and very small minorities themselves. Many of them are politically active homosexuals whose organizations have endorsed his candidacy, and the rest are the residue of the radical and counterculture movements."[19]

ISSUE #4: While black politicians are closely scrutinized for racial objectivity, coverage of white racism is often lacking.

During Harold Washington's mayoral run in Chicago, the media picked up on his supposed racial failings but wasn't nearly so vigilant about blatant white racism in the campaign. The *Tribune*'s endorsement of Daley claimed that Washington's campaign was "racially polarizing." But that same newspaper barely mentioned (on page 18, as part of another story) what the local Democratic party chairman said at a meeting the weekend before the election. "It's a racial thing. Don't kid yourself. I'm calling on you to save your city," he said. "... We're fighting to keep the city the way it is." Steve Neal, the *Tribune*'s political editor at the time, told the media-issues publication *Extra!* that he downplayed the episode "because the election was becoming increasingly racial and we didn't want to stir things further."[20]

In another instance, Republican House leader Robert Michel made racially polarized comments during a taping for the now defunct "USA Today: The Television Show" in September 1988—but the show sat on the interview until after the Presidential election. Michel imitated the character Kingfish from "Amos and Andy" and complained about not being able to sing the original lyrics (which include the word "nigger") to the tune "Old Man River." Michel had a history of playing the race card. In May 1988, he told the *Washington Post*: "It will be surprising, I think, to some people when they look at the Democratic National Convention and see one-third blacks in that composition of delegates." There was no fallout from these statements. The *Chicago Tribune* ran an editorial in November of that year lauding Michel for his "warmth and candor"; the *New York Times* felt he was qualified to write an op-ed about "ethical standards of behavior," which ran on June 18, 1989. As at least one article pointed out, the media's lack of attention to Michel's remarks is in sharp contrast to Jesse Jackson's "Hymietown" remark in 1984. Too often, if African-Americans make racial gaffes, it's "racism"; when whites do, it's "candor."[21]

A corollary of this might be called *the only right minority is the white minority.* Many African-American politicians have been branded "un-American" in their pursuit of minority rights. But at the same time, several of black politicians' most severe critics support minority rights—when the minority is white. Columnist Lally Weymouth, the daughter of the owner of the *Washington Post* Company, condemned Lani Guinier as anti-majority rule. Then Weymouth herself came out against majority rule—when it came to black South Africans. In a May 1993 article on Guinier titled "Radical Justice," Weymouth claimed that the law professor "intends to abolish one of the cornerstones of American democracy—majority rule. . . . The outcome? Minorities, potentially, would enjoy vastly increased influence."[22] Then, in a July article, Weymouth advocated Guinier-style protections for South African whites, stating: "There can't be democracy in South Africa without a measure of formal protection for minorities."[23] (Weymouth isn't the only one concerned about white South Africans. Patrick Buchanan, while a Presidential candidate in 1992, voiced the same opinion.[24]) The lesson? Majority rule is bad—if it applies to blacks. "Radical justice" is good—if it applies to whites.

Case Study: Anatomy of a Racial Smear Campaign— David Duke

David Duke, a former Klan member who won the majority of the white vote in his unsuccessful 1991 campaign for governor of Louisiana, embodied African-American voters' worst fears, and played on every fear and stereotype of blacks to win white votes. Duke's transition from fringe to mainstream politics, and the number of supporters he found, should remain a warning to media experts who declare American racism a thing of the past. Although Duke's racial history is extreme, the issues and battles of his campaign provide a useful measuring stick for the broader problems of race in politics. Duke's brief rise is a particularly poignant statement on how little progress we have made given that, a century before, an African-American briefly served as acting governor of Louisiana. That achievement required a level of racial open-mindedness in the state almost unthinkable now.[25] Both candidates in the 1991 race for governor were far from ideal; Duke was the Republican contender, while the Democrats nominated scandal-plagued governor Edwin Edwards. When the votes were counted, the majority of whites—fully 55 percent—had voted for Duke. In all he won 40 percent of the vote, kept from victory only because of the determination and organization of the black community, which mounted get-out-the-vote rallies and registration drives. Ninety-six percent of African-Americans voted for Edwards.[26]

Worries about potential boycotts may have helped keep Duke out of office. Some Louisiana residents worried that the state would lose business, much as Arizona did after the state refused to honor the national Martin Luther King, Jr.'s Birthday holiday. From the time the holiday was rescinded in January 1987 until November 1991, Arizona had groups and conventions representing over 134,000 visitors cancel, with a net loss of $77 million. They also lost the 1993 Super Bowl, which could have brought in $150 million.[27]

Duke was able to rely on stereotypes about African-Americans to milk white fears. The candidate consistently made statements that didn't fit the facts. "[M]iddle class families have difficulty affording children of their own right now and yet we are financing a very high illegitimate welfare birth rate," he said. Yet the average size of a family on welfare is just two children and their mother. On "Larry King Live," Duke said: "I mean when you take a test for the post office in this country right now and you're white, you're very likely to have your test score dropped fifteen or twenty points and if you are a minority you are liable to have it raised fifteen or twenty points." Actually, there is no race-norming for post office tests. Only veterans receive an advantage of five points, ten points for disabled veterans.[28]

Duke had a clear record of stating that African-Americans were inferior. Before his run for governor, Duke said blacks are "more primitive in a lot of ways [and] much more closer to the jungle."[29] He built solid support among America's blatant racists. Said Jean Harrington, Duke's operations director in Monroe, Louisiana: "You've got to realize that years ago the Klan . . . was like police. . . . They were formed to keep law and order, regardless of what color you were." Another local supporter said that belonging to the NAACP and belonging to the Klan were the "same thing."[30]

It's not just fringe politicians like Duke who manipulate African-American images for political gain. There is a clear pattern of mainstream politicians using blacks as symbols of social ills, crime in particular, to either scare or impress white voters. During the 1988 presidential campaign, George Bush and his political allies made a symbol of Willie Horton, a black murderer who raped a white woman and assaulted her husband while on furlough.[31] Said Bush's research director Jim Pinkerton: "The more people who know who Willie Horton is, the better off we'll be."[32]

During the 1992 presidential election, Bill Clinton approved the execution of Ricky Ray Rector, a black man who killed a policeman. But Rector lobotomized himself when he tried to blow his brains out as police closed in on him the day of the shooting. At the time of the execution, he didn't even understand he was going to die. Some commentators suggested Clinton approved the electrocution of this profoundly retarded man to show he was not "soft on crime."[33]

In 1990, Michigan governor James J. Blanchard ran a re-election ad about a "boot camp" prison alternative that features a white instructor yelling at a black inmate. Before the election, Blanchard paid no attention to the program, and at first he aired the ads only in mostly white areas of Michigan, not in majority-black Detroit.[34]

Case Study:
The Media's Hall of Mirrors—
The Lani Guinier Incident

In early 1993, President Clinton nominated Stanford law professor Lani Guinier to head the Commission on Civil

Rights of the Justice Department. Then a *Wall Street Journal* editorial titled "Clinton's Quota Queen" blasted Guinier's scholarly articles on voting rights, and the press went wild.[35] When Guinier refused to withdraw her nomination, Bill Clinton withdrew it for her.

The lesson to be learned from this incident concerns the ways in which conservative opinions about Guinier were accepted by members of the media as fact, and how quickly these initial media reactions were picked up by organizations across the country. In other words, a relatively small number of individuals influenced the information the rest of the country was receiving, no doubt heavily swaying public opinion. Negative public opinion also influenced President Clinton's decision to withdraw Guinier's nomination, at which time he called her writings "anti-democratic" and "difficult to defend."[36]

An October, 1993, *Columbia Journalism Review (CJR)* article tracked the cannibalization of old stories which helps stereotypes become accepted conventional wisdom. The spin on Guinier began when the law professor was cast as a "quota queen" in an April 30, 1993 *Wall Street Journal* op-ed by Clint Bolick, a former official in the Reagan Justice Department. Bolick himself was "tipped off" to Guinier by conservative Boston University political science professor Abigail Thernstrom. The quotes that Bolick used in his article, including some taken out of context, were then recycled at publications ranging from the *Washington Post* to *Newsweek* to the *Los Angeles Times*. Many other publications, even if they did not rely on Bolick's initial article, relied heavily on other summaries rather than on a reading of Guinier's work for themselves. For example, the *CJR* article says, "Stuart Taylor, Jr., a columnist for American Lawyer Media, says he received several 'frantic' calls from reporters asking for a quickie summary of Guinier's articles."[37]

In reality, Guinier's writings are not only far from "anti-democratic," many of the voting remedies she suggests are practiced in democracies around the world. The kind of "proportional representation" that Guinier suggests to remedy black underrepresentation exists in Germany, Spain, Ireland, and Israel. As with all democracy, proportional representation still guarantees majority rule.[38] Even the American legislative system has an element of proportional representation. In the U.S. Senate, each state is represented by two Senators regardless of population: tiny Rhode Island has the same pull as Texas.

The Future of
_____ Black Political Participation

As with many of the other crucial issues on which blacks and non-blacks disagree, the degree to which the American political system has become equal and open to voters and candidates of all races is hotly contested. As is quoted at the top of this chapter, a *Newsweek* column on Guinier stated: "The trouble with Lani Guinier is that she believes it *is* 'us versus them.' In her writings she extrapolates from anachronistic Southern situations—and assumes, against the evidence of the past quarter century, that white racism is structural, unyielding and insuppurable."[39] Unfortunately, there is evidence that racism in politics can be structural, unyielding and insuppurable. In 1992, the conservative-dominated Supreme Court ruled in favor of local governments which, faced with blacks in a position of political power, change job descriptions to take that power away. Each commissioner in Etowah County, Alabama, used to have full authority on spending the funds allotted to their district. But in 1987, after an African-American was elected a county commissioner, the majority-white commission voted to centralize funding—effectively stripping the black commissioner of control. The Supreme Court specifically ruled that this instance and a similar one did not violate the

Voting Rights Act of 1965.[40] Just as barriers to black political participation seem to fall, they rise again. Only if all Americans remain vigilant about keeping our political system open and fair for all citizens can we be assured that our goals will be reached, and another racial friction point diminished.

Notes to Chapter Seventeen

1. Joe Klein, "Principle or Politics?" *Newsweek* (6/14/93).
2. Joint Center for Political and Economic Studies, "Political Trend Letter," in *Focus*, vol. 21, no. 10 (Washington, D.C.: October 1993); and David S. Broder, "North Carolina's 12th," *Washington Post* (7/7/93).
3. Thomas B. Edsall, "Conflicting Trends Seen in Whites' Willingness to Vote for Blacks," *Washington Post* (12/9/93).
4. Andrea Stone and Patricia Edmonds, "Politics of Race vs. Just Politics," *USA Today*, (11/5/93).
5. Joint Center for Political and Economic Studies, "Political Trend-Letter," in *Focus*, vol. 21, no. 4 (Washington, D.C.: April 1993).
6. Joint Center for Political and Economic Studies, "Political Trendletter," in *Focus*, vol. 21, no. 9 (September 1993).
7. Charles V. Hamilton, "Promoting Priorities: African-American Political Influence in the 1990s," in *The State of Black America 1993* (Washington, D.C., Urban League Press: 1993).
8. *New York Times*, "Highlights of Term" chart (7/6/93).
9. Doug Ireland, "Press Clips" column, *Village Voice* (5/25/93).
10. E. J. Dionne, "In Poll, Blacks Defy Political Stereotyping," *Washington Post* (July 9, 1992).
11. Author's reporting for *Newsweek* (10/93); The Christian Coalition, press release "Christian Coalition Survey Shows Strong Support in Minority Community," (9/9/93).
12. Scot Lehigh, "Media Coverage of Minorities Hit at Harvard Forum," *Boston Globe* (5/5/90).
13. Courtland Milloy, "The Media's Unfair Coverage of Black Politicians," *Washington Post* (7/5/90).
14. Robert Entman, "Representation and Reality in the Portrayal of Blacks on Network Television News," *Journalism Quarterly*, 71, no. 3 (Autumn 1994): 509–520 (Northwestern University Department of Communications, 1993).

15. Howard Fineman, "The Go-Between," *Newsweek* (October 25, 1993): 26–28.
16. Albert R. Hunt, "Ron Brown, His Own Worst Enemy," *Wall Street Journal* (10/14/93).
17. Gary Rivlin, "The Election of Harold Washington," *Extra!* (July/August 1992).
18. *Newsweek* cover, "The Power Broker: What Jesse Jackson Wants" (March 21, 1988).
19. Alexander Cockburn, "Media See Whites-Only White House," *Wall Street Journal* (3/24/88).
20. Rivlin, "The Election of Harold Washington," *Extra!*
21. Lionel McPherson, "Focus on Racism in the Media," *Extra!* (July/August 1992).
22. Lally Weymouth, "Lani Guinier: Radical Justice," *Washington Post* (5/25/93).
23. Lally Weymouth, "Mandela, deKlerk and the Future," *Washington Post* (7/15/93).
24. Cathy Burke, "Pat Worried by Black S. Africa Vote," *New York Post* (1/13/92).
25. Lerone Bennett, Jr., *Before the Mayflower: A History of Black America* (Johnson Publishing Company, 1986): 492.
26. *Wall Street Journal* (no byline), editorial "Little Comfort in Mr. Duke's Loss," (11/18/91); and Lynne Duke, "Blacks Mobilized to Defeat Duke," *Washington Post* (11/17/91).
27. Roberto Suro, "Duke Campaigns on Distorted Facts Despite Rebuttals and Clarifications," *New York Times* (11/12/91).
28. Suro, "Duke Campaigns on Distorted Facts Despite Rebuttals and Clarifications."
29. Tom Shales, "Scrutinizing David Duke," *Washington Post* (3/3/92).
30. Bill Nichols, "Support Solid in 'Duke Country': Message Heard, Past Overlooked," *USA Today* (11/11/93).
31. Anthony Lewis, "What is a Man Profited?," *New York Times* (10/27/88).
32. Sidney Blumenthal, "Willie Horton and the Making of a Campaign Issue," *Washington Post* (10/2/88).
33. Nat Hentoff, "The Race Game—Anybody Can Play," *Village Voice* (10/26/93).
34. Paul Taylor, "Governor Blanchard's Prison Camp Ad Draws Fire from Three Sides," *Washington Post* (5/24/90).
35. Clint Bolick, "Clinton's Quota Queen," *Wall Street Journal* (4/30/93).
36. Doug Ireland, "Press Clips" column, *Village Voice* (6/15/93).

37. Laurel Leff, "From Legal Scholar to Quota Queen," *Columbia Journalism Review* (October 1993): 36–41.
38. Ibid.
39. Klein, "Principle or Politics?" *Newsweek.*
40. Ruth Marcus, "Court Relaxes Voting Act Restraints," *Washington Post* (1/28/92).

Eighteen

Who's Making What News?

News is what is exceptional. To a white in a dominant white society, being black is unusual. Having a black mayor is unusual. . . . [R]ace is the basis for deciding what is unusual, and what is, therefore, news.

—Ohio State University journalism professors Lee B. Becker, Thomas A. Schwartz, and Sharon C. West.[1]

Washington Post *magazine editor Jay Lovinger, interviewing black writer Jill Nelson for a job in 1986: "The Metro editors . . . were intrigued by your perspective."*
Nelson's mental reply: "I'm not surprised. Two white males running the Metropolitan desk in a 70 percent black city that is also the nation's capital are probably in a constant state of intrigue."

—paraphrased from Jill Nelson's book on her experiences as a black writer at the Post magazine, *Volunteer Slavery: My Authentic Negro Experience* [2]

I N August 1993, two thousand black reporters gathered to hear recalled Clinton civil rights nominee Lani Guinier speak during the annual conference of the National Association of Black Journalists. Guinier analyzed how her views were consistently misconstrued and sensationalized in the media, then, quoting another author, chided journalists for being "stenographers to power." Rather than become offended by that statement—after all, it was a jab at the chosen career of almost everyone gathered—the audience greeted it with fervent clapping. Either it was a moment of unquestioning humility, or, despite their positions, the black journalists gathered were clapping heartily because they did not consider themselves part of "the media" being criticized.

Black journalists weren't the only ones at the NABJ conference. White managers, editors, and writers showed up to look for fresh talent (or, as some black journalists suspect, to look like they were looking). Among the recruiters was a *Washington Post* staff writer, Richard Leiby, who recounted his time as a minority-majority in a column titled "White Like Me." Sitting in a seminar, he wrote: "I suddenly feel blonder, paler, and more thin-lipped than I ever have in my life." His solution? To blend in. "And so you start dropping the 'g's' on your 'ing'-verbs in a phony jive," he continued, ". . . 'like I was sayin' to him'—and even trying out 'dis' and maybe even 'yo.' " When a colleague tried to introduce Leiby at a dinner by telling everyone he'd written a story on Bob Marley, he bristled. "I think I might have been patronized," he fretted. But before long, the conference was over, and everything was right again. "Flying back to Washington, I'm in first class, courtesy of my employer," he concluded. "There are a dozen white faces in first class, one black. I settle comfortably into my seat. For some reason, I feel like I'm already home."[3]

Events like the NABJ conference make clear just how deep the rift between African-Americans and that perceived monolith "the mainstream media" is. Only five percent of reporters in the United States are black, making journalism one of this country's most segregated professions. That's a shameful statistic in and of itself—but just as important is how it affects the news. The dearth of black journalists is one of the key reasons why the media consistently overreports the violence and weaknesses of the black community and underreports black everyday life and its strengths. The body of overwhelmingly white reporters don't seem willing or able to locate hardworking African-Americans but are able to hone in on urban deprivation, which they at least know where to go to find. The media's constant attention to certain stories—like crime—in the black community borders on obsession; the trend of ignoring others—like black community watch groups and self-help—borders on true pathology. And too often, news organizations are smug about their strengths, blind to their weaknesses, and surly when these weaknesses are pointed out.

Overview: Black Representation in the Media

Looking at the many African-American television anchors on local stations and reading the strong black columnists who have joined media's comfortable upper ranks, it would be difficult at first to see just how skimpy the African-American presence in the media is. The reality? Although progress has been made, television and print media are still unwilling or unable to hire and retain black journalists—and are especially bad on promoting people into positions where they actually can influence the news America sees and reads. Here is an overview of the present and past of African-Americans in the broadcast and print industries.

Broadcast

In the broadcast industry, only six percent of management jobs are held by African-Americans.[4] Although most major cities now have at least one black news anchor, without black counterpart producers and managers, they too often have little control over the tone and content of the news.

Just three decades ago, the picture for black broadcasters and black viewers was grim. During integration, for example, WLBT-TV in Jackson, Mississippi, was so blatantly anti-black that it was rebuked by the Federal Communications Commission in 1965. In 1969, the station's license was revoked.[5] And at the 1965 convention of the National Association of Educational Broadcasters only five of the 1,600 attendees were black.[6]

Black broadcasters made great strides in the 1970s and early 1980s, when, for example, the late Max Robinson became the first African-American to co-anchor a nightly national newscast. But during the Reagan years, the picture for black broadcasters dimmed some. Carole Simpson anchors ABC's weekend broadcasts, sometimes sits in for weekly anchor Peter Jennings, and also hosted one of the 1992 presidential debates. In the 1980s, Simpson summed up the disappearing opportunities by stating, "We're not voguish anymore."[7]

Even in areas which would seem "naturals" for black representation, like sports broadcasting, African-Americans are underrepresented. In 1989, for example, of the sixty sports producers and directors at ABC, NBC, and CBS only one was black.[8]

Today, black anchors and co-anchors are standard on the nightly newscasts in most major cities, but there are no regular black anchors on network nightly news.

Newspapers and Magazines

According to the American Society of Newspaper Editors, only five percent of newspaper reporters are black.[9] Only 3.1 percent of newspaper managers are black.[10]

Forty-five percent of all newspapers do not employ *any* non-white reporters. And even major metropolitan dailies often employ shockingly few reporters of color. For example, only 15 percent of the staff of the *New York Times* is non-white, though the city is "majority-minority." Only 19 percent of the *Washington Post*'s staff is non-white, though the District of Columbia is 66 percent black. Both of these prominent papers are national in distribution and scope. But their small rosters of non-white journalists contribute to the alienation of many readers in the cities in which they're based.[11]

Many prominent newspapers are family-owned and -run, which limits the chances that outsiders will reach top management ranks. The *New York Times*, for example, is owned by the Sulzbergers; the *Washington Post* Company (which also owns *Newsweek)* by the Grahams. Not only are the very top management positions passed from one generation to the next, but the broader group of people at the highest levels are picked to "fit in" at the organization, and are often selected in part because of personal referrals and recommendations.

In the magazine industry, which is both smaller than the newspaper industry and even more reliant on word of mouth and connections, only two percent of the senior ranks were African-American.[12] Media giant Time Warner, which owns a stable of thirty magazines, including *Time* and *Sports Illustrated,* had no black top publishing executives in its magazine division until 1993. That year, Kieth Clinckscales became president of the newly published hip-hop magazine *Vibe,* a joint venture between Time Inc. and musician/producer Quincy Jones.

Black reporters and writers were generally confined to black publications until the urban unrest of the 1960s. By the mid-seventies, about 100 black journalists were working in mainstream publications. By the mid-eighties, that number had jumped to 3,000.[13] For example, in the 1950s, pioneering black journalist Bob Maynard got nearly 300 letters of rejection because of his race. When he deleted all references to race in his inquiry letters, he would get interviews. But when he showed up for those interviews, he was dismissed out of hand. In 1983, he became editor and publisher of the *Oakland Tribune,* the first time an African-American had owned a "mainstream" newspaper.[14] Before his death in 1993, financial difficulties forced him to relinquish control of the paper.

Despite the checkered opportunities available to black journalists, many have succeeded spectacularly. Well over twenty African-Americans have won Pulitzer Prizes in the past decade, including Les Payne of *Newsday* for International Reporting (1992), and two-time photography winner Michel duCille of the *Miami Herald* (1986 and 1988). Photographer Moneta Sleet of Johnson Publications was the first African-American to win a Pulitzer, in 1969.[15] Among those African-Americans in prominent positions in the newspaper and magazine industry are Jay Harris, editor of the *San Jose Mercury News*, and Joel Dreyfuss, editor of *Information Week* (and former editor of *PC* magazine).[16]

Race in the Newsroom

Many African-American journalists struggle with the "inside-outsider" status the job confers. In the "White Like Me" column, Leiby speaks of attending a book signing for Jill Nelson's *Volunteer Slavery*. "Many whites at the *Post* view the book as mean-spirited, one-sided, even paranoid. Can race possibly be so transcendent a factor in one's job experience? Why is she so angry?"

"Why are they so angry?" is a common managerial chant about African-American reporters, who, it is not so secretly believed, should be deeply grateful for the opportunities white editors give them. Less well-explored is the anger of white reporters who've lashed out at the "special preference" they imagine black reporters have. At the *Boston Globe* in 1991, white reporter Peter Howe acted as a "deep throat" for a column in the rival daily on white *Globe* reporters' anger over "special treatment" for blacks. Among those specifically skewered was African-American journalist Fred Biddle, who was promoted to the state house—the same beat as Howe—after being courted by the *Washington Post*. Biddle pointed out that no one complained when *Globe* sportswriters won higher salaries after being courted by the (now-defunct) sports daily *The National*. And no one pointed out that Howe was hardly an objective observer—at the same time he was venting about an "alleged double standard," he may have been feeling the pressure on his own beat.[17]

During the Los Angeles riots in 1992, black *Los Angeles Times* editor Linda Williams was quoted as stating that the paper was "bussing minority journalists into the city to use as cannon fodder."[18] Lower-ranking reporters and trainees, including the minorities Williams was speaking about, often get their start in suburban bureaus; if there's "urban unrest," they get to make a guest appearance on the choicer Metro beat. The 1992 riots were an ironic statement on how little things change. Three decades earlier, during the Watts riots, black copy boys were instantly promoted to reporters to fit the media's needs.

A 1993 study by the National Association of Black Journalists found widespread disagreement between blacks and white managers on career opportunities. Among the findings: Only half of black journalists thought their news organization made a serious effort to recruit black journalists; 91 percent of managers thought they did. Just under one-third of black journalists thought that bringing up racial issues damaged their chances for advancement. In July 1994, the National Association of Black Journalists hosted the first-ever joint meeting of African-American, Hispanic-American, Asian-American and Native American journalists. Each of the four journalism groups has expressed a belief that race-based reporting in some way helps stereotype their communities and a desire to increase the representation of minority reporters at America's newspapers, magazines, and television stations.[19]

Myths of Black
Media Influence

Time and time again, journalists (usually African-American ones) have documented pervasive trends of biased coverage in the media. Yet, dishearteningly, the industry seems to have changed little in recent years.

In 1990, David Shaw did an extensive series on race and the media for the *Los Angeles Times*, criticizing coverage by his own and other papers. As he pointed out, "[A]part from truly major stories—a big election or earthquake ... what's newsworthy is largely an arbitrary decision made by mostly white editors."[20]

Myth: *Even if African-Americans aren't heavily represented among members of the media, black viewpoints are represented—if anything, overrepresented.*

Reality: Black viewpoints are consistently underrepresented in the mainstream media, and sometimes journalists are shockingly honest about their perceptions.

Said "60 Minutes" executive producer Don Hewitt at a speech at the University of California, Berkeley: "Listen, you got a whole section of America that talks sort of blackspeak that white America doesn't understand ... even when they don't say 'Ax!' they say, 'Hey, man!' And if no one understands it, you can't tell it very well."[21] "60 Minutes," of course, is considered one of America's more evenhanded media outlets.

The lack of African-American journalists and African-Americans as sources in the media has a profound effect on coverage of black issues. On April 6, 1990, the Associated Press ran a story titled "Bush Foresees Black as President." The body of the story was far different: it focused on how angry black leaders were about Bush's attempts to gut civil rights legislation.

Another example: On March 27, 1987, public television aired "Street Cop," a documentary on drug crime in Boston. They only aired footage from black neighborhoods, showing black dealers and users.[22] The reality of drugs in America is far different. The commander of the Boston Police Department's Drug Control unit admits: "We've arrested people from every town in the metropolitan area for buying drugs in the city. The majority are fully employed white males in their thirties."[23] The "Frontline" documentary ignored drug crime in white areas and, most important, the white suburban consumers who drive into the city for their fixes and keep the trade alive. America rarely sees these white users, even on public television.

Myth: *News about African-Americans is not disproportionately "negative." Journalists would be "going out of their way" if they tried to publish more "positive" stories.*

Wrote *Washington Post* columnist Bob Levy: "Should visible columnists . . . go out of their way to publish positive news about black people, and should they label black news as such? I say heavens, no."[24]

Reality: For most columnists, the vast majority of whom are white, black America *is* out of their way. Columns are powerful and incisive because they tend to be personal and anecdotal—but they are limited for the same reasons. Journalists, as might be expected (but is usually not acknowledged), tend to write what they know. To provide better coverage of African-Americans would not be a matter of "going out of their way"—it would be a matter of journalists knowing their weak spots.

Despite the presence of columnists like the *Washington Post*'s Pulitzer Prize–winning William Raspberry, the vast majority of newspapers do not give African-American journalists the power and latitude of top editorial positions. Until 1993, when the paper hired Bob Herbert, the *New York Times* did not have a regular black editorial columnist.[25]

Mainstream media misses big stories as well as small ones. Nelson Mandela finally gave his approval to ending economic sanctions against South Africa in October 1993; at the time he was in New York City and gave a press conference with David Dinkins. Yet neither the *New York Post*, *Daily News*, nor

Newsday thought it front-page news. And when the commandant of the Marine Corps said on national television that blacks and other minority officers were less proficient than whites, it was conveniently excised from the media. On the October 31, 1993, episode of "60 Minutes," General Carl Mundy was asked why blacks make up nearly a third of Armed Forces enlistees but only about ten percent of officers. Mundy said that "in the military skills, we find that the minority officers. . . . don't do as well." Yet the vast majority of national newspapers did not pick up on his comments, allowing them to stand virtually unchallenged.[26]

Case Study:
Some Pictures Are Worth a
_____ Thousand Wrong Words

On March 1, 1993, the nationwide newspaper *USA Today* took the bold step of apologizing for misrepresenting members of the African-American community. In this instance, the offending medium was largely pictorial—photographs of Los Angeles gang members. The young men were told they would appear in a story on exchanging their guns for jobs but instead appeared in a front-page, all-too-stereotypic story titled "Gangs Put L.A. on Edge."[27] It didn't mention the guns-for-jobs program, but rather speculated about the possibility of rioting after the second trial of the officers who beat Rodney King. It was a case of the facts being bent to fit the "news." In fact, when one of the young men showed up without a gun, the reporter, Richard Price, took the unusual and possibly unethical step of driving him to his mother's house to pick up his shotgun.

USA Today tried to play down the controversy at first. Two days after the article ran, the paper printed a one-sentence "clarification" at the bottom of a box on page one.[28] But eventually the paper was forced to bring the story out into the open. Los Angeles community activist CaShears, who arranged the guns-for-jobs photo op, was given the opportunity to write a long column on the aftermath. When he told the young men what had happened, CaShears wrote, he took "verbal abuse from my own people for bringing white guys into the projects to 'use and take advantage' of them again.... Yes, they were angry, but I saw more pain, hurt, and disappointment than anything else. Their trust had been betrayed.... I think you've done a disservice to my people who are very sensitive about a media portrayal of black males across America," he wrote in conclusion. "I feel that you've fanned the fires of racism, hatred and division."[29]

While it was certainly admirable for the newspaper to print CaShears's statement, there were signs that the editors were not quite ready to consider all of the implications of this case. "On its own, the photograph was accurate," wrote an editor in a parallel column to CaShears's. "None of the subjects in the photo have denied being gang members or having access to guns."[30] That statement ignores the story's other failings: that its premise was sensationalistic and misguided. Using black gangs as the pivot of a story on the riots doesn't mesh with the fact that the vast majority of those who rioted were not gang members, nor were the majority of those arrested even African-American. The constant emphasis on black potential for violence only heightens racial tensions and white fears.

The Big Picture

The positive side to the misrepresentations of African-Americans in the media is that they spur more and more

Americans to be critical of what we see and read. For example, a 1993 article in *Newsweek* about a brutal multi-suspect Houston murder was accompanied by a stereotypic picture of a menacing, scowling black man. In a subsequent issue, a reader wrote in: "Since five of the six defendants in the Houston rape/murder case were Hispanic, why did your accompanying photo picture only the African-American defendant? That doesn't seem to give a very representative portrait."[31] At the 1993 National Association of Black Journalists convention, actor Tim Reid put the need for monitoring media coverage in succinct terms. "If you don't react then shut up!" he said.[32] In fact, millions of Americans are deeply concerned that the media's failings are helping to drive the races apart. A 1994 Gallup poll found that over 40 percent of both blacks and whites felt that news coverage *worsened* American race relations. (Smaller numbers of Asian- and Hispanic-Americans felt the same way). Only 21 percent of whites and 19 percent of blacks felt news coverage helped improve race relations.[33] Refusing to talk about racial issues, particularly in the media, will not change things for the better. It's only if we take a stand and make our presence known that we can fight the hype.

Three decades ago, following the Watts Riots, Lyndon Johnson's Kerner Commission lambasted news organizations for being "shockingly backward" in not hiring, training, and promoting more African-Americans: "For if the media are to comprehend and then to project the Negro community, they must have the help of Negroes. If the media are to report with understanding, wisdom, sympathy on the problems of the black man—for the two are increasingly intertwined—they must employ, promote, and listen to Negro journalists."[34] Those words were prophetic when they were first written, and are still crucially important now. Unfortunately, it seems that the media will only show us the real face of black America when we compel it to do so.

Notes to Chapter Eighteen

1. "Notable and Quotable" column, *Wall Street Journal* (4/17/84).
2. Jill Nelson, *Volunteer Slavery: My Authentic Negro Experience* (Chicago: The Noble Press, 1993).
3. Richard Leiby, "White Like Me," *Washington Post* (8/1/93).
4. 1992 Federal Communications Commission employment survey.
5. Jannette L. Dates and William Barlow, eds., *Split Image: African-Americans in the Mass Media*, Second edition (Howard University Press, 1993): 421.
6. Dave Berkman, "Is Educational Broadcasting Segregated?" *NAEB Journal* (January/February 1966): 67–70.
7. Michael Massing, "Blackout in Television," *Columbia Journalism Review* (November/December 1982); and Robert Entman, "Representation and Reality in the Portrayal of Blacks on Network Television News," unpublished draft of article forthcoming in *Journalism Quarterly* (Northwestern University Department of Communications, 1993).
8. Norman Chad, "Balance of Power Affects Balance of Color," *Washington Post* (6/22/89).
9. "Newsroom minorities top 10 percent, ASNE 1993 survey shows," news release from the American Society of Newspaper Editors (3/30/93).
10. Ibid.
11. *Minority Employment Survey*. American Society of Newspaper Editors, 1994.
12. 1992 National Association of Minority Media Executives survey.
13. Dates and Barlow, *Split Image: African-Americans in the Mass Media*, p. 392.
14. Ibid, pp. 392–393.
15. Ibid, p. 397.
16. The National Association of Black Journalists, *NABJ Journal*, vol. 2, no. 4 (December 1993/January 1994).
17. Howard Kurtz, "Raises & Racism" *Washington Post* (11/2/91); and Kurtz, "Source of Leak Tracked Down At Boston Globe" (11/28/91).
18. Howard Kurtz, "Diverse Views of the News," *Washington Post* (3/2/93).
19. David G. Savage, "Minority Journalists Assail Crime Stories," *Los Angeles Times* (7/29/94).
20. David Shaw, "Newspapers Struggling to Raise Minority Coverage," *Los Angeles Times* (12/12/90).

21. Mark Zingarelli, "Ya Wanna Be a '60 Minutes' Producer, Eh?" *Mother Jones* (September/October 1993).

22. Kirk A. Johnson, "Can We Talk About Race," *Extra! Focus on Racism in the Media* (July/August 1992).

23. Holly Sklar, "Young and Guilty by Stereotype" *Z Magazine* (July/August 1993).

24. Bob Levy, "Bob Levy's Washington—A Need for Positive Black News?" *Washington Post* (9/17/90).

25. Pat Guy, "Columnist Keeps Style at 'Times,'" *USA Today* (7/19/93).

26. Howard Kurtz, "The Shot Not Heard Round the World," *Washington Post* (11/12/93).

27. Richard Price, "Gangs Put L.A. On Edge," *USA Today* (2/16/93).

28. Howard Kurtz, "Why the Press is Always Right," *Columbia Journalism Review* (May/June 1993).

29. CaShears, "Activist: 'Paper Has Done Disservice,'" *USA Today* (3/1/93).

30. Joe Urschel, "*USA Today*: Here's How It Happened," *USA Today* (3/1/93).

31. Sally Campbell of Houston, TX, letter printed in the 8/9/93 issue of *Newsweek*, referring to the 7/19/93 issue.

32. *The NABJ Monitor*, a publication of the National Association of Black Journalists' convention (7/22/93).

33. *USA Today* (no byline), "Racial, ethnic groups give mixed reviews to media," (7/26/94).

34. "The News Media and Disorders," *Report of the National Advisory Commission on Civil Disorders* (1968): 362–86.

INDEX

Schott, Marge, 160
Schwartz, Thomas A., 241
Science; blacks famous in, 94; education, 71–72, 74, 89
"Scientist's Report on Racial Differences, A," 67–68
Scott, Dred, 169
Seale, Bobby, 175
Seattle, Wash., 75, 225
Segregation: of affluent blacks, 47–48; of black college students, 90–91; current vs. past, 48–49; in education, 72–75; and employment, 105, 124–25; geographic, 15–16, 46, 47–48; and health care, 216; of higher education, 80–81; history of, 171–73; and home equity, 136–37; improving problem of, 57–58; media coverage of, 52–53; and power of black neighborhoods, 57; in sports, 160; and suburbs, 54; and teen motherhood, 29; of white ethnics, vs. blacks, 56
Self-employment, 126
Selma to Montgomery march, 174
Senior citizens, 3
Senna, Carl, 66
Sentencing, 191, 195–96, 197–98
Sentencing Group, 197
"Separate-but-equal" rationale, 169
Serial killers, 5, 200
Service sector jobs, 118
Sexual assaults, 156, 194, 201
Sexual behavior, 30–32
Shaw, David, 248
Shawmut National Corporation, 52
Shockneck, Kent, 205
Shoney's restaurant chain, 112
Signet Bank, 138
Silber, John, 209, 210
Silver Spring, Md., 74
Simi Valley jury, 199, 206
Simpson, Carole, 244
Simpson, O. J., xi–xii, xiii, 10
Single mothers, 16, 21–25, 27–32; and drugs, 212; incomes of, 40, 118
Singleton, John, 142, 144
"60 Minutes" (TV series), 129, 248, 250
Slade, Leonard A., 84
Slavery, 167–70; abolished, 170; and black athletes, 155; and black net worth, 135–36; and diet, 219–20; and out-of-wedlock births, 25–26; rebellions against, 177–78; significance of, 178–79, 181

Sleet, Moneta, 246
Smith, Tommie, 175
Smoking, 66, 218
Snipes, Wesley, 142
Snyder, Jimmy (the Greek), 154, 155, 159
Social Security, 42
Socioeconomic class, 17; and college degrees, 82; and crime, 193, 196–97; and drugs, 209, 211, 213; and health, 209–10; and racism, 185–86; and school expectations, 71–72
Solidarity Day March of the Poor People's Campaign, 175
Source, The magazine, 134
South, 16, 48, 67, 202–3
South Africa, 232, 233, 249
South Boston, 192
South Carolina, 169, 170, 171, 177
Southern Christian Leadership Conference, 176
Southern Poverty Law Center, Klan-Watch project, 187
Spanish-American War, 180
Special education classes, 71
"Special preference," 108, 246
Spelman College, 75
Sports, 154–62; broadcasting, 244
Sports Illustrated, 156, 245
Standardized testing, 70–71
Stanford University, 83, 96
Staples, Brent, 147
State legislatures, 171
State of Black America, The (National Urban League), 63
Stereotypes: and arts, 140, 143; of black politicians, 228–29; of blacks by whites, 184–85, 188; and college students, 80, 91–92; and criminals, 198–200; and drugs and health, 220–21; facts to counteract, 5–6; and media, 247, 250–52; and sports, 155–58; and welfare, 35–36; and white politicians, 233–35; and workplace, 110
Stock ownership, 135
Stokes, Carl B., 175
Stop the Violence movement, 148
"Street Cop" (TV show), 248
Stress of being black, 216
Stride-Rite Shoes, 125
Stuart, Carol, 7, 200–1
Student Nonviolent Coordinating Committee (SNCC), 174, 176